THE MYTH OF TWO MINDS

Books by Beryl Lieff Benderly

THINKING ABOUT ABORTION
DANCING WITHOUT MUSIC: DEAFNESS IN AMERICA
DISCOVERING CULTURE: AN INTRODUCTION TO
ANTHROPOLOGY (coauthor)

THE MYTH
OF TWO MINDS

WHAT GENDER MEANS
AND DOESN'T MEAN

Beryl Lieff Benderly

Doubleday

NEW YORK

1987

Library of Congress Cataloging-in-Publication Data
Benderly, Beryl Lieff.
The myth of two minds.
Bibliography: p. 295
Includes index.
1. Sex role. 2. Sex differences (Psychology) 3. Sex
differences. I. Title
HQ1075.B46   1987   305.3   87-5327
ISBN: 0-385-19672-5

Contents

"We have found that where science has progressed the farthest, the mind has but regained from nature that which the mind put into nature.

We have found a strange footprint on the shores of the unknown. We have devised profound theories one after another to account for its origin. At last we have succeeded in reconstructing the creatures who made the imprint. And lo! it is our own."

Sir Arthur Stanley Eddington
Space and Time Gravitation, 1920

THE MYTH OF TWO MINDS

PROLOGUE

Myths, Minds, and Near Misses

This book started out to be one thing and ended up, against its will, as something quite different. It began as a straightforward summary of the new evidence for three increasingly apparent scientific truths: First, despite the social changes sweeping America, men and women think, feel, and act differently. Second, these differences have definite physiological bases. Third, physiology explains the very different male and female roles observed in many cultures, and these differences therefore doom recent, well-meaning American attempts to narrow the gap in power and opportunity that now separates the sexes. I threw myself into reading the latest scientific literature, which, everyone said, ever more clearly affirmed these ideas. But a strange thing started to happen; the more I read, the uneasier I felt. I soon began to suspect, and finally came to know, that the three "truths" were false.

This wasn't easy. At the time, articles and books announcing newly discovered gender differences were fairly tumbling off the presses. From laboratories and computers across the nation came authoritative word that new chemical and electronic analyses could pinpoint sex differences in the brain. Meanwhile, the latest tools of evolutionary reasoning had tracked behavioral differences through our species' ancient past.

And these findings implied some important conclusions. The tissues that house intellect, emotion, and motivation, for example, appeared to differ by sex just like those that cover the pectorals or contain the genitals. Male and female behavior, therefore, didn't express different relationships to power or different memories of mother; they seemed to arise necessarily from different neural connections. And that meant that aggression, competition, trigonometry, and leadership come as naturally to one sex as whiskers and ejaculation; compassion, passivity, social graces, and submission come as naturally to the other as the soprano voice and the monthly period. Further struggles to equip ordinary girls and women to be astronauts, senators, CEOs were hopeless and therefore pointless. The same went for experiments to involve ordinary men more deeply in their children's lives. The traditional order of things was the natural one because "the brain," as one writer put it simply, "is a sex organ." There are two minds, a male mind and a female mind, as distinctive in form and function as male and female bodies.

For some months it seemed that every periodical from the scholarly journals to the comic pages proclaimed the new certainty; books expounding it filled the drugstore racks and the catalogs of university presses. You could feel the ground shift under the continuing national debate over sex roles. The brave assurances of the recent past, the apparently settled finding of social science—that experience and expectations accounted for most of what distinguished male and female minds—now had to bow to up-to-the-minute discoveries of neuroscience and endocrinology. *La différence* clearly owed more to hormones and cerebral hemispheres than to manners and mores. And beyond that, the new science of sociobiology, a reputedly revolutionary and undubitably Harvard-bred amalgam of anthropology, ethology, and population genetics, revealed the evolutionary reasons for these newly obvious physiological facts.

Ironically, just as American men and women had begun acting more alike than ever before, science was uncovering the physical bases for real behavioral, emotional, and intellectual distinctions. In only a few years, a push toward fundamental equality had transformed homes, workplaces, even firehouses, space capsules, and ships at sea, but that made no difference. The king was dead. Long live the king!

Eager to keep up to date, I started out, quite simply, to master and then summarize the new knowledge. From what I had read, from what well-informed people around me were saying, I could see that science was moving briskly toward a new consensus. I expected a straightforward drive down the superhighway that led there. But quite soon after setting out, I sensed something awry. The expressway to certainty had become a rutted path over hillocks of contradiction, a carriage track through thickets of controversy, a rickety footbridge over rivers of unknowns. Rather than the near unanimity reported in magazines, I found, down poorly marked byways, entire bodies of educated contrary opinion. Researchers fully as eminent as those quoted in the newspapers, professors teaching in the very same distinguished departments, held reservations about the new findings that ranged from serious doubt to undisguised scorn. For them, the notion of a female mind fitted for social life and nurturance (and unfitted for aggression and precision) had nothing to do with science and everything to do with ideology.

The skeptics' ideas, though, made singularly poor feature copy. "Re-analysis Faults Finding of Differences" or "Painstaking Attempt Fails to Replicate Influential Study" headlined no late city editions. "What We Still Don't Know About the Brain" and "Faulty Assumptions Weaken Chains of Evolutionary Reasoning" enthralled the readers of no slick magazines. "Scientists Urge Caution in Interpreting Statistical Data" blared from no Sunday supplements. Only the brainiest (and least read and viewed) media gave voice to the skeptics. These scientists, however, continued to publish for their accustomed symposia, colloquia, and festschriften; the community of academic researchers continued to know who they were and what their views counted for. Only the rest of us, who get our science from the evening news and brightly colored magazines, rather than from conference lectures and journals with eleven-syllable names, remained in the dark.

In most scientific discussions, of course, public ignorance of the various positions makes no difference. What actually happened in the first milliseconds after the Big Bang, which of several intracellular mechanisms actually triggers cancer, why the dinosaurs perished, have no practical bearing on the life of anyone not employed in a laboratory. When the experts have agreed, when the facts have emerged, the rest of us will find out in good time.

But how and why the sexes differ is not the kind of question that waits docilely in the seminar room while doctors of philosophy debate. Millions of individual destinies and huge financial and political interests ride on the decisions that society makes about this, the central social issue of our age. If science had a good answer, we would need to know it. But if science doesn't, as is now the case, we need to know that, too.

It's not, of course, that we lack information about gender. Never before have so many bits of knowledge about males and females been available for study. Experts from many disciplines, using their diverse jargons and analytical tools, have probed the bodies and behaviors of countless creatures, analyzing them as systems of interlocking molecules, genes, cells, enzymes, hormones, synapses, tissues, hemispheres, brains, nerves, glands, bones, instincts, drives, perceptions, strategies, needs, self-images, identities, and social units. We know about the mating habits of fish, the neural fibers of rodents, the nursery equipment of arctic birds, the sweat glands of tropical mammals, the secret messages of amorous fireflies. We know why certain reindeer mothers get their young through the winter, how certain bird fathers guard the nest, where certain fish suitors find their mates.

But we can't agree on what this mountain of facts adds up to in human terms. Society has split into hostile, name-calling factions. Science has reached no consensus on the answer; it can't even agree on how to ask the question. Each separate discipline—each coterie of scholars trained in a single tradition—has a distinctive idea of what the answer is and how to discover it. And each of them has a different stake in the outcome. Some produce data that fit neatly into magazine and news stories and get a lot of attention from reporters. Others struggle with the messiness of nuance and perception, and disappear into a fog of their own footnotes and definitions. And none of them speaks especially clearly to the others.

Even if the stakes were mere disinterested knowledge, this confusion would be intolerable. But this debate concerns concrete gain and loss in the lives of countless real people, so the confusion becomes actively pernicious. It permits the clever people to manipulate belief for particular social and political ends. It lets the wily people disguise self-interest as scientific truth.

Only clear understanding of what we really know and don't know can defend us against manipulation. That means we have to understand the meaning of gender in our society, and we can't do that unless we comprehend the meaning of human gender, period, in all its complexity. And those questions extend far beyond hormones and synapses into the furthest reaches of our history and the deepest reaches of our minds.

Like all living creatures, we stand atop an immensely long evolutionary past; countless generations of our human and pre-human ancestors lived, struggled, bred, and died. They survived in specific times and places, they faced specific challenges, they arrived at specific solutions that still shape our biological and social inheritance. From them arise our own possibilities—our mentality, our spirit, our emotions, our sexuality. And from them arises the living reality of contemporary males and females, the infinite variety of living male and female minds.

Science hasn't yet arrived at a complete understanding, but numbers of thinkers are working to hack clear the paths that may someday take us there. To follow them we have to journey back to the beginning, way past the headlines, far deeper than the magazine stories, to the place where knowledge comes from: the pointed question. Three such questions, answered in detail, will banish the myth that physiology determines what males and females may be capable of, that it imposes limits on our natures and our lives together. First we will ask: What *are* males and females anyway? Next, what are they *like?* And finally, what are they *for?*

To accomplish this, we'll explore many smaller questions that add, like tributary streams, to a growing river of knowledge and reasoning. Why do we have gender in the first place? How do human societies deal with this fact? And does this differ from what happens in other sexual species? What specific physical, psychological, intellectual, and behavioral differences are known to distinguish human males and females? What meaning do these differences have in human life?

The really big scientific questions, of course, finally blend into ideas that we more often regard as esthetic or even philosophical.

At a certain point, the issue of gender differences will become, at last, a question of symmetry—in both of the word's highly relevant senses. First, of course, we will reckon with the ancient meaning: two complementary, interdependent halves that look at each other across a dividing middle but together compose the whole of our species and its life. The second is a much newer, mathematical use: the notion that a valid, unifying theory applies equally in varying conditions. With this idea, Einstein unlocked our century. For him, as developed in his special relativity, symmetry required that the laws of physics had to predict equally the experience of an observer at rest *and* an observer in uniform motion. By the time his thought had culminated in general relativity, he knew that laws must even apply to an observer in accelerating motion. The search for symmetrical theories—those accurate both in our world and in others half a cosmos away—has become a major preoccupation of physics.

In just this way, a theory that would explain the facts of gender must take with equal seriousness the male condition and the female, must predict with equal accuracy the experience of both types of humans. No true law of nature distorts an astronaut's or a Venutian's reality in favor of an earthling's. Nor can the reality of one sex be distorted to answer the ideological needs of the other. The eternally incomplete process that framed our species works according to a single law, applicable to ourselves and to all life.

We won't penetrate the forest of that immense, ancient night all at once, but must proceed, as good science does, by the winding, backtracking, tentative steps of many small questions. Each chapter that follows asks a simple one and follows it to its hard and not always satisfying end. But there it always hooks up to another question that carries us a bit further along. At our present state of knowledge, we can't hope for a royal road to truth, neither the kind that religion provided our ancestors nor the kind the magazines and evening news promise us. But we can already travel far enough to see, perhaps, our goal burning dimly in the distance.

We can also see, far back in our unknown past, the now dimly glowing fires of our ancestors. Their mastery of fire was a major influence in making us what we are. It permitted them to cook their food, and thus vastly expanded their diet and the lands they could colonize. It permitted them to fashion tools and weapons far more powerful than those available to any competing lineage. And around their fires, in camps and on altars, they fabricated that other material central to human life: a tissue of belief about themselves and their place in the world. We don't know what myths they whispered as protection against the primeval dark, although we can make some shrewd guesses. But we do know that we still share that myth-making capacity. For generations, Americans have spun, among other stories we live by, the myth that male and female minds differ in some basic, inherent, irremediable way. We start now to unravel it by asking the most basic, and probably the most complex question of all. What, indeed, *are* males and females?

I

WHAT ARE MALES AND FEMALES?

1

What Is Gender?

Alice Smith was starting to worry. Her daughter, Mary Beth, a tall, long-legged teenager with flowing hair and a growing corps of youthful admirers, was coming along admirably—in every respect but one. She did well in school, she had many friends, her years of ballet lessons had given her a lithe, shapely figure that boys admired and girls envied. But still she had not menstruated.

A trip to the library allayed Alice's concern for a while. Menarche—she hadn't previously known the technical term for the onset of the monthly cycle—could occur at any time from eleven to fifteen, and in some especially athletic girls, even later than that. Probably Mary Beth's ballet, along with her new interest in cheerleading, qualified her for that category of late starters.

But more months passed, and still unused in the dresser drawer sat the box of pads Alice had bought Mary Beth when her friends one by one started to announce their periods. From time to time Mary Beth made some joking reference to it; a mother's eye saw the fear under the humor. "You know, honey," Alice would say, "a lot of women in my family were late starting. My grandmother didn't start till she was sixteen." But most girls started later in those badly nourished days, Alice's reading had told her. She hoped a daughter's ear didn't pick up the hollowness of the assurance.

At last Alice voiced her fears to her husband. "But you say she's still inside the normal age range," Tom said when he had heard her out.

"Do you think I should take her to the doctor?"

"Why upset her? She's certainly well developed in every other way."

And then Alice knew for sure. Mary Beth had developed well in every way that Tom could know about, but there was one that, not having seen Mary Beth undressed for a number of years, he had overlooked. Alice hadn't before connected it to the missing periods but now her mind's eye saw an illustration in one of the library books. The pubic hair, the caption said, was among the first signs of sexual maturity. Now, Mary Beth was outwardly as mature as a high school girl could be, but she had very little pubic hair. Indeed, she counted herself lucky for not having to undertake the awkward shave job that some of her girlfriends needed to look right in their leotards and swim suits.

The crease between Tom's eyes deepened as he listened to Alice explain. She saw the expression again as the doctor looked up from Mary Beth's pelvic examination. "We're going to need some more tests," he said steadily.

The frown was deeper still as he faced Alice across his desk a few days later. "I'm afraid my news will surprise you," he said. "Mary Beth is never going to have periods. She's never going to have babies." He paused and hunted for words. "The thing is that Mary Beth isn't really a woman—well, not in the complete physiological sense." He finally abandoned the attempt at scientific detachment. "You may not believe this, but in her genes, Mary Beth is a male."

Gender is physical fact, but not a simple one.

In a world of creatures going two by two, Mary Beth stands alone. She continued cheerleading and ballet, she dated many boys before finally marrying one and adopting children. Only her family and some doctors ever knew the truth about her body: that during the complex process that should have made her definitively either male or female, something had gone wrong and made her both— and neither.

The error happened at the very start. Months before the obstetrician confidently pronounced her a girl, years before the doctors peered at her cells through a microscope, an elegant, complex series of interlocking, microscopic changes should have gone forward to establish her sex. But a tiny genetic something had gone wrong, spoiling forever Mary Beth's chances of belonging unequivocally to one of humankind's two great divisions.

People in our culture—and most people everywhere—see this division as absolutely basic to our humanity; it's also fundamental to all our fellow mammals, all our fellow vertebrates, many lesser creatures too. But for the first six weeks of fetal development—almost a sixth of a full-term pregnancy—it scarcely exists. The genetic complement, of course, is set at conception by the luck of the draw—the configuration of the 23rd chromosome pair, the only one that's sometimes asymmetrical. The mother's ova—each carrying one member of every chromosome pair—all have an X in the 23rd space. Some of the father's sperm have an X, the rest a Y. A single sperm penetrates the ovum, uniting two genetic halves into a brand-new whole, and determines the genetic sex. Two Xs make a female, an X and the smaller Y make a male.

For six weeks, though, this microscopic difference is all that distinguishes a future girl from a prospective boy. The nervous system, the eyes, even the fingers are in place before any physical difference appears between those with the Y and those without. And the similarities are more than skin-deep; at this point, all embryos have the physical equipment to grow into either sex: identical rudimentary gonads and two rudimentary internal ducts—the Mullerian, poised to become uterus and fallopian tubes, and the Wolffian, ready to grow into the male reproductive tract. Nor will appearance tell you which of the identical sets of folds and bulges will grow into penis and scrotum and which into labia and vagina.

Shortly after Alice was sure she'd missed her period, long before the obstetrician announced, "It's a girl!," Mary Beth's indeterminate body should have become fully male. With an economy of means that any systems analyst would envy, our genes transmit the absolute minimum of information necessary to bend that dual potential in one and only one direction. So exquisitely engineered a system of differentiation, so powerful and pregnant a use of single binary choice, indicates an evolutionary process all but perfected over many, many generations. And the system does reach very far back into our evolutionary past; we share it in detail with all other mammals, and in slightly different versions, with sexual species generally. Mary Beth started out, unremarkably enough, with Alice's X and Tom's Y.

At the right moment, in the 6th embryonic week, the crucial decision was made. An as-yet unidentified gene on the short arm of the Y chromosome shunted Mary Beth's development onto the spur that should have led ultimately to manhood. Without this signal, the human body becomes female; the gonads become ovaries, the Mullerian duct matures, and the Wolffian duct withers. But right on schedule—by a process not yet understood—it made the primordial gonads grow into testes. So far so good for Mary Beth. Just when they should have, her new testes began secreting chemicals that made the Mullerian duct wither. The first stage of her growth into a male, defeminization, was complete.

A few weeks later, the second stage, virilization, began uneventfully enough. The testes now began a new secretion, probably of the hormone testosterone. And it's here that things started going wrong for the boy Mary Beth should have been.

To understand why, we need a short detour to make the acquaintance of that special class of chemicals, the hormones. The body's chemical couriers, they carry coded messages between sending organs and target cells. The glands resemble radio stations, broadcasting signals into the surrounding air. The target cells resemble listeners, tuning in to the programs they want to hear.

Radio listeners are choosy, picking an AM, FM, police band, CB, or shortwave receiver, depending on the information they want to hear. Hormone-sensitive receiving cells are even choosier; they have special antennalike receptor molecules, either on their surfaces or in their nuclei, that capture and bind particular hormone molecules. Only then can the chemical "message" enter the cell.

When the hormone meets the genes in the cell nucleus, particular reactions follow, resulting in specific molecules able to carry out special functions. These molecules include inert structural building blocks, enzymes to catalyze further reactions, and secondary hormones to carry new messages to other organs. We don't know exactly how the hormone affects a gene to cause a reaction, but we do know that hormone messengers get through only to properly equipped target cells. Breast cells, for example, respond to estradiol, the Leydig cells of the testes to the so-called lutenizing hormone (LH).

And it's the receiving cells, not the hormones, that determine the reaction. A single message on the police band tips off a criminal to flee and a squad car to pursue. Follicle-stimulating hormone, depending on where it alights, calls for sperm or egg follicles to grow.

The particular hormones germane to Mary Beth's drama belong to a large chemical family called the steroids, which include the so-called sex hormones, the androgens (literally, "male-producers") and the estrogens (literally the "frenzy-producers"—the first of many scientific distortions of female sexuality that we'll see). The two groups play so many crucial parts in reproductive anatomy, physiology, and behavior that it's probably legitimate to call them "sex hormones." But they appear in so many roles in so many places in both males and females that they are not "sex hormones" in the sense of belonging exclusively to one sex or the other. The testes, ovaries, and adrenal glands all produce both "male" and "female" types. Concentrations vary by gender, but also by species, age, time of day, time of month, and general state of health. For years, the richest source of "female" estrogens was the urine of stallions.

Chemically, all the sex hormones are close cousins in the steroid clan. Steroids regulate sexual differentiation and reproductive behavior, but also do jobs as diverse as responding to stress and retaining salt. But they all have a strong family resemblance; they descend from cholesterol, the complex fatty acid molecule. They all have a similar central structure of four carbon rings. The differences lie in the arrangements of the side chains. The pregnancy-supporting progestins have twenty-one carbon atoms, the androgens nineteen, and the estrogens eighteen. All these groups have several members, with very specific functions. And the individual hormones derive from cholesterol by a chain of small changes, each caused by the specific enzymes in particular glands and tissues. Testosterone frequently passes through several stages into estradiol, the main estrogen; this happens in the brains of rats and hamsters, and probably in our own as well. But this biochemical hide-and-seek vastly complicates attempts to track hormones or tie them to particular outcomes. Specifically, it has foiled many efforts to relate levels of circulating steroids to human behaviors and bodily states.

In fact, most of the chemicals really vital to gender routinely confound sexual typologies. Not even the H-Y antigen, long thought to be a basic male-maker, is exclusively masculine. In the laboratory, it turns human gonadal cells testicular, but chicken cells ovarian. What it really does is induce the gender that has two different sex chromosomes (the so-called heterogametic gender). In ourselves, that's the male, but in birds, it's the female. In all sexual species, the gender with two *similar* sex chromosomes (the homogametic) forms the ground plan of development, and the heterogametic gender is the detour.

Meanwhile, back at Alice's womb, the climactic event making Mary Beth a boy is about not to happen. Her newly activated testis is pumping out the requisite androgens. Receptor cells await the signal—most crucially, at this point, in the Wolffian duct, which cannot masculinize without it. Nor, in its absence, can other cells, biding their time in the brain, do so either.

And this is what did not happen: her cells took no notice of the androgen message. Years later, a sliver of skin from her fingertip showed doctors why: abnormal androgen receptors. A recessive trait on her single X chromosome produced faulty "antennae" in every cell in her body, leaving her totally insensitive to androgen. Ironically, she's even more insensitive than an XX woman carrying the same trait, who would likely have a normal gene on her second X. Some XY "women," with a slightly different defect, totally lack androgen receptors.

So Mary Beth's Wolffian organs didn't grow, depriving her of masculine innards. And her brain never became properly "primed" for manhood, depriving her of a masculine puberty. In that vast and dimly understood warren of cells, the androgen messengers failed to trigger another fetal function vital for future masculinity; scientists rather ambiguously term this process "organizing" the brain.

Vertebrate brains control, among other things, the immensely complex and varied processes of reproduction, and they normally come equipped with strategically located steroid receptors. Where these lie varies among species, but most often they cluster in sites related to reproductive behavior. Male songbirds can't court and mate unless they can sing, and the areas that control warbling and chirping, not surprisingly, respond to androgens. Rats are more silent, but no less ceremonious, suitors. For them, special postures invite and consent. The brain centers that control the male practice of mounting and the female one of lordosis (presenting the genitals for mating) respond to steroids as well.

But where do the androgens come to rest in the minuscule brain of a human fetus? We know that they bind to parts relating to reproduction, but can't entirely map these steroid-sensitive regions. Indeed, we know rather less about our own neural equipment than about that of many simpler creatures. Only by mutilating the brains and manipulating the hormones of living persons could we definitively map the neuroanatomy of behavior. And this lack of exact knowledge underlies the general confusion about what, besides very obviously reproductive functions, the "organizing" effect of fetal androgens might involve. We know this much for sure, though: the early androgens lay the groundwork for events that won't happen for more than a decade.

Months before birth, and a dozen years before puberty, the androgens "tune" certain cells to the hormones that will flood the body at sexual maturity. The sexes, of course, start out with the same androgen and estrogen receptors. But in early adolescence, like resistance fighters after patient years at their clandestine shortwaves, certain cells will rise to a long-awaited signal with the properly masculine response. At this point the human male will embark on his half-century career of almost constant reproductive readiness. And just as important, he will *not* embark on a female career. He will not begin to cycle—monthly among ourselves, biannually or annually in some other species. Midway between every two periods, a woman's pituitary releases a surge of LH. Part of an intricate chain of reactions among the hypothalamus, pituitary, and gonads that regulate the production of eggs (and sperm in men), this hormone spurt will trigger ovulation.

"The main difference between males and females," writes physician Susan Gordon, "is the absence of a surge of LH in the male."[1] Becoming functionally masculine, therefore, means suppressing this ability to cycle; clearly, therefore, one thing the fetal androgens do is suppress the capacity for the LH surge. In some species, androgens irreversibly suppress cyclicity. Others, including rats and some monkeys, retain a lifelong ability to cycle under proper hormone stimulation; without ovaries, though, they clearly can't ovulate. Neither can Mary Beth, despite the monthly LH surge (in an androgen-insensitive brain).

Puberty also brings other changes. The human body takes on one of two characteristic shapes. The pubic hair sprouts, in response to androgens. The reproductive organs come to maturity. In many species, the special behaviors involved in mating become frequent.

The androgen "tuning" is clearly an "extra" added to the basically female frame. An unknown something seems to protect fetal males from the large quantities of estrogens in their mothers' bloodstream, but fetal females have no such protection from any abnormal androgens that might get into their blood before or (in some species) soon after birth. Girls exposed to testosterone *in utero* masculinize to some extent. Natural and laboratory experiments have shown the same thing in rats, which make particularly good subjects because their sexual behaviors are so distinct. Females born in heavily male litters, and those located between brothers before birth, act more masculine than do those who spent the intrauterine time among sisters.

Can we see similar hormonal influence in our own actions? No question more sharply divides gender researchers. Everyone agrees that hormones have reproductive functions, but human action also comes under the much more complex and subtle influence of culture and consciousness. We don't—perhaps can't—discern the connection between prenatal chemicals and adult actions. Some theorists see hormones as instruments of command, exacting adherence to primordial social roles. Others see them as only one of many forces shaping our urges and actions. To see just how subtle the question becomes, consider a study that looked into the LH surge, that hallmark of the female brain.

What would happen if men could experience the spurt? To find out, researchers injected men and women with Premarin 4, an estrogen preparation, to mimic the mid-month spike. The two genders showed a "clear sexual difference in the LH response to Premarin."[2] But not all the men were created equal, apparently; the males also divided neatly—along lines of sexual preference. Men with strongly heterosexual histories showed one pattern; men with lifelong homosexual leanings showed another. No man showed a female response.

"This invites the idea," the researchers muse, "that there may be physiological development components in the sexual orientation of some homosexual men."[3] In other words, the developing brain may have been "primed" for homosexuality. Whether the same goes for less exclusively male-oriented men, the team cannot know. Still, a curiosity unhampered by scientific reserve can entertain tantalizing possibilities. Perhaps these men, and others like them the world over, represent—like Mary Beth—slight errors of the male-producing process. But like her, they're highly serviceable for most human purposes nonetheless.

Many a human body with slight defects gives a lifetime of worthy service. The survival of the species may depend on the ability to reproduce; the survival of individuals most decidedly does not. Scientists have isolated a number of these "sexual discordancy syndromes"—a bland term indeed for the mystery of Mary Beth. Hers is an extreme case; mismatches range all the way from such cataclysmic errors to slight, easily correctable genital anomalies in otherwise apparently normal persons.

Like Mary Beth's, their fate hinges on extremely tiny genetic or biochemical errors. The lack of a single enzyme can utterly distort the complex series of chemical steps that changes cholesterol into just the right hormone. Or a gland may malfunction, producing either too much or too little of a hormone, or the testes may fail to make the Mullerian-suppressing substance even though the androgen-driven virilization stage proceeds perfectly. That particular glandular lapse produces a normal-looking or almost normal-looking male who has, along with his standard-issue masculine reproductive gear, a uterus and fallopian tubes.

The virilization stage, while the male organs are taking shape, is even more vulnerable to error. Slip-ups here involve androgens, because estrogens are vital to life itself. An embryo without an adequate supply simply cannot implant in the uterus or survive even the few weeks until sexual differentiation begins.

Most common of the androgen failures is Mary Beth's, technically known as testicular feminization: apparent, though incomplete, female development in the presence of functioning testes. She had a shortish, blind vagina and no uterus at all. Surgeons constructed a usable vagina to permit her normal female sexual satisfaction, and also removed the useless testes to avoid possible malignancy.

Mary Beth embodies the most spectacular and covert gender error possible in a human being. Most others come to medical attention much earlier—at the moment when the obstetrician confronts obviously anomalous genitals.

All these conditions ring changes on Xs and Ys. An XY male with normal testes and androgen supply but cells partially insensitive to androgen has Reifenstein's syndrome. The Mullerian tract regresses normally, but too little of the androgen message gets through, leaving the Wolffian tract organs incomplete and the outer genitalia only vaguely masculine.

A roughly similar appearance can disguise a completely opposite history—congenital adrenal hyperplasia. A normally equipped XX female carries a recessive gene that upsets the adrenal cortex, producing too little cortisone and too much androgen. Internally she's female but externally she looks rather masculine. Surgery and hormones can produce normal-looking genitals and a normal puberty and adulthood.

Mary Beth's genes and hormones made her neither a girl nor a boy at birth, but her parents made her a woman for life. Cuddling her in a lacy pink quilt, Tom and Alice couldn't have known that they were assigning a social gender to a physical anomaly. But the parents of more obviously ambiguous children do know, and consciously choose their child's identity—usually the one that doctors can best mimic with surgery and hormones.

Children need to know very early where in our two-by-two universe they belong, so they can learn the skills and habits of their half. As early as one and a half or two, most kids have the idea. By three or four they suspect that their state is permanent; by five they know this for sure. Indeed, Jan Morris, the British writer who spent her first four decades as James Morris, the British writer, tells of knowing clearly, at the age of four, that, despite appearances, he was really a girl. Sitting under the piano in his childhood home, he realized that he was the victim of a cosmic hoax. No amount of contrary evidence—not boys' schools, not army service, not even fathering children—ever convinced him otherwise. His widely-known sex-change operation in middle age, and his immediate pleasure in life as a woman, merely confirmed a lifelong belief.

Morris's utter conviction of belonging to one sex and one only was not a psychotic delusion. It mirrors—if perhaps in a fun-house looking-glass—the nearly universal human trait of gender identity. Each of us knows, at the deepest level that we know anything, where we belong. Even delusional psychotics keep it straight; they think they're Jesus *or* the Virgin Mary, but hardly ever both or the wrong one.

But here human nature sneaks a wild card into the scientific deck. Although researchers can't know for sure, they believe this human phenomenon unique. No other animal possesses this fixed conception of itself in relation to its fellows; none other, indeed, seems to have the ability to entertain so abstract an idea. So every study relating physical features to behavior must, with its human subjects, consider this extra, and possibly confounding, factor. Does knowing make human experience simply incomparable to animal behavior? This is the crux of the nature-nurture debate.

Even so, "gender assignment" sounds very arbitrary, and sometimes it is. Parents and doctors pick a category and, through repeated acts of will, shape a person to fit. Viewers watching a film of the same infant saw "feminine" traits if they thought the child a girl and "masculine" ones if they thought it a boy. In one celebrated accident, twin boys underwent an experimental form of circumcision, which damaged one baby's penis beyond repair. With no hope of reconstructing a normal manhood, surgery, hormones, dolls, and frilly dresses ultimately made a satisfactorily "feminine," if sterile, girl.

The logic of these lives seems to derive from science fiction; on them hinges, though, one of the great debates about scientific fact. What, exactly, makes a human being a male or a female? Is Mary

Beth a girl because her body can't absorb androgens, or because everyone has always told her so? What makes CAH children into tomboys, too much androgen or too little confidence in the femininity of their odd-looking genitals? In laboratory animals, we can clearly track the hormones from the gonads, through specially sensitive portions of the brain, and on into unmistakably male or female actions. Some years ago, reports from the Caribbean promised to do the same in humans.

A group of related families in the Dominican Republic, it appeared, had involuntarily carried out the crucial experiment. They produced children whom they raised as females. In small villages of Spanish heritage, this meant a childhood learning to be helpful and submissive, a girlhood mastering the arts of modesty and allure. At puberty, however, these girls reportedly put away their dolls, grew phalluses, scrotums, beards, and body hair, and embarked on a youth of working, playing, and carousing with other young men.

"Hormonal influence proved!" announced the headlines. "Androgen overturns feminine socialization," declared the magazines. And indeed, the early reports did seem to indicate that children "unambiguously raised" as females could, with very little trouble and just a dose of androgen, fill the much more dominant and active social role of men. Biological scientists flocked to this tantalizing mystery and soon solved it: lacking a single enzyme that converts testosterone into the dihydrotestosterone needed to form the male external genitalia, these XY males did not appear at birth like the boys they were.

But social scientists followed too, and they made other observations. The genitals weren't exactly feminine, but as one observer put it, "profoundly ambiguous": a phalluslike clitoris, a pair of tiny scrotal sacs flanking a small opening, and inside the folds that in women become labia and in males become scrota, a pair of perfectly normal testes.

And observers noticed the villagers' lives in the humid tropics: small, crowded houses, with numbers of relatives sleeping in a single room; a rather casual attitude toward modesty in small children; communal bathing in a nearby stream. Could these children's very odd genitals really have escaped adult notice? Could relatives and friends really have regarded such babies as true females? And could the children themselves, as they grew up, fail to notice that they differed from other girls? Wasn't it just possible that a culture with a severe standard of masculinity and a strict division by sex simply assigned them to the category they most resembled, which was also the markedly less prestigious sex?

The villagers, it turned out, had not failed to notice. They even had invented names for this special kind of child, chiefly *huevadoce,* or "eggs at twelve." (Spanish slang uses "eggs" for testicles in exactly the sense that English uses "balls": it even has the same overtones of boldness and pride.) Others frankly spoke of *machihembras,* or "male-females." So the villagers knew, at least after the first few cases, that these weren't true girls and shouldn't be raised as such.

American-born children who carried out the same involuntary experiment produced an opposite result: girls who remained women even after their bodies became those of men. The scant privacy and strict role definitions of Dominican society imposed one solution, the more liberal U.S. conditions—where the social premium on manhood is rather smaller than in a poor, machismo culture—permitted another.

So the Dominican pseudo hermaphrodites, as the scientific literature calls them, prove not to be girls who become boys, after all. And the lesson, if any, that they can teach us about the uses of hormones in human life is also less striking than it first appeared to be.

Indeed, note Robert Goy and Bruce McEwen, leading students of this entire vexed question, "it has been argued that the effects of prenatal hormones on behavior [speaking here of animals] can be better accounted for by changes in peripheral organs than by modification of the central nervous system."[4] Large doses of testosterone shortly after birth give a female rat a clitoris that resembles a penis, whereas castration of a male at the same time makes him grow an inadequate phallus. Could these abnormal organs account for their owners' anomalous sexual behavior? If so, "no changes in the central nervous system have to be assumed."[5]

All the anomalies we've seen so far occur in persons with the normal number of sexual genes. The Y, with its small stock of genetic information, can't by itself map out a viable human being, but even a single X can and does. A lone X instead of a 23rd pair (usually written as XO) results in Turner's syndrome, a short, squat person with very low levels of androgens and vaguely feminine genitals. The literature generally considers these persons females, and they're assigned and raised as such. But they're not true physiological—or even genetic—women; though they have Mullerian internal organs, they have undifferentiated streaks in place of ovaries. And they have a particular form of mental retardation that, as we'll later note, has taken on theoretical importance as a presumably pure, if imperfect, example of X-chromosome mentality. But as psychologist Rhoda Unger observes, "they are defined as female simply because of the inadequacy of our dichotomous classification system for sex." She views them as "essentially neuter individuals whose external genitalia are similar to those of females."[6]

This isn't the only faulty deal off the chromosomal deck. Living combinations include XXY, XYY, XXXY, XYYY, and probably others as well. In the early 1960s, Richard Speck's ghastly murder of Chicago nurses splashed the XYY across the nation's tabloids. Scientists quickly linked the "supermaleness" of a double dose of Y to all manner of aggressive, violent, antisocial behavior. Large numbers turned up in prisons, often for repeated or horrible crimes of violence. (The fact that scientists looked on death rows but not in monasteries, universities, or the flute sections of orchestras may or may not account for this apparent propensity for mayhem.) We don't know the XYY frequency in the general population, but lots of them later turned up among the law-abiding, too.

One thing that multiple-Y men do seem to share is uncommon height; they may show up as often on basketball teams as on chain gangs, one observer suggests. Long extremities go with the Y, as witness Mary Beth's tall, leggy figure—what her admirers regarded as her most womanly trait. A more typical woman is shorter and rather short-legged. Androgen-insensitive XY individuals, ironically, make very handsome women, at least by the standards of a society that admires a long, coltish frame.

We may not have learned what gender is, but we've gotten insight into what it's not: simple, straightforward, and absolute. Some of us don't even know where in the two-by-two parade they belong.

We can't say for sure where gender resides: in the genes, or in the hormones, or in the brain, or in the eye of the beholder. There are clearly more than two ways to be human.

But still, the great mass of our species marches in the same two-part parade as all our close or inconceivably distant cousins, the mammals, the birds, the vertebrates generally, even the earthworms and snails. We step to a tune that sounds in nearly faultless variations across great stretches of time. It echoes through our entire past as communicating creatures, as upright creatures, even as creatures that crawl or slither on land. We step to a tune that sets the melody and rhythm of our lives, both as animals and as social creatures.

Each of us has heard this tune all our lives, and all the life of our species. Nothing seems more obvious and natural. But of all the puzzles this book will try to untangle, or all the mysteries we try to explain, the greatest is also the simplest. No one knows for sure why living things have gender at all.

2

Why Is Gender?

The short answer is that nobody knows for sure.

Scientists have spun a good many long answers in the 13 decades since Darwin, winding through disciplines and theories, weaving among cases and facts, but, always ending up with some loose ends dangling. We've yet to find a neat reason why so many species reproduce in so singularly costly and complicated a manner.

We used to think we knew, but even before Darwin, the accepted answer didn't wholly satisfy. Genesis reports that the Lord made Eve to provide Adam company. That's an argument for another person, not another *kind* of person. Of course, the Lord also made the first couple to be fruitful and multiply; but the Creator of a whole universe out of nothing, the Designer of the exquisite differentiation mechanism we just examined, could certainly solve the far less taxing problem of fashioning creatures who simply popped out copies of themselves. Indeed, so inventive and powerful a deity hardly needed help from His creatures at all.

Graham Bell, a deep student of the problem, finds this all intensely frustrating. "Sex would be merely a curiosity," he writes, "if it were not so widespread amongst animals and plants." But nearly everyone does it, he finds, from critters that creep on the ocean floor or root permanently in lonely crevasses, up to and including ourselves. If that weren't puzzling enough, we all do it in just about the same way; our chromosome sets split apart and, in an elaborate gavotte, sort themselves into partial sets that eventually join up with other partial sets. Ultimately each chromosome ends up with a new partner and each offspring with the same number of chromosomes as its parents. "The combination of intricacy and uniformity makes it impossible to interpret sexuality as other than a highly adaptive character," Bell muses, "precisely sculpted by selection to fulfill a function of central importance in the economy of a multitude of species."[1] The only trouble is that he doesn't know what that function may be.

To further complicate the issue, Bell believes that any reasonable discussion must clearly distinguish sex, gender, and reproduction, each of which occurs separately in the minuscule world where gender first arose. By "sex" he means genetic recombination, the dance and shuffle of the chromosomes; by "gender," the distinction between males and females, where it exists, which is not everywhere; by "reproduction," the making of new individuals.

In creatures like us, these three go together like the proverbial horse and carriage. But they didn't first evolve in large, complex, multicellular creatures like us. To reproduce, a simple creature need only pack up a clear copy of its chromosomes along with sufficient protoplasm for a start in life. The ability to make the copies is built into the helical structure of DNA, the basic stuff of genes. Thousands of tiny species simply knock off a second set, surround it with some protoplasm, and split, bud, or throw off a complete second self.

True sexual reproduction requires something more—the knack of making haploid cells (called gametes) that contain half the normal number of chromosomes (one from each pair). But sex in this sense doesn't require a partner. The first sexual creatures practiced what the evolutionary geneticists call automixis: they combine two of their own haploid cells. They somehow hit on a scheme that, for only a small investment of extra effort, offers a useful advantage: more diverse offspring than stamping out carbon copies could possibly produce. The next evolutionary step, amphimixis, involves sex but not gender. Two separate individuals combine their haploid cells. But there's no egg, no sperm, no male, no female; everyone simply ejects structurally identical cells into the surrounding sea.

We don't reach gender, in fact, until we reach creatures sufficiently complex and sufficiently committed to sex to need—and afford—a bit of specialization. One parent, the female, tacks on a supply of food, making a rather larger, but also longer-lived, gamete. The other parent, the male, produces a stripped-down version equipped to hunt down a slow, cumbersome, moving target. The female, because she packs more into each cell, produces fewer, but more durable, gametes. The male continues high-volume production of the economy model.

Gender, therefore, has both large advantages and substantial costs. It permits quite complex, highly variable offspring who enjoy a period of protection they need for a good start. But it cuts by at least half the number of offspring each parent could produce if no one needed a partner. It even cuts the number possible under amphimixis. Instead of everyone churning out young as fast as they can absorb the necessary nourishment, now an entire class, the males, must waste most of their gametes in a futile hunt for the suddenly scarcer eggs.

And this is what has stumped generations of scientists: What's the advantage of reproducing so expensively? The arrangement that Darwin called "nature's masterpiece" appears to fetch a very high price. But the one thing that everyone agrees on is that advantage there must be. The logic of post-Darwinian biology demands that changes in the basic economy of life happen only when they confer some benefit in the struggle to keep on keeping on.

That this is so is the basic postulate of the theory of evolution, and thus a statement about the way the world works. Pious ignoramuses to the contrary, there is nothing "theoretical" about this understanding of how life functions on this planet. Its factuality rests on a gigantic body of interlocking evidence from sciences as diverse as geology, anatomy, and biochemistry.

In simplest terms, the theory of evolution says this: heritable features of living things change through natural processes that alter the distribution of genes in populations. A number of processes, prominent among them natural selection, might be responsible. Organic evolution affects only traits that individuals possess and can transmit through their genes. Thus, in a simple and famous example, a population of English moths became darker and darker as factories went up in the neighborhood. Highlighted against the town's new film of soot, light-colored moths made easy prey for birds, whereas darker ones found themselves helpfully camouflaged. The proportion of dark genes naturally grew.

So we can explain changes in reproduction only by finding what made the proportion of sexual or gender genes increase in given populations. We know lots of reasons why the change didn't happen. It didn't happen, for example, to lay the groundwork for more advanced creatures like ourselves. As our example makes clear, natural selection is arbitrary and capricious. A town clean-up campaign might well have produced a lighter moth. Evolution doesn't drive toward any particular goal, it has no impetus to create "higher" life forms or "improve" a breed. Secondly, change doesn't take place in order to create new traits. Selection can choose only from among the traits already present. Finally, change doesn't happen to help a species. Selection works on individuals, only rarely on whole populations, and then only when they all have the trait being selected against. Individuals live or die, individuals reproduce or not, individuals keep their offspring alive or fail to. Evolution doesn't occur "for the good of a species." Indeed, it doesn't occur "for" any purpose whatever, any more than gravity exists "so that" furniture won't go flying off into space.

Basically, evolution has this result: over time, and in an environment that doesn't change too drastically, genetics and selection combine to produce creatures that live and reproduce fairly efficiently.

But exactly how does sex help? (We start with sex because it's an even stiffer puzzle than gender.) The moths on the fence give an important hint: some survived because they had a color that proved unexpectedly useful. Parents with only one kind of offspring put all their genes in one selective basket.

But making several different kinds means that each offspring gets a different combination of the parental genes. A parent practicing apomixis—not making haploid cells but simply passing on, intact, carbon copies of its own genes—can't produce variety. It can't even produce offspring that express all the variation theoretically possible from its own genetic complement, because its genes can never occur in new combinations. Recessives permanently married to dominants, for example, can never be expressed.

Even automicts, which shuffle their own haploid cells into different combinations, can produce a moderate degree of diversity. Long-hidden recessives can become living traits. But more of the offspring will die as lethal or undesirable recessives produce individuals that can't survive. (Geneticists call this "inbreeding depression".)

Amphimicts—joining haploid cells from two parents—are the real diversity champs, but also the biggest spenders of their reproductive resources. So here's the real poser: when the first amphimictic parents sent their gametes out into the great world to find mates, that world was already full of long-established, self-fertilizing (parthogenic) competitors gobbling up what nourishment and sunlight the primeval sea afforded. Our newcomers could survive only by wresting their share away from more practiced opponents. They could prevail only by wresting *more* than their share. Hindsight tells us that they succeeded. The question is: How?

Exactly how, in other words, did they overwhelm rivals that greatly outnumbered them? What the parthogenics lacked in variety, they more than made up for in the sheer quantity of offspring they could cheaply and relentlessly grind out. Nothing could beat them on that score, not even the self-fertilizing automicts, which had to turn out two reproductive cells per offspring, to the apomict's one. Amphimicts also faced the immense cost of finding a mate; even today, millions of human sperm perish for every one that turns into a full-term baby.

Obviously, sex could take hold only in a situation where its advantages heavily outweighed its tremendous costs. And the problem that has bedeviled generations of theorists becomes clear: What combination of circumstances could possibly favor those advantages long enough for the new system to become established in the face of more efficient competitors? "Biology is not physics," Bell reminds us; "our abstractions must not refer to supposed universals, but instead must be tailored quite precisely to the curious details of what, from an infinity of possibilities, has actually evolved."[2]

We can quickly discard some long-cherished possibilities. Regardless of what your eighth-grade science teacher said, sex didn't evolve for the ultimate good of any species or to prepare living things for an uncertain future. We can also reject the notion that reshuffling, by producing more heterozygotes, allows a population to rid itself of undesirable recessives. It's true that automixis—the earliest form of sex—does permit this to happen most rapidly. But the species sloughs off bad genes only by sloughing off the individuals who carry them; it's just another name for a higher death rate.

Of course, combining gametes does also produce homozygous carriers of the best genes. Could these outstanding specimens produce huge numbers of offspring to counteract other losses? Probably not, because such a huge advantage implies very strong selection in their favor, and that implies a radical change in the environment just as they appeared on the scene. But radical changes don't appear often enough to explain why sexuality is so common. So far, instead of sweeping the world, sex ought to have simply died out.

But, Bell points out, a slight variation in any number of things—the temperature, or the amount of light penetrating the water, or the chemicals found at a certain spot, or the numbers of other creatures nearby, or the strength of a current—would spell a very big difference to something small enough. If we imagine the world from the standpoint of a tiny creature afloat in the ocean, where conditions vary over very short distances, we can begin to understand how having variable offspring might mean a real advantage—as long as sex didn't cost too much. And at this level, it doesn't; the parent merely combines two of its own haploid cells.

Now, this tiny creature competes with others much like itself, except that they reproduce by cloning; entire populations consist of absolutely identical individuals. Wherever the asexual clones are best adapted, the sexual individuals can't get a toehold; as a group —and for the most part, as individuals—the sexuals are less perfectly adapted. But in a rather variable environment, such ideal spots are scarce and sought after. In them, all the identical clone siblings compete with each other.

But in spots less desirable to the clones, the sexual brood has a chance of putting forth a member or two better adapted than any the clone can produce. And the sexuals needn't compete as fiercely with their own siblings, which are not as ideally equipped for this particular niche.

If the sexual creatures in such an environment can fairly cheaply and continuously produce large numbers of varied offspring—and small automicts decidedly can—then it is conceivable, and mathematically demonstrable, that they can overtake the breeding power of an asexual competitor. The clones have a single shot at adapting to the new environment. But the sexual species can turn out endless new variations until some of them hit the bull's-eye.

And so, points out pioneer researcher George Williams, sexual reproduction does have selective advantage for highly fecund creatures. Ironically, though, that doesn't include us mammals. Our numbers come nowhere close to exploiting our theoretical ability to throw off countless somewhat different offspring. Indeed, large, slow breeders with gender pay such high costs that we would quickly lose out to any direct competitor that could breed more cheaply.

So why do we remain sexual? Because evolution chooses only among the variable traits of reproductively active creatures. And the presence of sex is never a variable trait among the reproductively active members of sexual species. Every mammal, bird, insect, and fish must possess sex to reproduce in the first place, so we have absolutely no chance of developing a capacity to reproduce asexually.

So the benefits of sex and gender to creatures like ourselves turn out to pose no mystery at all. The mystery arose simply because we asked the wrong question and looked for something that doesn't— and never did—exist. We large creatures are not sexual because sexuality confers advantages on *us*. We're merely the descendents of distant, microscopic ancestors who found sex so very advantageous to *them* that they lost the option of ever reproducing in any other way.

So we were not even a gleam in evolution's eye when sex first appeared. Still, sexual species succeeded in colonizing countless niches everywhere. At some point, some of them stumbled onto the idea of tacking a food packet onto the gamete, and invented the egg. Incidentally, this CARE package also increased the reproductive chances of the gamete that mated with the egg.

Where there had previously been only one successful strategy— shoot out as many gametes as possible—there were now two. A would-be parent could either continue in the old way, producing the equivalent of sperm, or turn out somewhat fewer of the much better equipped new-style eggs. In the new system, each gamete cost more, so egg producers were putting their genes into even fewer baskets. But the increased survival chances from an on-board food supply must have hedged bets sufficiently to make this an effective gamble in many, many environments.

The eminent scientists who elaborated this theory didn't mean, of course, that tiny worms or protists with the merest speck of neural matter analyze their prospects and make a conscious choice. Much evolutionary writing does seem to imply just such sophisticated judgments by some of the world's least intelligent creatures— or perhaps by their totally insentient genes. What the writers really mean is that some creatures act in ways that turn out advantageously and so get to pass their genes on. And if their choice of that behavior depends at all on the genes, then future generations will tend to make the same choice too; if advantageous enough, the choice may come to predominate.

This rather messy and costly process of false starts and high mortality is what serious students of evolution mean when they use expressions like "adopting the optimal strategy." They could not mean otherwise, knowing that in most species, leaving descendents that reproduce is the exception. Only plants make new food; every other organism on earth survives by eating someone else's descendents. But evolutionary theorists don't study the daily struggles of individual organisms; they consider gene distributions in whole populations. And they think about them mathematically, using a particular verbal shorthand to report their results in English. In this language, words like "strategy" and "response" refer to mathematical abstractions, not to the motivations of animals or plants.

Still, our two main strategies don't work without suitable tactics. Consider the odds against finding a mate by simply scattering your gametes into the surrounding water. Clearly, with lots of species-mates nearby, the best bet might be to turn out as many sperm as possible, because the odds of running across a mate fairly soon are reasonably good. That, of course, is the male approach: a shotgun blast of the cheapest shot possible. But living farther from your fellows calls for gametes that can survive for a while; the female approach of packing a picnic makes sense there. Clearly, then, individuals in patchy environments, not having much control over their locations, have the best chance of passing on their genes if they can size up their circumstances and act accordingly.

Consider, therefore, the cautious nematode, a type of tiny unsegmented worms that start life without any particular gender and go out into the world to seek their fortunes as parasites on insects and plants. They quickly get a worm's-eye view of gender, which comes down to two ways of filling their bellies. A male can get along on fairly little food, because making sperm doesn't demand much energy. But a female needs lots of calories to pack into her eggs; she has to be bigger and so needs a bigger food supply. So where food competition is stiff, a worm is better off as a male. Thus, an unformed youngster lost in a crowd faces a choice. "It can become," report biologists Eric Charnov and James Bull, "an average male or a below average female."[3] So nematodes solve the food problem neatly: those that find crowded hosts become male, but those in easier circumstances adopt the more luxurious strategy of the female.

This strategic worm isn't alone in its wait-and-see approach to gender. Bonellia, a marine invertebrate, also has large females and small males, but only the males are parasitic, living frankly, and literally, on the females. "Larvae that settle alone become females," note Charnov and Bull, "those that attach to females become males."[4] The big egg-layer aggressively fends for herself; the little sperm-producer goes along for the ride, always on the spot when his services are needed.

This pattern of the large, aggressive female and the small, dependent male occurs again and again among marine animals. In many sea-born environments, a female's main competitors for food and other resources are not, as on land, the males of her own species, but other females and their young.

The amphirion solves this problem very neatly. It must live on a particular kind of sea anemone that occurs only on widely scattered coral reefs. Waiting for a mate to happen by could thus spell extinction. But, report Hans and Simone Fricke, the female amphirion meets all her reproductive needs through the elegant device of controlling "production of [competing] females by aggressive dominance over males."[5] Amphirions are monagamists and live *en famille,* sort of. Their social groups consist of "a large female, a single smaller male, and a varying number of subadults and juveniles, none of which is offspring of the adult pair."[6]

Young amphirions—they all start out male—leave home at a tender age. Most anemones are already taken, so they usually have to join an established household, despite a rather cool welcome. The largest and oldest member—always a female—dominates each group, attacking, with her mate's help, any smaller, lower-ranking male that gets out of line. The beta male (second in the group but first among the males) particularly keeps his eye on the pretentions of the next-ranking gamma male, which, like all those of lesser status, is "psychophysiologically castrated" by continual abuse. As long as the top couple stay together, nothing changes. But when alpha dies, the largest male—generally beta, her mate—promptly takes her place, turning female in the process. The long-suffering gamma now reaps his reward as the new beta, the only sexually active male and mate to his former nemesis. Thus, in a system that neatly maximizes the production of eggs and keeps on tap a constant stag line of eager swains, "females control the procreation of other females. They restrict the size of the breeding population and actively suppress males which are likely candidates for future females."[7]

Amphirion transsexualism is a one-way proposition. If two males find themselves paired off, the larger becomes a female. If fate casts two females together, however, the smaller has no way back to the comparative safety of maleness. Instead, the larger simply does her in.

Another coral reef fish, the *Anthias squamipinnis,* bases a similar approach on opposite logic. Here, everyone starts out female. Social groups consist of a single male and several females; at his demise, the largest female turns male. The change, write Goy and McEwen, leading authorities on the neurology of sex difference, is "surprisingly rapid," considering that it includes "transformation to the color pattern, gonadal histology, and behaviour of the normal male."[8] But even more surprisingly, the other females apparently play a vital part in the change. Before a human observer can detect any signs, they know it's coming; they've already begun treating the changer as a male. Indeed, report Douglas Shapiro and Ralf

Boulon, *Anthias* chroniclers, the change seems to require a group of at least three adult females in the chorus. In some mysterious fashion they stimulate the understudy to step into the new role. Shapiro and Boulon even believe that peer pressure itself somehow causes the change, through links to "a particular value of behavioral interaction within the group. When the value of that measure for any individual changes beyond some critical amount, that individual would change sex."[9]

The subtlety and complexity of amphirion and *Anthias* sexuality indicate a long evolutionary past. But to us they seem to violate the very nature of gender, which is permanence; in fact, they only exploit the advantage of less than total specialization. Piscine genetic systems retain possibilities that mammals lost long ago.

Unlike our own, both the X and Y chromosomes of a fish retain enough information to produce a new individual. Hormone manipulation can even make an XY fish embryo a functional female. Mated to an XY male, she can produce the usual XY and XX offspring, but also viable YY males. Some species, like platyfish, have even more options. Their three possible sex genes produce five combinations: XY and YY males and XX, WX, and WY females. (WW doesn't occur, because only females carry W.)

Before our distant ancestors had genders, they had a single version of the chromosomal blueprint for reproduction. As gender developed, plans for the second strategy became encoded as well, and in some evolutionary lines different information became strictly segregated on two distinct kinds of chromosomes. Somewhere along the immensely long pathway separating fish from mammals, therefore, our ancestors lost much of the primordial Y's information; across species and even phyla X chromosomes resemble one another much more closely than do Ys. Different lines lost different information from their Ys; these losses may well have coincided with the process that finally committed the mammals' ancestors to inalterable gender determined at conception.

What we gave up in flexibility, though, we more than got back in specialization. Simple creatures can rapidly change gender because their gender doesn't entail much commitment. Both males and females simply eject gametes from their bodies, and apart from perhaps scaring off obvious predators, do little to protect or nurture their young.

But large or complex offspring need time, and food, and safety. And animals in environments favoring size do well to produce larger, more costly eggs that can safely grow into larger, more complex young. Higher unit cost of course implies smaller numbers; so it makes sense to protect the investment.

Animals find wildly different solutions to this common problem. Pipefish and seahorse fathers carry fertilized eggs in a special broodpouch, nourishing them through a placentalike attachment to the fathers' own bloodstream. Emperor penguin fathers, on the other hand, valiantly cuddle their mate's single egg through the ferocious Antarctic winter. The young spend the long season of killing cold growing inside the shell; no small creature could possibly retain enough heat to survive. The egg is sizeable, therefore; it must provide several months' food. The fathers' feat of endurance uses their feet—and a special insulated pouch just above them—to balance the egg off the bare, frozen ground. Only the warmth of his own body keeps the chick from freezing.

But this strategy condemns the fathers to near starvation as they huddle together, unprotected, against the brutal wind. The Antarctic winter affords them no nourishment at all, and they survive until spring on the rapidly dwindling stocks of fat built up the previous summer. The females, meanwhile, spend a relatively temperate winter feeding at sea. They must abandon their mates and young for the sake of posterity: if they spent their fat wintering at home, they wouldn't have the energy to produce a viable egg the following summer.

We have a term for the selfless devotion of those emperor fathers: mother love. But that's our mammalian bias speaking, flowing from a long-ago choice to protect and nourish our young inside the mother's body. Among many mammals, in fact, she's completely on her own through pregnancy, birth, and rearing. The father may contribute nothing more than half the genes of the offspring and often competes with the mother for food. But certain males not only father the young, but partially mother them too.

One such paragon, surprisingly, is the wolf, no heartless philanderer, despite his reputation, but really the most devoted of family men. Wolves live with lifetime mates in mixed-sex packs. Each year a female member bears several cubs, whom all the adults help rear. The mother nurses for a few weeks while the others provide food. Right after weaning, she resumes her true career as a hunter. Pack members babysit, bring food, help to teach hunting skills.

Canines apparently became "wolves" when they joined forces with Homo sapiens. Male domestic dogs, observes biologist Roberta L. Hall, have lost "the ability, interest, or training to participate in pair bonding and the rearing of offspring."[10] Perhaps two wolf parents caring for a litter inconvenienced humans in need of reliable hunting companions willing to relinquish their catch. Perhaps human help partially replaced the males. However it happened, female domestic dogs took over the responsibility their wild ancestors had shared with others. This drastically changed the whole economy of their lives; male dogs and female wolves can still produce—but not rear—viable pups. She isn't the full-charge mother he expects; he isn't the nurturing father she needs.

Still, no one who has watched a pet dog bear and rear a litter can doubt that she understands at some level deep in her being what she must do: find and prepare a safe place to give birth, whelp her pups alone, carry them safely in her mouth, nurse and clean them, keep them corralled, wean them, and then return to her other life without regret. She even knows roughly how many of them there are. How can a creature that needs many trials to learn the simple connection between dinner bell and feeding time carry out this exacting performance faultlessly on the first try? And how did her first domesticated ancestors elaborate practices that differ so markedly from those of their own wild forebears, the wolves?

The answer, on one level, is easy: selection—certainly helped along by humankind—shaped the domestic dog to her new circumstances. To argue that just the right mutation came along when needed violates both the logic and spirit of evolutionary theory. Some wolf mothers must have taken better than average care of their cubs, and some wolf father worse. By selectively breeding for these desirable traits, human beings made them the norm in the domesticated breeds.

But on a deeper level, this simple answer only begs the question.

How does evolution, a process affecting gene distributions in populations, come to affect the behavior of an individual organism? What accounts for the "remarkable and supremely efficient fit between behavior and the demands on a species" that struck William Redican and David Taub as they studied many animal parents?[11] Perhaps, in the case of a dog, it's "instinct," or, in the more fashionable jargon of the computer age, "hard-wiring," in the animal's nervous system. But some theorists advance this argument about human mothering and fathering too. Does it also hold good for us?

Of course, certain categories of our behavior may well be "hardwired." We clearly have a natural propensity for language, for symbolic communication. (Some of our great ape cousins appear to have a bit too.) But it's the *capacity* for language that's built in, not the irregular verbs. It takes years to master a mother tongue, and few people can learn a second language with native fluency beyond middle childhood. And there are some who never properly learn a tongue; but feral children and the severely retarded don't become less human for being nonverbal.

And even though it's a safe genetic bet that a baby born today will be speaking fluently three years from now, we have no genetic means for predicting whether it will be in Bhil or Bantu or Brooklynese. To pin that down, we need to know the details of a particular biography. Only they will reveal why someone drops terminal *r*'s or uses sentence structure showing the influence of rural Swedish.

"There is absolutely no factual justification", observed the great student of animal behavior, Theodore Schneirla, "for the conclusion that the adaptiveness of such group behavior [as wolf packs caring for their young or human beings using creole French or army ants migrating in response to food depletion] accounts in any way for the events in individual behavior through which it works."[12] In other words, the fact that our species *needs* us to speak doesn't explain how we acquire a working knowledge of the subjunctive.

Schneirla is making a subtle distinction—but one that becomes crucial in the discussions ahead—between two senses of a common word, "innate." Geneticists use it to mean that you can predict an individual's traits if you know the distribution of traits in the parental population; in a two-legged, language-using group, chances are good that any newborn will have two legs and learn to talk. But other sciences use "innate" to mean something entirely different, what animal behaviorist Daniel Lehrman calls "developmental fixity," the fact that a trait is "impervious to environmental effects during development."[13] To say that language is innate in this second sense would amount to predicting that the child must speak American English of the Middle Atlantic variety because its parents are from Philadelphia.

Does it make any more sense to argue that parental behavior, clearly crucial for species survival, arises from animal genes and "hard-wiring"? Evolutionary theorists and others who know more about computers than about animals often think that it does. But close students of animal behavior have their doubts. Famous studies of primates and "cloth mothers" have shown that animals deprived of good mothering grow into incompetent mothers themselves.

Even animals as unintelligent as male ducks have to *learn* that most basic skill of reproduction, picking a suitable mate. A drake favors females of the species that raised him, even if not his own. A female, though, usually favors her own species regardless of who reared her.

This paradox has a good evolutionary explanation. Each species' males have brilliant and distinctive plumage; females can easily be "hard-wired" to seek a certain bar at the shoulder or pattern on the back. But all adult females have dull, indeterminate, "cryptic" plumage that is difficult to see, let alone identify, at any distance. So only the finer points can lead males to genetically suitable objects of their affections.

Thus, Lehrman argues, the fact that a trait (such as a male duck's desire for lady ducks) is hereditary "by no means demonstrates that the *same* characteristic cannot be influenced by environment."[14] He offers as exhibit B that old friend from high school biology, the fruitfly, *Drosophila melanogaster,* and a particular mutation that causes abnormal wings; the exact configuration depends on the ambient temperature during growth. Thus, "different flies of a single genotype [that is, with identical genes] may be able to fly normally, weakly, or not at all, depending on the temperature at which they were raised," Lehrman notes, in another clear case of environmental influence on a selectively important hereditary trait.[15] But, he goes on, suppose that the flies bearing this mutation happened to live in only a narrow range of temperature. Well, scientists would clearly conclude that environment had no influence on wing development, even though in fact it did. They would not have established the trait's imperviousness to experience, only their experiment's inability to tell the difference.

We have to bear this possibility firmly in mind, because Redican and Taub do not in the least exaggerate the wonder of animals' behavioral adaptations. Birds present a particularly dazzling array of possibilities for keeping young alive. Either sex, or both, or neither, may build a nest. The New World cowbirds and African indigoes build none at all; the female simply lays her eggs in the nests of unobservant neighbors, who obligingly rear the young interlopers as their own. Canary females build a single nest. The male European wren builds several, which he shows off to his lady love. She chooses the one where she will lay her eggs, first giving it a soft lining of her own feathers.

But laying the eggs only begins the work of avian parenthood. The embryo must stay warm until ready to hatch. Among songbirds, fowl, and hummingbirds, the female incubates by sitting. Dove and parrot couples share the duty, with the female on the night shift. Sanderlings lay their eggs in two clutches and one parent incubates each. Rhea and phalarope fathers bear the sole responsibility. The male bush turkey also goes fatherhood alone, but doesn't take his responsibility sitting down. In a unique display of technological extravagance, he opts not for a nest but for central heating. As breeding time approaches, he, like other birds, starts collecting vegetable matter. But unlike them, he puts his into a compost heap. As it begins to ferment, he carefully tests the temperature with his beak, stirring and mixing until satisfied that it's just right. Only then does he allow his mate to lay her eggs atop it. Then he covers them carefully with sand and she goes away. He maintains a solitary vigil until the chicks hatch, monitoring the temperature of his pile and even regulating it by adding or removing sand as needed.

Mating behavior varies just as widely. Some birds are faithful lifelong monogamists, others the wildest libertines, mating as often and as widely as their fancies dictate. Some males fashion elaborate bowers where they attempt to entice nubile females. Others form immense stag lines, where they strut, prance, caper, and fight to attract a lady's eye. Some achieve their goal through gorgeous plumage; others live a happy home life in feathers of dull gray-brown. And, as we've seen, even closely related mammals also take strikingly different approaches to breeding and rearing. What can account for such vast variety in what began as two simple strategies?

"In all sexually reproducing species, and especially among verte-brates," writes anthropologist Melvin Konner, "several facts about males can be predicted from the degree to which they participate in or abstain from direct care of the female's offspring."[16] Monoga-mous family men (in what biologists call "pair-bonding species"), faithful to a mate through a season or a lifetime, help with the chores of parenthood: carrying the young, feeding them, some-times even chewing their food. Their dowdy style matches their homebody ways; the sexes are alike in size and appearance, and neither has elaborate ornaments. Like the penguins or the seahorses, certain males even have special body parts designed for nurturing.

But some creatures are enthusiastic playboys (technically known as "tournament species"). They don't form durable bonds with fe-males, but simply "score," and certain individuals rack up consider-ably higher scores than others. In extreme cases, as among elephant seals, a small number of heavy hitters can account for half, even three-quarters, of the copulations in their neighborhood during an entire breeding season. Their disappointed rivals must content themselves with milling, disgruntled, on the sidelines. A single seal has been known to father more than two hundred young during his four-season career as champion.

As the name implies, members of these species compete ardu-ously, even dangerously, for the attentions of females. Reindeer, mountain sheep, and seals literally joust—ramming, biting, battling until victors emerge. Other species achieve the same end by es-thetic means; the males grow spectacular ornaments or stage pro-duction numbers (called leks) to catch the female fancy. Like Phila-delphia mummers on New Year's Day, decked in brilliant feather fans, ruffs, and spangles, they gather at a river bank or a certain grove of trees. Their audience, the receptive females, assembles nearby. Before these exacting connoisseurs the males dance, sing, cavort through the air—whatever is their own species' way of showing off beauty and agility to best advantage. Some species even present two-man acrobatic acts. The females then choose, lining up if necessary to await the services of a particular star.

But neither the dandies nor the toughs count for much on the home front; indeed, their fine feathers would endanger the helpless young by attracting attention to the nest and its delicious and vulnerable contents, which the incubating females, in their dull cryptic (literally, "hidden") plumage, endeavor to keep safe from predators.

Indeed, a striking feature of the tournament species is just how different the males and females look. Males are often much larger than females—double or even triple their weight, as among elephant seals. They may also have appurtenances and appendages that females lack. The reindeer's majestic antlers, the peacock's lavish tail, make sense only as parts of the intense annual competition for copulations.

The bucks or cocks that can out bash or out flash their rivals get to leave their genes to the next generation. Continued over even a few generations, let alone the thousands in the archeological record, the tournament system obviously favors the traits most germane to competition: size, weight, great horns, huge antlers, lavish plumage. Darwin called pressure for competitive advantage "sexual selection," and he concluded that it affects males far more than females. In most species, he surmised, a fertile female gets to mate as often as she wishes, so none produces an enormously larger number of young than the others. Theoretically, therefore, the degree of difference between the sexes in the sexually selected characteristics (the difference in tail size between a peacock and a peahen, or in horn size between a ram and a ewe, or in body size between a bull and cow seal) ought to reflect the difference between their potential numbers of offspring. The less faithful the males, the larger they and their antlers and muscles and tails ought to be.

In the 1970s, during the heady early years of sociobiology, an innovative young theorist named Robert Trivers carried this theory a step further. He related the degree of sexual dimorphism—the clear differences in appearance, structure, behavior, or whatever, within a species—to what he called parental investment: the percentage of an individual's total reproductive potential that he or she devotes to each offspring. A female that spends months or years bearing and rearing her few offspring, he reasoned, has more at stake in each of them than does a male that spends a few minutes in casual copulation. Each existing progeny is a real obstacle to the mother's bearing and caring for others; she'd simply have to subtract some of the time, care, food, or whatever that she'd spend on newcomers from that available to older siblings. Natural selection should favor mothers that take good care of the relatively small number of offspring they can efficiently manage. But the father who contributes nothing to his offsprings' care has almost no investment in them. They impose no obstacle to his continually fathering more. So in tournament species, Trivers reasoned, selection ought to favor the genes of tournament males that did just that.

In pair-bonding species, though, the father can make a real difference to his offsprings' survival. And by limiting himself to a single mate, he puts all his genes in her basket; his potential progeny are no more numerous than hers. So it makes sense to devote himself to protecting his investment by guarding, feeding, carrying, or whatever.

This extremely elegant and compelling, if somewhat circular, argument has had a huge influence on evolutionary thinking in the past decade. Seeing a species' adaptation as a seamless whole composed of environment, body, and behavior, it goes far toward unifying an immense number of small mysteries into a single, comprehensible phenomenon. But it arises from a particular set of assumptions about the nature and mechanics of evolution, and it flows directly into sociobiology; indeed, it forms one of the major tributaries of a current of thinking that has swept across the intellectual landscape.

Later on we'll look more closely into the philosophical and empirical complexities of sociobiology and its explanation of behavior. For now, we need only note, with Donald Symons, himself a leading sociobiological writer on sexuality, that parental investment is "not the whole story. . . . Sexual selection is also a function of the extent to which the particular ecological and environmental circumstances make it economically feasible for an individual to monopolize multiple mates or the resources critical to gaining multiple mates."[17]

Animals, in other words, live in concrete environments, not in mathematical models; we can't explain everything they do as ideal strategies for maximizing descendents. Some adaptations—perhaps even gender itself—happened because a species ventured too far out on an evolutionary limb to get back.

Our old friends the elephant seals are a prime example. They spend most of their lives at sea, but they're really mammals descended from land-living ancestors. They've adapted so well to the ocean that they couldn't easily go back to their landlubber ways, having become such slow and clumsy walkers that they can't compete with terrestrial species. They come ashore only on small, protected islands that other mammals can't reach. Still—or, perhaps, because they have this safe terrain—they mate and give birth on land, just as their forebears did. This annual necessity to haul out and lumber around on rocky ground enables the large bulls to keep the cows away from the smaller males—who would surely win on speed and agility if they could fight in the water. Males of mammal species that mate at sea don't outweigh the females—because they don't engage in battles that revolve on heft. The earth's largest living creature is the female blue whale. "Among mammals," Symons concludes, "environmental circumstances may be more important determinants of the intensity of sexual selection than parental investment is."[18]

But even if parental investment can't clarify everything, it does, as we shall shortly see, explain a good deal, if not precisely in the terms that Trivers suggests. It helps us view gender and reproduction in the expansive frame of a species' total adaptation; and it will help us to keep in perspective an element crucial and unique to our own species' adaptation.

This chapter began with a simple question. After touring the animal kingdom, we still have no answer. We can't explain gender as a necessary feature of organic life. It certainly doesn't provide advantages to any living individual. It has no consistent rules that apply across species. There are countless ways to be male and female.

The best we can do is consider it one of many legacies of our evolutionary past, along with—among other things—warm-bloodedness, the opposable thumb, and the propensity to live in groups. Each species has just such a grab-bag inheritance—the ability to breathe under water, for example, or to support one's weight by the tail, or to invest sounds with meaning. And each species must use what it has to fashion a design for living.

Now, the limits of our bodies—the fact that we come in two kinds, the fact that one kind bears live young—powerfully shape the lives that human beings can make. We must come to terms with those two facts as surely as any bird or ape or reindeer. But like them, we do so in a specific time and place. And nothing in the physical facts we've seen so far—not the workings of our own cells and hormones nor the workings of the forces of evolution—suggests that there is only one human solution to this universal problem, any more than there is one canine solution.

And something else enters the human equation. The neuroscientists Goy and McEwen, of all people, came across it midway through their consideration of the neurology of gender, and an improbable find it seemed. It spoils some of their neatest explanations. "For some highly social species, like human beings," these neuroscientists observe, "culture may define the types and limits of sexual dimorphism. Worse luck yet, the individual human being may be forced to learn to acquire those dimorphisms that, like the sex-reversing *Anthias squamipinnis,* the behavior of his or her peers thrusts upon him/her."[19]

That strange little fish becomes male because her fellows want her too; somewhere in the depths of piscine neurology and biochemistry there's a power that molds behavior to the needs of the group. And two eminent biologists seem to be saying that there's a power that does the same thing to us. That's what we'll look into next.

3

What Do People Make out of Gender?

Every day the sun rises and sets: a plain physical fact with no inherent purpose, a coincidental biproduct of the earth's axial spin. Flowers and molluscs and lizards and moles all note it; they wake and sleep, open and close, stay home and venture out according to the amount of light in the sky.

We note it too. Thousands of years ago on the Ganges plain, curious humans began to draw some conclusions. Clearly, they saw, the days didn't occur in isolation but formed part of a recurring pattern. Fifteen days, careful observation showed, formed a natural unit, the *paksa*. Each *paksa* (which, after slight numerical tinkering, dropped about half a day) marked the time a new moon needed to wax full or a full moon needed to wane. Adding the bright *paksa* of the waxing moon to the dark one of waning equaled a month, the period from full moon to full moon. Two months equaled each of the year's six seasons. The resulting 354 days (adjusted by a leap-month added after every thirty months) was a full year, from the parched infertility of one *Caitra*, through the monsoon-fed green and cool seasons to the next time of heat and dryness. So obviously does this system express the reality of time that Hindus around the world still reckon their holy days by counting the passing *paksa*s.

But the Indians, of course, were not the only inquiring intellects scanning the skies. Some hundreds of years later, Middle American observers wrote down their conclusions about the nature of time.

Every day had two markers: one of thirteen recurring numbers and one of twenty recurring signs. Today might be, for example, three lizard or nine crocodile or fourteen snake. This count fitted, like one cogwheel, into another counting system that meanwhile turned, like a second cogwheel, on its own independent axis. In this second count, every twenty days were a month and every eighteen months a year; five extra "evil days" at the end brought the annual total to 365. Once in fifty-two years the systems intersected; the same dates and signs of dread portent coincided in the two counts. During each of these *xiuhmolpilli* or "year knots," the world hung in the shadow of catastrophe. Not until the next sunrise did the terrified people know whether the priests had saved the planet for another fifty-two years.

Halfway around the world, during each Mayan night, residents of the Fertile Crescent also quizzically watched the dawn. We, their spiritual descendents, already know what their days naturally added up to: a seven-day week, six days for work and one for rest. And we know why their days fell into this obvious order: the Lord created for six days and rested for one, and we, in His image, do the same to mark our distinctiveness from the beasts. For three or even four thousand years, at least since Moses came down from Sinai, the civilization that we inherit has marked time in recurring blocks of seven days. And we've learned about the days: the blueness of Monday, the thank-Godness of Friday, the good luck of the child born on the Sabbath. Tuesdayness is as integral to our experience of today as the humid warmth and the overcast sky. Try thinking of some past event without remembering whether it happened on a weekday or a weekend. Try locating some event in the near future without thinking of the day of the week it will fall on. If you're like most of us, you can't.

Still, when you read of *Caitra* and *xiuhmolpilli*, you instantly understood that they correspond to nothing in the natural world. It should be just as clear that Thursday afternoon doesn't either. But that's a bit harder. We humans, unlike every other species, not only live the fact of days, we impose form and meaning on it.

Here's another plain physical fact: there are two kinds of humans, one that bears children and one that doesn't. Some modern thinkers, of course, explain it with the theories in the last two chapters, but those explanations don't rule our lives any more than knowledge of astronomy erases the reality of Friday. For millennia, around hearths and altars and deathbeds, people have told and retold other, simpler stories, stories that put humanity at the center of creation. We Judeo-Christians, for example, know how, on the day before resting, the Lord made Adam and Eve; and how they soon lost the right to live in His perfect garden. But other peoples tell other stories. The Seneca of upstate New York explained physical gender this way:

Before the world began, a woman named Ancient-Bodied lived with her husband and daughter in the sky. But her husband doubted her fidelity and, in a rage, tore a hole in the sky and ejected mother and child. Ancient-Bodied, though, snatched a piece of the sky-stuff and, as she fell through space, also got hold of some corn. Eventually the two exiles alighted on Turtle's back. Using the heavenly flotsam, Ancient-Body created earth fit for farming and planted corn. She called the sun and stars into being. Eventually her daughter, pregnant by Wind, bore two sons, one normally and one through her armpit, the former good and the latter bad. The good son, in a battle with his half-brothers, Wind's other sons, captured the animals, which he released in the forest near home. He and Ancient-Bodied named them, she naming the large ones and he the small.

Few of our contemporaries take either of these accounts literally any more, but that doesn't make them mere fiction. The Constitution of the Five Nations, a code of law transmitted orally among the Seneca and their sister tribes, said this about the daughters of Ancient-Bodied: "Women shall be considered the progenitors of the Nation. They shall own the land and the soil."[1] And Tertullian, a father of the Christian church, said this to the daughters of the hapless woman in the garden: "Do you not know that you are Eve? God's sentence hangs still over all your sex and his punishment weighs down upon you. You are the devil's gateway."[2]

Do pious pronouncements make any difference? Well, among the Seneca and other peoples of the Iroquois nation, the women descended from Ancient-Bodied ran the farms, presided at religious rituals, and named members to the national assembly. Meanwhile, in the neighboring "civilized" white villages, the women descended from Eve lived their whole lives as legal minors, forbidden to stand in the pulpit, enter the voting booth, or even dispose of their own property.

Up to now we've considered gender as something we are. But it's also something we know about. We can't tell if knowledge—as opposed to cerebral hard-wiring—affects the survival of other animals, but in Homo sapiens, the knowing hominid, it stands at the center of our species' adaptation. The anatomical features distinguishing our skulls from our close ancestors'—the more delicate jaw, the high forehead, the arching braincase—have to do with the astonishing organ of knowledge housed within. Several hominid species once stalked grasslands and forests, but only we survive. This attests to the power of our sapient adaptation and its speed at filling every niche where a bipedal, manually dextrous, symbolically communicating primate could possibly eke out a living.

Our ancestors had a good deal of knowledge quite early in their career as humans. They had fire and weapons, and all the subsidiary understandings they imply. To survive as foragers, they knew hundreds of plants and animals by their seeds, tracks, droppings, bark, and roots. They found their way accurately and efficiently across trackless wilderness and located safe places to camp, drink, cache supplies, and collect raw materials. They understood the physical properties and heat tolerances of numerous minerals, woods, and fibers. They predicted the trajectory of a spear, the paths of migrating herds, the growing seasons of trees and plants, the life cycle of their own kind. They made carved and painted images, they disposed of their dead ceremoniously, they arranged special possessions in recurring but not utilitarian patterns; they obviously tried to divine much larger answers as well.

And they possessed the forerunner of our brain, so they understood these things as we do: not as jumble of facts but as interrelated systems of ideas stored and expressed in symbols. They must have accumulated knowledge, memorized and shared it. Their skeletal remains permit no other conclusion. Without the tremendous advantage that symbols gave them over competitors, selection could not have favored an information organ as complex and costly as our brain.

And the human brain is very costly indeed. It grows so large that it can pass through the birth canal only quite early in its development, even though the human female has a very wide pelvis for her size. Years of care and training must follow. Such immature young forced human adults to organize their lives around the longest dependency in the animal kingdom.

Even so, this extremely high initial investment pays off handsomely, producing a creature of such power and flexibility, a competitor so ingenious and adaptable, that it survives in nearly every environment on earth and holds its own against life forms from viruses to whales.

No other primate, no other mammal, has enjoyed success on our scale. We moved from the African savannah, where we first emerged, to make homes in deserts, mountains, steppes, beaches, tundras. We live wholly on animal food, wholly on vegetable, and on every combination in between. We get food by hunting, gathering, herding, fishing, farming. We live at sea level and above the tree line, in tropical heat and arctic cold. We go naked and drape ourselves in animal fur and petroleum fibers. We retrieve food from treetops and seabeds. We travel across sand dunes, oceans, and air.

We can drastically change our way of life without changing our "hard-wiring." We simply run a new "program" on a mental "operating system" of astonishing power and versatility, as for example, the Plains Indians did several centuries ago when they first caught stray horses that had escaped from the Spanish explorers. Mounting the curious foreign beasts as they had seen the white men do, they suddenly found themselves lords of a world previously closed to them. No longer pedestrians on the margins of the treeless plains, they could now chase down the herds of bison that stretched to the horizon. It took only a couple of generations to devise the technology and organization for efficiently plundering the vast, moving fields of wealth on the hoof. So perfectly did they learn, though, that whites encountering the mounted hunters a century or two later concluded that they had lived on horseback since the beginning of time.

We are talking, of course, about culture. To understand Homo sapiens we must understand an essential point: this particular adaptation, this trick of creating symbols and a shared memory, has played a role as central in species survival as the penguins' insulated pouches. The ability to live culturally is not an "extra" added on to a basic human physical structure. It was built in at the beginning, as integral as hearing or sight.

Living culturally does not mean only—or even mainly—that we follow customs or make artifacts. It means that we understand symbolically and act systematically. In a systematic world, events have causes, acts have meaning, and like things resemble one another. Culture is the tool that lets us make order of a world infinitely full of facts and phenomena.

Here's one with far-reaching consequences: male genitals permit intercourse with an unwilling partner, but female genitals do not. In their heyday, the Great Plains mounted warriors used it to prevent female adultery; a cuckolded husband might punish his wife by inviting his friends to gang-rape her. The Gusii of Africa used it to enforce male authority; every honeymoon began with the bridegroom battling his resisting wife into submission, sure that nothing less would win her admiration.

But the Mbuti pygmies of the Congo jungle believe that it illustrates depravity; any violence among tribe members of either sex indicates mental aberration. And the Kaulong of Papua–New Guinea pay no attention to it at all; they expect the woman to pursue the man, and the man to resist her advances, in literal fear of death.

Obviously, then, a Gusii husband predictably acts differently from a Kaulong, and a Comanche husband from a Mbuti. Unaware of all the others, each man regards his own behavior as natural, normal, and correct. We Americans more closely resemble the Comanche and the Gusii than the Mbuti and Kaulong in the incidence of forcible rape, and side with them on what the physical fact means. For us, rape happens because of the way our private parts are built.

Anthropologist Peggy Reeves Sanday locates the cause somewhere else: in the way our brains are built. We can't survive alone, and we can't live together unless we can count on predicting one another's actions. Every group needs specific, enforceable ideas of the behavior it can accept. And every person needs those ideas to fit into a coherent picture of the nature of the universe.

This sounds like a very tall order: to live contentedly, men and women need to know that all their trips to the supermarket and days in the fields and chats with neighbors and family reunions reinforce the way the world really works. If we can push our cart along the aisles or plod behind the plow or gather at the campfire because it is our very nature to do so, because all heaven and earth wish and expect us to, then our lives take meaning from the world as we know it to be. At the deepest level, this is culture's job: to give us reasons to go on living, and to connect them to the innermost workings of reality.

In one community, life is about the honor of the family name; this calls forth a fierce and jumpy pride. In another, it's about individual happiness or spiritual salvation or the perfect harmony of the group; each calls forth its distinct response. These basic notions about the meaning of life, says anthropologist Clifford Geertz, form a people's "symbolic templates," their outlines of worthy action. And we use them, as carpenters use templates, to reproduce a desired form.

The symbolic template gives shape to experiences otherwise "without form and void." What does it mean to be an adult, a householder, a citizen, a human being? The symbolic template— our group's set of basic, perhaps unconscious, answers—explains the nature of causality, the essence of humanity, the purpose of living. And very prominent among a society's basic ideas is "a sex-role plan—that is, a template for the organization of sex-role expectations. . . . [These] help men and women orient themselves as male and female to each other, to the world around them, and to the growing boys and girls whose behavior they must shape to a commonly accepted mold."[3] Tertullion had one ideal outline, the Seneca another.

Thus the immense power of Eve and Ancient-Bodied. These tales don't merely beguile the imaginations—although they fail at their cultural task unless they do. More importantly, they lay out the ultimate causes and basic definitions that explain life as we find it.

They tell us what human beings are like, and just as importantly, why.

This insight is hardly novel; nor is the notion that human societies hold immensely diverse ideas about males and females. In some places males unquestionably command and in others the sexes amiably share power and authority. Generations of social scientists have tried to test propositions about gender by a sort of worldwide head count—tallying the numbers of societies that fall into each category.

The numbers decidedly favor the theory that males are meant to rule. In some of the most extreme cases, a preadolescent boy's opinion outweighs that of a woman of mature years. Statistically-minded investigators have more than once concluded that this preponderance represents the species' natural bent. Something that most people do, they argue, must serve an essential human purpose. The biologically-minded go even further, concluding that male dominance is *the* evolutionary necessary pattern of human relations.

But Sanday argues out of a different intellectual tradition. Hers—American cultural anthropology—emphasizes, even cherishes, the integrity of special cases. And the rules of logic add weight to her objection: any exception, no matter how tiny or obscure, refutes a universal statement. And because societies without male dominance do exist—the Seneca and Mbuti, to name only two—it cannot be universal and therefore must not be biological. "Sex-role plans are cultural and not biological," she concludes. "If [they] were derived from the human biological structure, we would not find the variety of plans that do exist."[4]

But a catalog of examples—Iroquois matriarchs engineering political deals, Ashanti queens ruling over the women's world as equals of the kings who rule the men's—only confuses the issue. Indeed, the study of gender has long lacked a conceptual architecture to organize widely scattered observations. But Sanday, in her way, clears away as much conceptual clutter as Darwin. Sanday even begins with a Darwinian observation: bodily organs don't evolve at random, and neither do sex-role plans. In fact, they come in a limited number of types: In societies, "the sexes are either merged or they are segregated; the power to make decisions is either vested in both sexes or dominated by one."[5]

And a sex-role plan relates to many other features of a culture. Here she stands Trivers' dictum on its head: we can predict much about a culture from how its members organize themselves to care for their young. Just as Trivers predicted, this relationship unlocks the deepest workings of gender. But for Sanday, human gender is as much symbolic as genetic; in the microcosm of each individual birth, she finds the macrocosm of the birth of the world.

In Western memory, the word of the Lord brought the cosmos into being. The Seneca believed that the world arose from the combination of natural forces and the efforts of a woman. The Semang people of Bali believe that a woman and her grandson together formed the world and its inhabitants. The Ashanti of Africa believe that two couples, one from the heavens and one from the earth, conceived and brought forth the first people.

In the great array of fantastic founders and outlandish feats, Sanday finds only two basic stories. In one a masculine being, like the Lord of the Bible, creates the world; in the other, females, couples, or even bisexual beings do. Very deep differences divide these two plots. And in those differences lie the lineaments of the universe, hidden but imminent, like a child in the womb.

Female creators and couples bring life into being as the Seneca founders did, through the natural processes of human—specifically female—fertility. The primordial humans emerge from a living womb, or from the earth, or from water, or from some other enclosure that resembles a human birth.

But male creators, lacking the womb, can't give life in the female way. Instead, they create magically, in ways unavailable to ordinary mortals. The Lord of Genesis brought the world into being simply by stating His intention. He made man from a lump of clay ("Adam" means "earth" in Hebrew), breathing life into inert matter. He made woman (in the second but far more influential of the Book's accounts) from a dispensable bone in Adam's body. Then Eve led Adam, and humanity, into sin and sorrow, and the Lord sentenced her to exercise her female function in agony.

The Genesis account could, indeed, serve as archetype for the male-oriented creation tale. It begins with a Creator producing life by remote control, using means that no living human beings can hope to emulate, and it ends with woman subjected to the will and spiritual superiority of men. In some versions the women suffer a straightforward punishment; in others the men or male divinities win through violence, cunning, or chicanery.

Origin tales make concrete the group's deepest assumptions about men, women, and the creative forces that sustain life. If people look back to female or couple creators, then every childbirth reenacts the creation of life itself, every mother participates in the universe's central mystery, every woman and girl bears within her the force that drives the world. (In these stories however, the primordial mother almost always shares her creative power with a male figure; she becomes pregnant by the sun, or the earth, or the sky, or some divinity.)

If we believe in male creators, then women stand apart from the power of the universe. They can't touch, reenact, or even aspire to creativity. Eve can never emulate the creative act of her Creator (she is not even made in His image) and her own poor powers of creation serve to punish, not exalt, her. A woman in such a universe merely "bears" or "carries" a man's—or, in a single, exemplary case, God's—child. Western religion knows only one Mother, "alone of all her sex," who achieved exaltation, and she only by transcending, through utter submission to supernatural masculinity, the essence of her nature as a physical woman. (This sacrifice of hers, incidentally, didn't redeem all women from the specific fall of Eve, although the sacrifice of her Son redeemed all men, and women too, from the fall of Adam. But her Son, as God Himself, ever and always possessed the power of redemption. She cannot be God and thus cannot acquire it.)

Symbols organize experience, and these symbols organize the overpowering experience of human reproduction. "There is a puzzling contradiction between belief and reality in the notion that people are made magically by a masculine supreme being," Sanday observes.[6] But it becomes less puzzling and less contradictory when we realize that this notion simply mirrors the group's daily life. For men in these societies, birthing and rearing are woman's work, apart from and beneath the concerns of men. Here wives literally "present" men with heirs, as nineteenth-century novels put it. They enter a frequently all-female seclusion ("confinement," the Victorians called it) and bring forth their baby out of the fathers' sight. The separation continues as the child grows; men take little or no part in care. In forty-seven societies that believe in male-oriented creation, Sanday found only eight that expect regular, close contact between fathers and infants.

A magic trick performed by a distant male is one way to experience human birth. A natural process growing in and from the bodies of women or couples is another. And, naturally, stories of creation by a female or a couple organize the experience of childbirth quite differently. Societies that emphasize the creative power of women value childbirth and childrearing as imitations of the divine. Fathers spend time and effort on young children, quite apart from providing material support. And they often witness birth itself, so they can't dismiss it as a clean, distant conjuring trick but respect it as a painful, taxing struggle full of strength and danger. They may even take its pain and peril—and power—on themselves, like the Pacific island husbands who bleed their penises to replicate menstruation and, through the rituals of the couvade or mock pregnancy, take to their own barren childbeds.

An origin tale tells in shorthand how a people stands with the creative power of the universe. Significantly, Sanday notes, masculine tales place the physical source of that power far from the ordinary precincts of human life, usually in the sky. A masculine attitude, what she terms an "outer" orientation, emphasizes distant forces that work through males. Female or couple tales place creation in the human realm, in the human body or the earth. A feminine attitude, what Sanday terms an "inner" orientation, emphasizes organic forces that work, at least in part, through females.

Life everywhere mirrors art, and daily life, more often than not, resembles the creation myth. Women of inner-oriented groups both symbolically and individually wield public and private authority. They speak in political councils and religious rituals; ceremonies often require some element that only they can provide. Valid worship often can't occur without them. They may also formally or informally control certain realms of the economy. Iroquois women, as descendents of the first cultivator, held a monopoly on agriculture. The men, as descendents of the twin grandsons, occupied

themselves with hunting. Inner-oriented societies may produce matriarchs, but not the matriarchies of science-fiction fantasy. Where
females hold power, they share it with men; female authority does
not seem to depend on denying the strength or mythic potency of
males.

A dual monarchy ruled the Igbo, for example, a West African
farming people. Power culminated in the person of the *obi,* his title
rather misleadingly translated as "king." In theory he ruled the
entire nation, but in practice he limited himself to the male sphere.
He shared power with the *omu,* and to call her a "queen" even
more seriously violates reality. Unlike the queens of our experience, she held power in her own independent, female right, and
not through marriage or in the absence of a male heir. She ruled
through her own cabinet, and her own pyramid of officials oversaw
specifically female interests at all levels of society.

In societies with outer orientations, daily, temporal life operates
through males; like the creator they emulate, males control the
levers of power. They dominate politics, economics, and ritual.
They exclude women from the prestige of public honor. Is it only
coincidence that two symbolic changes happened in a single American generation: fathers began to witness and assist in the birth of
their children, and progressive religious denominations admitted
women to long-forbidden sacral functions?

It's a cardinal error to ignore symbols in human affairs, but a
bigger one to overestimate them. Symbolism explains a great deal
about behavior, but circumstance explains much more.

Our own culture has a strongly "outward" or masculine orientation. Our religion runs straight back to Genesis. Our patriotic holi-
days celebrate the founding fathers (and ignore the mothers, like
Abigail Adams, who ran the farms and businesses and freed the
men to fight battles and frame laws). Our classic American literature also chronicles the exploits of men—subduing nature on land
and sea; escaping the snares of mothers, aunts, teachers, sweethearts
to find their destinies. But there are some dominant, assertive
women on the margins of our symbolic life. They reach mythic
proportions only in our own century, and only as new voices, rising
from other memories, joined the literary chorus. In black and Jew-

ish-American writing, the hero also struggles for his manhood—but not against the frontier, the white whale, the brave bull, or the river, and not only against a prejudiced society. Between him and his destiny often stands a strong, demanding woman: a mother who would control him or a lover who would devour him.

Andrew Young, an intimate witness to the twentieth-century civil rights movement, once unwittingly puzzled over this fact. "We had a hard time with domineering women in SCLC," he says of an organization run by ministers but galvanized by the defiance of a seamstress. "Martin [Luther King, Jr.]'s mother, quiet as she was, was really a strong, domineering force in the family. She was never publicly saying anything but she ran Daddy King, and she ran the church, and she ran Martin." What lay behind this "problem in the early days," the inconvenient tendency of certain females to "run" things? Why didn't the women, from Mrs. King, Sr., on down, simply accept the notion—which was dogma during the United States of the 1950s—that political actors are male? Three centuries of aspiring to white models and yearning for a biblical redemption had surely erased memories of the West African past—especially among highly educated families like the Kings. Young mused a bit longer on the enigma of unwomanly women and then ventured a suggestion: "This is a generality, but a system of oppression tends to produce strong women and weak men."[7] He could more accurately have said: oppression can produce women more dominant and men less dominant than the American ideal. It produces individuals who violate the categories that define American gender. But that's because their lives have violated other American categories too.

For generations we Americans divided our daily life between two spheres: the public one of marketplace, church, and politics; and the private one of home. Until very recently, we believed each sex was naturally suited to one domain. The front door divided man's work from woman's work, manly pursuits from womanly pastimes, the masculine traits of dominance and acquisition from the feminine ones of nurture and conciliation. A bridegroom carried his bride across this symbolic divide, delivering her safely into the private world of his protection.

But what if life divided up differently, into three realms, not two?

Then we'd live according to the cultural categories of the *shetlach* (singular, *shtetl*), the small Yiddish-speaking towns of Eastern Europe. Men held undisputed sway in the prestigious world of synagogue and study hall, of the sacred Hebrew language and the holy rabbinic texts. At home, women ordered family life. But in the third realm, the marketplace, both sexes and all ages struggled for a usually meager living.

Under Russian rule, a harsh outer reality governed *shtetl* economic life: the secular law excluded Jews from most respectable and lucrative trades, including farming. Many workers pursued marginal handicrafts, petty trading, manual labor, or the life of the *luftmensch*, the "air person" who lived solely by his wits.

A revered inner reality governed the *shtetl* religious life: tradition defined sacred scholarship as the highest calling, life's most sublime goal. Unlike their Christian neighbors, however, pious and learned Jews upheld no ideal of celibacy; marriage and parenthood were universal religious duties. Scholars had families, though few scholarly careers produced a liveable income. A man without the means to support him and his children could not hope to live for study.

Luckily for some, well-to-do families sought the prestige of learned sons and sons-in-law, and some scholars lived in comfort on happily supplied lifelong allowances. For the rest, only one person could earn the family's bread: the scholar's wife.

So stringent was the economy, though, that many ordinary, hardworking husbands also failed to earn a living. Their wives, too, joined the labor force, helping in his trade or shop; running a tiny grocery or notions business from the front room; making cakes to sell door to door; peddling food or dry goods from a cart in the market; teaching girls, if she herself had any education; arranging marriages for a fee; attending at childbirth; cooking, sewing, washing, babysitting, or cleaning for more prosperous women. Observe Mark Zborowski and Elizabeth Herzog in their classic study of *shtetl* life:

> The earning of a livelihood is sexless and a large majority
> of women . . . participate in some gainful occupation if
> they do not carry the chief burden of support. The wife of
> a perennial student is very apt to be the sole support of

her family. The problem of managing both a business and a home is so common that no one recognizes it as special.[8]

But bearing the breadwinner's yoke is not without its compensations. "As a full participant in . . . economic support, the woman escapes the burden of a sheltered life. If anyone is sheltered, it is the scholarly man: women and girls move about freely. . . . But everyone assumes that she can take care of herself."[9] Women might not have known Hebrew and Talmud, but they often knew gentile languages and the ways of the marketplace better than their men. They may have deferred to male authority in matters of form, but the money they brought into the family gave their opinions weight.

Indeed, *shtetl* culture was ambivalent about the proper role of women. Deeply knowledgeable about the Bible, its members acknowledged the two Genesis creation stories. In the second, God created Adam and then Eve, but in the first, "male and female created He them." The Talmud interprets this ambiguous line to mean that God made bisexual beings and only later divided them into two separate entities. Neither half, however, could ever attain completeness without the other, just as no Jew could attain holiness in celibacy.

So on paper (parchment, actually) the culture reserved all important positions to men, but actually afforded women wide latitude. (Anthropologist Susan Carol Rogers found a similar situation among poor villagers of Mediterranean Europe. While the men guarded their honor in the public forums of the church, café, and marketplace, the matrons shaped public opinion outside the formal channels of control—just like their favorite divinity, a Mother like themselves, who, through irregular powers of persuasion, worked a woman's will in heaven.)

The contradiction disappears when we define the social features that constitute true male dominance. From a worldwide sample, Sanday distilled seven. A truly male-dominated society excludes women "from political and economic decision-making"; it turns a blind eye to "male aggression against women"; it fosters "the expectation that men should be tough, brave, and aggressive"; it supports male-only institutions and meeting places; it permits "frequent quarreling, fighting, or wife beating"; it expects rape; and it permits raiding for wives.[10] Clearly, American society, which meets every criterion except bride capture, is markedly more macho than the *shtetl* ever was.

The *shtetl* community's formal councils excluded women, but their opinions still helped mold public opinion; and, anyway, no Jew of either gender took any political decisions affecting gentiles. The religion utterly disdained aggression (although it must have occasionally happened nonetheless) and encouraged women to work outside the home. (The psalmist's "woman of valor," praised at every Sabbath dinner, traded actively in the marketplace.) The community's subservience to harsh gentile rule combined with its own religious values to devalue physical toughness and bravery as measures of manhood. The operative value exalted *menschlichkeit*, humaneness, an ideal open to both sexes. Males absolutely and exclusively controlled the synagogue, study house, and law courts, which ruled in matters concerning only Jews.

Altogether, therefore, *shtetl* culture fully met only one criterion of male dominance. Not surprisingly, it produced an image of manhood radically different from the one encountered at Ellis Island. A generation later, the immigrants' lack of apparent heroism puzzled and offended some of their Americanized sons. Still, observe the literary critics Irving Howe and Eliezer Greenberg:

> A culture that has been able to resist the temptations of worldly power—or has been blocked at the threshold of those temptations—will naturally favor an image of heroism very different from the one we know in Western literature. Few Yiddish novels or stories contain heroes who satisfy the Aristotelian formula [of *hubris*, fall, and eventual humility]. . . . Rejecting the whole ethos of historical aggrandizement as it has come to us from Greek drama and been colored by Christian expansion, the Yiddish writers express through the theme of anti-heroism their admiration for those who do not exert their social will but live and endure in silence, as well as their contempt for what the outer world takes as greatness but which they often felt is no more than an appetite for blood.[11]

Tevye the milkman, perhaps Yiddish culture's greatest single gift to world literature, embodies "the anti-heroic Jewish hero whose

sheer power of survival and comment makes the gestures of traditional heroism seem rather absurd."

So we must modify Young's remark further. Oppression doesn't
make weak men, but men and women who are strong in ways that
the very masculinist general American culture does not value.
Young's own ancestors, living under a particularly brutal oppression, present an even clearer example. The explicit goal of Southern slaveholding culture, after all, was unmanning black men. This
both guarded against rebellion and reduced competition for white
men's free sexual access to black women. The downtrodden East
European Jew at least ranked as "Christ-killer," an epithet implying
the respect due an ingenious if depraved foe; the downtrodden
Southern black man was nothing more than a "boy."

But the paranoid ravishment fantasies dear to white racists didn't
deceive; the slave system was sexual to its core. The socially
neutered black male still sprang from an African descent, supposed
source of a powerful sexuality. Thus, he perpetually threatened the
symbolic purity of white womanhood, which stood guard over
property rights in a society that reckoned slavery essentially
through the female line. For her part, the presumably helpless
white woman lived under white men's protection; as the vessels of
their men's family and racial honor, they embodied the delicacy
and passivity of ladyhood.

But the system stripped black women of any support or protection, either from their own men or from the code of white chivalry,
which applied to white women only. No black woman could aspire
to the lace-and-lavender ideal; instead, the supposedly inborn wan-
tonness born of the same African descent (rather than the over-
seers' whips and enticements) drove her indiscriminately into the
arms of men.

Generations of this savage hypocrisy denied black women (and
men) any hope of attaining the surrounding society's cultural ideals
(which, not coincidentally, encapsulated all but one of Sanday's
male-dominance criteria in a prevailing ethic of violence and female
sexual repression). Robbed of their ancestral cultures and exposed
to a debased form of Western Christian thought, the slaves also
suffered enforced illiteracy, geographic dispersion, and extreme
poverty. Together these hampered them from elaborating an ex-

plicit verbal code reflecting their own needs and circumstances. Within these bitter limitations, though, they made their own great gift to world artistic expression, an utterly original vocal and instrumental music proclaiming the heroism of those who simply endure.

The *shtetl* man, barred from manhood in the masculinist terms of the surrounding culture, at least could pour his energy and his dignity into the honored realm of religion. Among his own people he could aspire to, and achieve, a recognizably worthy manhood. The male slave, however, had not even that hope. Plantation culture permitted only one version of manhood, the violent, sexually aggressive slave owner with his veneer of gentlemanly manners, his military code, and his hair-trigger honor.

Even more than the *shtetl* wife, therefore, the slave mother (often prevented from marrying licitly) had no choice but to see to her own and her children's survival. She had no standing as head of a family; she was simply an economic asset (which must produce an economic return) and brood stock to increase her master's wealth. Even after slavery, Southern society still denied large numbers of black husbands and fathers the economic opportunity to support a wife and family decently.

A small number of educated men like King and Young, however, did achieve standing in the general culture, but the images of manhood and womanhood they found there clashed with their own people's history and habits. (Is it any wonder that King defeated white violence through the "soul-force" of freely accepted suffering?)

In earlier times, of course, black women used to "running things" were not a "problem" but a necessity of life. Paula Giddings observes in her searching exploration of race and sex in America that black women college graduates are "more confident of their own abilities" than their white counterparts. Three-quarters of the black women, but only half the whites thought their personalities "suitable to careers as business executives." Black women who pursue professional careers generally grow up in homes of working mothers, whose jobs often entailed higher educational attainment and social status (but not necessarily higher pay) than their men's. White women professionals, on the other hand, often see themselves as rejecting the benighted domesticity of their mothers. "Black women expected to have to work, whether they were married or not."[12] They did not, and indeed could not, view their jobs as "supplemental to those of their husbands." And most significantly, black professional women are much less troubled than whites by worries that careers make them masculine or unwomanly. A femininity that limits women to the home is quite simply a luxury that generations of black families could not afford.

So gender comes down to what life revolves around anyway: earning a living. In the abstract, all humanity faces the same problem: wresting food, warmth, shelter, and safety from an indifferent world. But in the concrete, the struggle takes a thousand forms.

Some of us, like the Mbuti, live in a perennially fruitful forest. The lush verdure and teeming wildlife provide an ample, if simple, living essentially free for the taking. In this silent green world, life is hospitable, fate forgiving. The Mbuti speak to their bountiful jungle as to their mother and father; like a loving parent, it supplies all their wants. Men and women skillfully gather plant foods that may vary with the season, but never fall short of need. They also capture various kinds of small animals. They live in harmony with the forest, and, to preserve its prosperity, feel compelled to live in harmony with one another.

But other places teach other lessons: that the world is a careless stranger or an implacable foe. Humans also coax their food from stony ground or cull it from herds of beasts vulnerable to hunger and thirst. They struggle to fill their children's bellies, plus those of the domesticated animals that depend on them, and on whom they depend, for survival. Farmers must feed dairy and draft stock through each winter or dry season; herdsmen must endlessly find new pasture and water as the herds exhaust the old. Men may even purchase their families' livings at the risk of their own lives, tracking and killing crafty and deadly large animals.

Experience teaches us what to expect of the forces that rule our lives. And this knowledge, Sanday believes, deeply colors outlooks —and habits. "Environmentally induced vulnerability (as in the hunting of large game) results in an outer orientation manifested first in the distancing of fathers from infants and second in beliefs about outer power." Hunters work in quiet and stealth, far from the noisy demands of children. They live by their wits and stamina, but mainly by luck—a power outside themselves and beyond their control. They spend their psychic energy devising ways to harness it, or, failing that, to keep it from turning against them.

Conversely, "the sense of security gained from a lush environment, where food is derived from the earth, results in an inner orientation manifested in nurturing fathers and beliefs about inward power."[13] How well people live depends on how diligently they gather the dependable fruits of the earth; disciplined human effort, not the unfathomable caprice, seems to determine destiny. The fertility of the human group, as embodied in its female members, their swelling figures, and the babies they produce, assures continuing prosperity.

So here we yoke the human capacity for understanding experience to the principle that population genetics discerns in animals, and we discover that the quality and quantity of parental care meshes into an entire system for wresting a living from a particular patch of earth, air, and water. How men and women divide the work of earning that living, and thus its privileges and responsibilities, structures relations between sexes, generations, kin groups.

And the fit, as among Redican and Taub's animals, is often strikingly exact. For the Hazda of East Africa, social form follows economic function so closely that it fluctuates with the seasons. In the bountiful wet season men and women forage for plant food and small game, living relatively amicably in small, scattered bands. But the dry season imposes a harsher reality. Small streams and waterholes vanish, and the Hazda must cluster in large camps near the few remaining water sources, where they also vie with thirsty animals. The parched land makes for poor foraging, and human numbers become too large to depend on trapping the depleted supplies of small animals.

Only hunting large game can efficiently produce enough food. A cloud of peril and foreboding gathers over the congested dry-season settlements, as the men now struggle for their precarious living against arbitrary forces beyond their control. The sureness of a guess, the trueness of a spear, the bravery of a comrade can spell the difference between prosperity and disaster. Luck and chance now obsess the men and they play out their obsession in endless gambling. To further protect their luck, they segregate themselves from the women, and impose strict taboos on contact with menstrual blood, so like the blood of wounded prey.

The Hazda, like many peoples who live by luck, see danger in the monthly bleeding. (The Mbuti in their jungle, meanwhile, joyfully celebrate a girl's first period as a harbinger of coming life.) Hazda youngsters spend the dry season with their mothers, because the hunters can't care for them; sexual segregation also limits contact between fathers and children. Relations between the sexes remain tense and hostile until the returning rains liberate the people from the confining large camps.

As a general principle, women enjoy equality when—as in the Mbuti jungles or the Russian pale—circumstances permit them to contribute conspicuously to group prosperity. In the nonurbanized world, that generally means an economy heavily weighted toward plant foods, either foraged or cultivated. When large animals enter the picture, either as big game, domesticated herds, or beasts of draft and burden, dominant power usually slips to the men who hunt, drive, or herd them.

In the California desert every adult Washo Indian adult collected his or her own food, gathering nuts and roots, fishing, or joining with others to trap jackrabbits in nets. They hunted nothing larger than deer, and then only very occasionally. Women worked alongside men, sharing in both leadership and celebration of the two great festivals, the one in honor of gathering and the other in honor of hunting.

Tiwi women of Africa also provide at least their share of the food, accounting for more than half of what the people eat. But their contribution consists of plant foods and small animals, while the men, concentrating exclusively on big game, bring in much more meat. The men dominate the society, although the women have power too; they're influential, for example, in politically significant marriage arrangements.

The Eskimo are the instructive exception to the generally more egalitarian habits of the foragers. Almost nothing edible grows in their frozen homeland; virtually everything they eat, wear, and use comes from animals, some of them extremely dangerous, that must be tracked and killed with courage and ingenuity in as unforgiving a landscape as human beings inhabit. On the male hunter and his luck hang the family's sole hope of survival. And here, alone among foraging peoples, we find very dominant men, very submissive women, and no acknowledged female power.

Exactly why women so rarely hunt or herd large animals is a controversial question for a later chapter. But in failing to do so, they abdicate the immense prestige that comes from bringing in goods desirable and plentiful enough to trade outside the immediate family. Many peoples must live mainly on seeds, fruits, roots, and grains; the huge wad of protein and calories in an antelope or bear or giraffe carcass is a very valued good indeed. Week after patient week of collecting produces only the same humdrum meals. A single lucky arrow can mean whole days and nights of feasting.

Meat equals prestige because feasting always includes persons outside the immediate family; no small group could possibly eat or preserve a large catch before scavengers or spoilage claimed most of it. Even so small a bag as a Thanksgiving turkey meant, in the days before refrigeration, that a whole clan or neighborhood assembled. A large carcass, hundreds or thousands of pounds of buffalo or seal or giraffe, inundates a small community. There's generally even a special etiquette for cutting it up—a particular part for the hunter who felled it, and a part for his wife, his parents, his other relatives; a particular part for the man who owned the spear, and for the one who first spotted the quarry; and certain shares for the others in the hunting party, and for their relatives; and shares for kinsmen standing in certain relationships to all of them. In a small foraging community, that will mean more than enough for everybody.

Ordinary vegetable food is rarely the stuff of celebration. It's protein and calories in much less concentrated form. It stays put, keeps fairly well, and needn't be felled all at once. It doesn't occur in sudden, thousand-pound windfalls. And, except for particular delicacies, it is every day's staff of life, not the banquet we remember forever after.

A straightforward economic fact illustrates the immense symbolic and practical power of large animals. In many male-dominated societies, the men provide the high-prestige calories, but the women do the great majority of the productive work. Day in and day out, they forage or garden for plant food, they collect firewood or drinking water, they make clothing and household articles, and even, among the migratory beduin—as masculinist a society as exists on earth— the women load the camels and erect the tents each time the group moves. The men, too elevated for such "women's work," spend their time preparing their tools and weapons, or speculating on the whereabouts of game or pasture, or guaranteeing safety and success through religious practices, or discussing the best plan for the next move, or vying for political advantage, or performing rituals, or preparing for war.

War, that most masculine of occupations, occurs among many but not all human groups. The anthropological data are quite clear; those who wage war always meet certain social criteria. First, they possess something that others covet. Immovable wealth like fields, gardens, or towns; or wealth on the hoof, like herds, have for millennia attracted envious interest. Societies that view women and their reproductive potential as male chattel rather than as female power see unprotected women in the same light. Warmakers also need an economic system that provides the wealth and frees the manpower to undertake so chancy, wasteful, and essentially frivolous an enterprise as combat.

Simple foragers own nothing they can't carry with them. They lack both the means and the motive for war. They rarely even settle personal scores violently if they can help it; small numbers of widely scattered people can't enforce their will on one another, and may later need each other's help. They are the exception proving that wholehearted mayhem doesn't arise from our primitive urges, but from the demands of certain social organizations. Only with civilization, in fact, does it become widespread and effective.

Richard Leakey, scion of the world's first family of archeology, has looked deeply into this question while examining the mortal remains of many ancient people. He bemoans the widespread misapprehension that "the violence and aggression that we see so much of today is because our ancestors behaved in this way. [People] believe that the killer ape idea is basically correct, that there's an instinctual drive on our part to kill and kill again."[14] He traces

this "powerful, popular, and compelling" notion to the specula-
tions of Raymond Dart, who in the mid-1950s analyzed the bones
found at Makapansgat, a South African cave. Dart found bones
sharpened by hominids living two million years ago, and concluded
that they were weapons meant for other hominids. Given the hid-
eous—and then recent—memory of death camps and cities bombed
to rubble, and the even more hopeless prospect of the Bomb,
Leakey argues, Dart could easily discern a precursor of his generation's anguish in stone and bone axes and daggers.

But, Leakey insists, the ethnography simply doesn't support this
picture. "Our species has a very long history," he says, "and for
most of our time we have existed on the basis of cooperation and
close communication. There is no evidence that this aggression, this
division that now separates many of us, is in our genes. It's something that has surely come about recently, perhaps merely in the last
ten thousand years."[15]

Through the research of anthropologist Richard Lee, Leakey believes, we can see how the change might have happened. When the
elders among today's !Kung people of Botswana and South Africa
were children, they lived as nomadic bushmen foraging in the
Kalahari desert. Today, encouraged by governments, they live as
settled, small-scale farmers, plowing the ground and keeping cattle
and goats. Their lives still mix the old, cooperative ways of
bushdwellers and the new stinginess of landowners. The !Kung will
give mongongo nuts for the asking, just as they did in the bush. But
they part with the new staples of goat meat or brewed beer only for
cash on the barrelhead. Lee observes:

> There's a different logic to the cash economy, to the herd-
> ing economy, than there is to the hunting and gathering
> economy. And so we get some interesting contrasts. For
> example, the women brew beer. They buy the sugar in
> the store, brew the beer, and they sell it to their kinsmen
> for five cents a cup. They will not take credit. On the
> other hand, after the beer has been drunk and the cash has
> been collected, they will share their mongongo nuts with
> their customers of a few moments before.[16]

Even more striking has been the change in the attitudes toward women and violence. In the bush, groups made decisions collectively; men and women whose opinions merited respect commanded respect. But:

> No government in the world is going to be able to deal with a committee of 70 or 100 !Kung. There must be spokesmen, or spokespersons, so that inevitably a hierarchy is developed. When these hierarchies develop, they're almost inevitably male, because that is the way most governments work, sadly, today. And so from a situation . . . where men *and* women participated in decision-making, they're moving rapidly towards a situation where the decision-making is more in the hands of men.[17]

And many of those men now have military training, thanks to the South African army. Systematically taught violence, this "formerly relatively unaggressive people" experienced a tenfold increase in homicides in one two-year period.[18]

War, even more than economics, brings men—and the values of male dominance—to the fore. Most warmaking societies protect women as the hope for future generations: some also disdain them as weaklings. Societies generally try to sacrifice only their most expendable members, the young men, especially those without families. It may be a deep sorrow to lose them, but no threat to the community's survival; the nations of Europe hemorrhaged an entire male generation into the trenches of World War I but reproduced to fight even more bloodily on another day, almost exactly a generation later.

Still, there's nothing inborn or genetic about the distinction between women and warriors. The nineteenth-century Dahomeans, a dual society rather like the Igbo, fielded a half-female army; of the king's 12,000 troops in 1854, fully 5,000 were female. An elite unit of women formed the palace guard, responsible for the king's personal safety. Forcible chastity lasting into middle age rendered them reproductively superfluous.

But the young men who constitute the bulk of the world's soldiers might come to resent being considered expendable, and even refuse to sacrifice themselves for someone else's notion of the common good. Against this threat, though, stands a mighty fortress —the values of male dominance in mythic form: the belief that violence is permissible, that mayhem is meritorious, that physical courage represents the highest expression of men's nature as males and human beings, that heroes fight and fighters are heroic. A society that needs soldiers or big-game hunters, therefore, exalts the virtues of the battle and the hunt: stoicism, aggressiveness, daring, respect for authority, a touchy sense of honor and, most especially, the differentness from women that mark a man among men.

Sanday's sample showed a striking correlation between male-dominated social structures and histories of stress and conflict. The groups that exclude women from decision-making, that countenance interpersonal violence, that accept rape as a natural, if regrettable, aspect of human nature, share a common experience with the communal jitters. They inhabit highly seasonal, unreliable environments. They have taken, or held, their territories through force of arms. They believe that they face continual external threats. They trace their roots to faraway places and their communal beginnings to battle.

The gentler virtues of emotional expressiveness, tenderness, caring, and forgiveness bring home neither the bacon nor the enemy's scalp. It cannot be coincidental that the few societies in Sanday's sample that still cherish these values have no military tradition whatever. They live in stable climates that unfailingly supply their wants. They lack any experience of invasion, either as invaders or defenders. They trace their mythic origins to the very lands they now inhabit (which are often too poor, remote, or difficult to tempt enemies).

So physical gender doesn't constitute a pair of immutable physical molds that inevitably shape human behavior. Some societies utterly reject even the immutability of the number two. Numbers of American Indian tribes, for example, permitted males and females to adopt the social roles of the other sex—not as deviants, like homosexuals among ourselves, but as respectable married persons and spiritual leaders. Some of these cultures posed stringent standards for manhood, but permitted another option for those unwilling to meet them. Others capitalized on the wisdom of women past childrearing.

White observers from the fifteenth through the nineteenth century recorded these customs with horror and dismay, and often totally misinterpreted them as institutionalized perversion. (They called the custom of men becoming quasi women *berdache*, from a North African word for homosexual boy prostitution, and thus ignored the institution's essential respectability.) But these cultures did not ignore the physical differences between the sexes; they merely uncoupled gender role from physique.

So, rather than peering into the genes for answers, we can profitably view gender as a screen where people project their own hopes and fears, where men's and women's actions trace the outlines of dreams and nightmares. But few peoples seem to know that they have imposed a social construct on a physical fact. "Frequently, . . . all the differences [between males and females ascribed by a society] will be taken together and appear to be based on biology," notes anthropologist Marilyn Strathern. "In most societies, gender thus has the appearance of being a straightforward representation of natural sex characteristics."[19]

When people believe that their habits represent "nature," sex differences become the most powerful of symbols—"a kind of language for talking about other things as well—for example, the respective prestige of certain occupations, or the correct relationship between a human and his deity."[20] In a male-dominated society, woman's work—be it loading heavy bales onto camels, as among the beduin, or knitting, as among ourselves—demeans the man who does it. Never mind that among ourselves, hefting luggage is a male prerogative—indeed, it demonstrates strength, another male prerogative—and among the Laymi of Peru knitting is. In their Andean villages, the right to knit the patterned caps emblematic of each community descends in the male line. (Beduin men also used to pass the long hours with their herds by knitting.) Male occupations, be they medicine in the U.S. or high school teaching in France, carry great prestige; female occupations, such as medicine in the U.S.S.R. and high school teaching in the U.S., carry much less.

And so, Strathern argues, Americans see ambition and business acumen as masculine not so much because only males possess them, but because we value them so highly. The *shtetl,* on the other hand, rated book learning (slightly suspect as womanish in modern America) as the highest male attribute; every market woman had a certain knack for turning a kopek. "Achievement motivation as an index for gender discrimination in fact tells us as much about our society as it does about sex differences," Strathern believes.[21] In societies obsessed with dominating nature, men aspire to dominance and toughness; but men shrink from violence in the few remaining societies obsessed with preserving the group's harmony with the forces that sustain it. In societies where manhood requires dominion over women, Sanday found, men's "intrinsic nature" permits them to rape. In societies where manhood includes respect for the special powers of women, it does not. The sons of Adam violate the daughters of Eve markedly more often than the grandsons of Ancient-Bodied would dare violate her daughters.

Here we close the first part of our inquiry, an attempt to discover what males and females *are.* We've considered them as actors in the great pageant of hominid evolution: as reproductive organisms, as members of the human species, and as members of human groups.

Now we ask a second, more sharply focused, question: What are human males and females *like?* We shift our attention from the species and its adaptation, to the individual and his or her lived experience, from gender as a pair of categories to gender as two sets of individual characteristics. We'll explore the talents and tendencies that seem to distinguish men and women, that shape such different lives. Are these differences inborn or imposed? Are they permanent or subject to change?

But before we do, we must answer two questions far more basic: What do we even mean by a difference? How do we recognize a difference when we see one? A digression into philosophy may seem a distraction here, when straightforward facts can tell us what we want to know. Of course, we won't lack for facts; we'll sift through scores of them. But we can't expect single, hard nuggets of truth. In the issue of gender, as in every issue with large interests at stake, the facts dissolve into the complicated, elusive, controversial findings of a dozen disciplines; the detailed, contradictory results of a hundred methodologies; the confusing, contrary products of deep but unspoken assumptions. Behind each fact lurks its author's notion of what a difference is and what differentness means. Only by first defining these can we finally understand what the facts mean.

II

TWO DIGRESSIONS
ON METHOD

4

What Constitutes a Difference?

The dictionary says, "The condition of being unlike."

The real answer is, "It all depends."

To see why, let's eavesdrop on a Martian spy reporting on earth's dominant life form.

"So, MS-12, you'd say that these medium-sized creatures that locomote on their lower protuberances—the so-called 'people' or 'human beings'—are the major active species?"

"Definitely, sir. They're found in nearly every habitat. Considering the state of their technology, they have made some fairly ingenious adaptations. They've mastered most of the simpler sorts of transportation and communication—jet propulsion, laser beams, that sort of thing. And they're the only species that exhibits any technology at all."

"So we have a uniform, fairly primitive population. . . ."

"Oh, no, sir, they're not uniform at all. They come in various colors, sizes, trim options, and two main functional models."

"Oh, really? But you say they're one species?"

"No question about it. They interbreed freely, and produce all sorts of intermediate models."

"Breed, MS-12?"

"I'll get to that, sir. Really, in 'human beings' you see lots of superficial variations—different trim packages and the like—but there are really only two basic types, what they call 'male' and 'female.' Both types are necessary for reproduction. They have all sorts of elaborate procedures for sorting out which two are going to cooperate on a particular offspring. That's what they call 'breeding.' "

"It takes two to reproduce? Remarkable. But is it difficult to tell the two types apart? Our landing parties will need to know."

"It takes a little practice, sir. Some of the optional accessories can get in the way. The first thing I noticed was that one group, the males, were larger. But that didn't seem to be the whole story. The two groups also seemed to differ in the shape of the torso and some other minor features."

"Torso?"

"Yes, the middle part of the body. The smaller group, the 'women,' have a less rectilinear outline, nipped in at the part they call the 'waist,' and then there are often a pair of protuberances on the ventral surface."

"Well, that certainly seems straightforward, MS-12. A large specimen with a rectilinear outline is a 'male.' "

"But there's more to it than that. At first I didn't notice, because of course I started out working in the surface perception mode. But the subjects themselves kept referring to certain differences that I couldn't locate. They said that these occurred in what they called the 'private parts.' I finally realized that they meant certain areas of the body that were almost always encased in artificial coverings— what they call 'clothing.' Well, using the interior perception mode I easily discovered what they meant. The area between the legs shows the greatest difference. In fact, if I hadn't already established that I was dealing with two subsections of the same species, I would have thought they were two different species."

"I don't understand, MS-12."

"It is a little hard to grasp at first, sir, but these pictures will help. You see, sir, in your 'male' you have this special appendage. In your 'female' there is this type of indentation."

"Remarkable. Truly remarkable. You've done an outstanding job, MS-12. If I may sum up, the main life form of earth, the 'human being,' occurs in two varieties. The 'male' is large, rectilinear, and has this appendage. The 'female' is small, more curved, and has this indentation instead."

"Well, not exactly, sir."

"I don't understand."

"Well, sir, the males are not always larger and more rectilinear."

"They're not?"

"No, sir, sometimes a female is larger, and not any more curved. That is, some of the men are as curved as some of the women."

"Then there's no clear demarcation? Some of the males are larger, more rectilinear, and have the appendage, but sometimes the opposite is true?"

"No sir. That is, a female never has the appendage, even though she may be large. 'She' is how they refer to females, sir. A male always has the appendage, even if he's smaller and fairly curvy."

"Puzzling, MS-12."

"Yes sir, at first anyway. It takes a while to get used to a life form as varied as 'human beings.' "

"So they're not really two distinct groups, a tall straight one with the appendage and a short, curvy one with the indentation."

"Well, they are two distinct groups, sir, but only the presence or absence of the appendage gives you a positive identification."

"Can they tell each other apart?"

"Oh yes, sir, virtually without fail."

"But how? You said that the appendage and indentation are nearly always covered."

"Yes, sir, but the males are larger and the females are curvier. . . ."

"I don't understand, MS-12. Your sentences are perfectly clear, but the ideas are not."

"No sir. I mean, yes sir, I know."

MS-12 and the commander would do better if they'd study, along with the physical traits of earthlings, something of earthly logic as well. Then they'd recognize that MS-12's statements, like human beings, fall into two sets. The two kinds of statements look alike on the surface, and both express widely recognized and easily verifiable facts. But this outer similarity, like the unisex clothing that so puzzled the Martian, masks a deep divergence. In fact, the two kinds of statements belong to different orders of description and call upon different canons of proof. No wonder they confounded the commander.

The sentences about appendages and indentations define a type of difference known as "dimorphism." Our species harbors two distinct, normal, and mutually exclusive versions of genitalia. Every individual has one and only one. Either an "appendage" or an "indentation" is normal in the right circumstances, but there is simply no middle ground.

The statements about height and shape discuss something entirely different, what statisticians call the effect of sex on variation. Human height is highly variable. A difference of almost a yard separates the tallest human adult from the shortest. More women, though, cluster toward the short end of the range and more men toward the tall. Still, some perfectly normal women tower over most men, some equally normal men look up to most women and most members of both sexes fall in between. There is simply no single right height for a man or a woman to be. Almost any position within the wide range of possibilities is normal for someone. Identifying an individual's sex from appendages and indentations is a virtual certainty, but predicting it from height is never more than a guess.

As MS-12 and the commander discovered, confusing these two categories can turn true statements false. When we say "females produce ova and males produce sperm," we define a dimorphism, two mutually exclusive categories. Some anomalous individuals produce neither, but no male produces ova nor any female sperm.

But when we say "men are better at math than women," we define nothing; indeed, we need further definitions even to understand what we've said. We don't mean what the previous statement about sperm and ova did, that every male without exception is better at math than any woman. We mean only that more men earn high scores (or, perhaps, that most men earn higher scores) on the mathematical sections of intelligence tests. Still, a few women score very high indeed, and more than a few men do very poorly. What we really mean is, "the average man does better at math than the average woman," or perhaps "the average male performance is better than the average female performance," keeping in mind that the average man and woman are statistical constructs, not human beings.

MS-12 and the commander aren't alone. A long, sad history of pain and mischief follows from their kind of confusion. Racial stereotypes, to take only one example, assign to all members of a group traits possessed by only some (and probably by nonmembers as well). Gender stereotypes are even more mischievous. The human races aren't hard and fast groups; in their original homelands, racial groups shade into one another over vast continental stretches. Interracial couples produce children with traits midway between the parents'. Only in discredited theories and tyrannical legal codes do racial groups constitute either mutually exclusive or exhaustive categories.

But in certain respects, males and females always do. Reproductively, at least, they're utterly distinct. They never shade into one another and unions don't produce intermediate individuals but a person just like one of the parents. In any universe of cases where everyone must be either a male or a female, they're reproductive opposites.

This initial, but quite limited, oppositeness encourages us to see others. And so does our cultural tendency, inherited from the ancient Greeks, to discern dualities of quality: good and bad, ugliness and beauty, old and young. In real life, of course, reproductive gender, and the oppositeness it implies, form only part of a larger identity. We can't, Strathern observes, "define a mother as a nonfather,"[1] or even a boy as a nongirl. The larger categories of parents and children define overriding similarities. Male and female *persons* can't be opposites; they share many, many traits in common.

But that's an easy point to forget, even among those who should know better. Consider, for example, the body of research that finds a statistical difference in the attention that baby boys and girls pay to objects and people. Given a forced choice between toys and pictures of faces, more males favor the mechanical and more females the social. "Surprisingly enough," muses psychologist Rhoda Unger, "no one ever considers alternate tendencies in the same study with the same subjects." Do the children who respond well to human images respond poorly to interesting objects? Do those fascinated by gadgets ignore smiles and frowns? Of course not; the two interests become opposites only when an experimenter artificially opposes them. Obviously, "interest in both the objective en-

vironment and the subjective environment is highly adaptive."[2]
Only autistic children systematically withdraw from major features
of their surroundings.

But the experiment embodies certain assumptions about males
and females, if only because our society uses gender as the major
marker in the division of labor. It assigns very different powers and
functions to the two sexes; thus it hunts assiduously for differences
and is inclined to see oppositeness.

But suppose science had arisen among a people with other assumptions. The cap-knitting Laymi of Peru, for example, see sex
differences as relevant to reproduction, but not to very much else.
In their high, cold Andean villages, Laymi men and women both
farm, herd, make textiles, carry out religious rituals, and contribute
to decisions. Boys and girls grow up seeing both parents doing very
similar work. Would Laymi scientists constructing the objects-ver-
sus-persons study phrase the results as sets of opposites or overlap-
ping ranges of variation? Would the question even occur to them in
the first place?

We'll never know, because, of course, science didn't develop
among the Laymi. It grew into an instrument of immense power
and precision among ourselves, and so it incorporates our habits of
mind. That statement surprises, even disorients, persons raised to
respect science as *the* unbiased method for finding truth, not as one
of several competing systems that have contended for control of
our culture. But, despite all the triumphs that have remade (and
may unmake) the world, that is what it remains.

What distinguishes it from other approaches to knowledge isn't
its method of making inferences; every intelligent person draws
conclusions from the evidence of experience. Nor does its unique-
ness lie in subject matter; many pseudo sciences—astrology, al-
chemy, creationism, phrenology—have shared substantive interests
with authentic sciences. No, science's special strength lies in its
method of testing statements through rigorous experimentation.
And that means that any question that can be phrased experimen-
tally can become "scientific." What's the speed of the ether? How
far apart are the canals of Mars? These are only two of the more
famous nonphenomena that have absorbed the earnest efforts of

legitimate, honest, even distinguished scientists. Science doesn't assure that the questions we ask correspond to reality, only that the conclusions we draw reflect the result of an experiment.

To see why, let's follow an idea from rumination to research paper. Picking up his car at the service station, or babysitting his infant niece, or attending a colloquium, or just walking down the street, a scientist wonders why American men generally show more talent for machinery than American women. Perhaps there's an inborn male affinity for gadgetry, as some have suggested. And he thinks, "If it exists, it ought to show up early in life. I wonder if baby boys show more interest in mechanical objects than do baby girls."

But turning this spark of curiosity into a scientific finding will take several more steps. First, the scientist must boil the question down to a statement he can test objectively. He might reason, "If I offer toy trucks and rag dolls to babies, the boys ought to show more interest in the trucks than do the girls." Of course, it's not so easy to tell what interests a baby, "but I'll define interest as reaching for the toy when it's presented, or smiling, or cooing, or not turning away. I can videotape the babies and then count up the number of times they show interest." Eventually, he states a tentative hypothesis: "There will be a statistical association between the degree of interest a baby displays in a doll or toy truck shown to it and the child's sex."

But he still hasn't arrived at a scientifically testable proposition. A statement is susceptible to testing only if it can be refuted, and nothing short of searching the entire universe can logically prove that something—the tooth fairy, or the fountain of youth, or a statistical association between sex and a taste for toy trucks—doesn't exist; the single, refuting example may lurk in the very next place we look. Searching the whole universe, of course, would exhaust researchers' patience and their research grants, so standard research design lets them off the hook. They simply transform the hypothesis into a negative statement that they can easily test: "There will be no association between the sex of a baby and its preference for dolls or toy trucks when offered both." This new statement, in a form known as the "null hypothesis" (for "null" or nonexistent association), is logically simple to refute; a sole counterexample does the trick.

Our scientist is now ready to begin the actual experiment. He'll use statistical formulas to determine how many babies offered how many dolls and trucks constitute a fair sample. He'll seek cooperative parents, visit toy shops, design an experimental environment free of biasing distractions. Finally, he'll show the dolls and trucks to the babies and record their reactions.

Next he'll analyze the results. Do the data show an association between sex and interest in trucks? His first computations seem confirmatory. Is the association stronger than might occur through chance or through choosing an unrepresentative sample? Certain very detailed and widely used statistical measures promptly provide these answers. If the findings survive their scrutiny, if the association still appears solid, convention permits him to conclude that he has disproven the null hypothesis. This means, as his journal article will shortly announce, that an association between sex and toy preference does in fact exist.

To this logically watertight procedure we owe much of the knowledge that has built our modern world. But, believes psychologist Anthony Greenwald, it still isn't a perfect instrument of truth. The very way it's phrased can disguise—and even foster—"a prejudice against the null hypothesis," a discomfort at finding no difference. Chemist Ruth Hubbard and biologist Marion Lowe concur. "Through their training, scientists learn to define and describe differences better than commonalities and to find them more 'interesting.' Indeed, a finding of 'no difference' often is considered so insignificant that it is not worth mentioning."[3]

A scientist has an "investment in confirming his theory with a rejection of the null hypothesis," Greenwald believes. Refuting the null hypothesis, after all, proves the existence of a difference or association. Confirming the null hypothesis (or, more accurately, failing to refute it) proves nothing, it being logically impossible to prove that something does not exist. Repeated failure does provide strong circumstantial evidence that no association exists, but can never establish nonexistence as a fact. Failures therefore make much less newsworthy journal articles and conference papers. And thus researchers may overlook "the possibility that the observed x-y association may be dependent on a specific manipulation, measure, experimental setting, or some combination of them," Greenwald believes. Did our researcher consider, for example, that the different colors of dolls and trucks might explain the children's reactions? Did he find out whether the boys had already received many trucks and the girls many dolls, and thus found them more comforting? "In his eagerness to proclaim a general x-y relationship, he has been willing to attribute his previous false starts to his (or, better, his research assistants') incompetence, and on this basis does not feel it necessary or desirable to inform the scientific community about them."[4]

There's another reason why our researcher prefers to find an association (and thus, a difference). It more clearly fits into the scientific enterprise. He undertook his study of babies and toy trucks to clarify a larger issue—the superior mechanical ability of American adult males. Scientific truth may advance more rapidly when erroneous theories are overturned, but scientific careers advance more rapidly through bold assertions of previously unnoticed associations. "One well-published positive finding [is] remembered," observes Oxford psychologist Hugh Fairweather, "where a score of subsequent failures-to-replicate are forgotten."[5]

So we've found one bias, at least: a preference for finding differences. The mere existence of a difference tells us nothing about its practical consequences—it can be real enough, but too small to mean anything in real life. Let's suppose that a scientist studied the effect of eating rutabagas on human growth. He followed two groups through childhood and found the tuber-eaters consistently heavier than the abstainers. As they began to toddle, as they graduated from junior high, and again on their twenty-first birthdays, the rutabagas eaters, both individually and as a group, always weighed more. Every rutabagas eater, on every trial, outweighed the controls by one percent of body weight!

A sophisticated statistical test would show that the association could not result from chance; in statistical terms, it is not only significant, but strong. But does the difference actually affect any aspect of anybody's life? Does weighing one and a third pounds more at age twenty-one make any *practical* difference? Of course not; in statistical terms, the "strength of association" or "measure of effect size" is very weak. Still, a devotedly pro-rutabagas researcher, convinced of the vegetable's importance in the human diet (or in the pay of rutabagas interests), might still publish the study without even calculating effect size. He did find a legitimate difference, even if it doesn't affect anything. In the sex-differences literature, the chi-square test for statistical significance (which measures the possibility that difference results from chance) appears in nearly every published study. The much less popular omega-square test for effect size shows up in relatively few.

But if our researcher is really after what a difference *means*, no statistical test provides much guidance. He didn't undertake his study to find out if baby boys enjoy trucks; he wanted to tie a certain fact into a wider web of knowledge. He was looking for an infant preference that foreshadows an adult discrepancy.

Looking for just such a large connection, psychologist Herman Witkin and his associates spent decades testing young adults on two puzzles, the rod-and-frame test and the embedded figures test. The first shows the subject a movable rod that pivots inside, but independently of, an illuminated frame. The task is to set the rod to true vertical, regardless of whether the frame is askew. The second test asks subjects to isolate a particular design from a surrounding pattern of similar designs. On the average, men surpassed women at both tasks.

But why should an able researcher devote his career to testing two such obscure abilities? Because, for Witkin, each was a tiny, visible tip of an immense psychological difference. Setting rods and spotting patterns, he believed, were only two measures of a crucial tendency that determines a person's entire cognitive style. He believed he had discovered a new trait, "field independence," or the capacity to disregard distracting stimuli irrelevant to the task at hand. A field-independent individual—one able to discriminate essentials from trivialities—ought to face the world, Witkin thought, more analytically, less emotionally and, ultimately, more effectively. The field-dependent person, on the other hand—constantly distracted from basics by ephemera—would respond to his (or, as it usually worked out, to her) environment in a more "global," less analytical manner lacking precision and initiative.

Now there's a frontier worth spending years to conquer. "The field-independent cognitive style has been characterized as 'differentiated, self-reliant, analytic,' as opposed to the field-dependent style, which is considered passive and conforming," other psychologists report. Mightn't it account for really big differences—maybe the male supremacy in science, requiring high degrees of both analysis and enterprise? Maybe even the male mechanical advantage? Witkin never shrank from such a conclusion in any of his many writings.

It wasn't until the late 1970s, in fact, that some psychologists noticed that "field independence, and not field dependence, has been associated with positive values in our culture."[6] And only then did the huge and influential literature note a relationship between field dependence and "interpersonal orientation."

Now, suppose that Witkin's original team had consisted of people who, unlike most university professors, value the arts of personal relationship over the craft of statistical analysis. Mightn't they have discerned the trait of "field sensitivity" leading to supremacy in the valued skills of negotiation, nuance, and intuition? Mightn't they have bemoaned the inadequacy of the "field-insensitive" approach to modern life?

Witkin's work stands for an entire approach to gender—what sociologist Anne Oakley calls the "which has the bigger foot" school of research. It "is based on the assumption that sex differences matter—that they matter more than sex similarities. In this way, scientific work starts from and reinforces the status quo of everyday beliefs about the roles of men and women."[7] So, the questions that we ask about gender, the differences that we ascribe, may indeed tell us more about our own assumptions than about the potential of men and women.

Indeed, if most gender research shows the status quo writ large, it shows the shape of science writ larger. The Gordian tangle of data appears to concern hormones, synapses, genes, and genetic fitness. But at its core twists a question far more troubling: Can we even explain human behavior at the level that this debate implies? If we study ourselves with tools made for nonhuman species, can we trust the results? Won't our unique habits of self-consciousness and culture cloud the outcome?

But this question troubles surprisingly few researchers. For all their technical power, few scientists have the training to answer—or even to consider—it; and those who do command that knowledge generally command little respect in the lab or computer room. So majestically has science—physical and biological science—advanced against human impotence, so decisively has it driven all competitors from the field of educated discourse, so completely has it captivated the intellectually ambitious, that it is our age's metaphor for knowledge itself. Fields of study that once tapped independent sources of truth—biblical commentary, psychological introspection, literary criticism, philosophy—have painfully remade themselves in the image of physical science. The uniform may chafe, the trappings may bind, but scholars concerned with values, qualities, and nuances have struggled into scientific garb and trained themselves to speak in quantities.

The masquerade succeeds in inverse proportion to their tolerance for things that can't be toted up. The great liberating insights into human behavior—Freud's, Durkheim's—pierced through to the meaning hidden behind the arbitrary, the nuanced, that which is inexplicable except in terms of itself. These thinkers saw that human beings live and die by symbols, not by facts. Tens of millions of men and women have willingly given their lives for the crescent or the cross, for a particular form of the cross, for a single- or double-headed eagle. Brothers have slaughtered one another for the difference between the Stars and Stripes and the Stars and Bars. A vocabulary for explaining human action must speak fluently about the utter concreteness of metaphor.

But hard science speaks in math, not metaphor. And mathematics —expressly invented to strip away allusion, to lay bare the girders of logical relationship—has no words to discuss this kind of fact, whose truth lies not in schemata but in detail, not in abstraction but in that which anthropologist Clifford Geertz calls "thick description."

Does it matter, for example, that American middle-class men and women experience the rod-and-frame test differently? The team of subject and experimenter works alone in a darkened room. Only the experimenter touches the rod, adjusting it according to the subject's instructions. The abstract, "objective" reports in the journals give the dimensions of the frame and the size of the sample. But a "thick" description—the kind that never appears in print—would delve into the meanings of darkness and closed doors at this moment in this culture. It could explore the relative power of the seated young woman and standing older man. It might wonder about her ability and desire to insist that he complete the task to her exact specifications. It ought to compare her thoughts to a young man's. And only then would it present statistics that gave a true picture.

Persons trained in "hard" sciences generally see the social sciences as very poor excuses for science, indeed. And that's precisely what they are—bodies of inquiry forced into often inappropriate shapes. They don't function like physics or chemistry; chemists don't argue out the nature of the molecule before each experiment. But the social sciences have continuously debated basic concepts for a hundred years.

And the findings of soft sciences don't always build on one another, and the studies often don't replicate; an insight about the Gusii may not hold for the Mbuti, and you can't replay a race riot to test your hypothesis. Their data are evanescent and notoriously impure; informants have their own biases, events their own inescapable historical contexts. And these sciences express themselves in the clatter of English rather than the pure tones of calculus or linear algebra. In short, they are sciences only by courtesy. For many "hard" scientists, therefore, what they know is barely worth knowing.

What *is* worth knowing, in these scientists' view, comes from the "harder" disciplines that produce more "basic" results. The idea that "hard data" explain human behavior has become the "ruling ideology" of the scientists who study the brain, believe neurobiologists Hilary and Steven Rose. Labs around the world search for the physical counterparts to mental events—the location of anger or the chemistry of altruism—in the belief that locating them also explains them.

Two assumptions support this effort. The first holds that "sciences are arranged in a hierarchical order, varying from high-level disciplines such as economics and sociology to lower-level ones such as biology, chemistry, and, at the base, particle physics." Traveling down the ladder toward "hardness" (which is also up another ladder toward prestige) takes one even further from the messy unpredictability of human action and closer to unambiguous physical interactions.

The second assumption justifies the first; "events in higher-level sciences can be reduced on the basis of a one-for-one correspondence to events, and hence laws, appropriate to the lower-level science." Thus, hormone or enzyme A triggers synaptic event B resulting in mental state C and social behavior, custom, or belief D. (The sociobiologists would add that genes Z explain the action and existence of A.) So the laws of chemistry and physics, if pursued far enough, could ultimately account for Zen Buddhism, matrilineal land tenure, and the Boer War.

Vexing questions of human behavior, in the reductionist view, yield easily to the techniques of hard science. No longer need psychologists and sociologists seek causes of alcoholism in family dynamics or personality structure when the answer really lies in the aberrant reactions between enzymes and the molecule C_2H_5OH occurring in the cells of alcoholics. But does biochemistry truly explain the mystery at the heart of addiction? Do cellular processes tell us why an individual voluntarily persists in behavior that imperils and ultimately kills valued relationships? Can enzyme analysis distinguish those persons with the courage and faith to break their chemical bondage from those who permit it to destroy them? Can it even reveal why one susceptible person succumbs in the first place but another resists for a lifetime?

Most decidedly not, the Roses insist. Laying out the chemical and enzymatic reactions, they argue, are "not *causal* but *identity* statements." They can't reveal the origins of drunkenness, but merely call it by another—and no sweeter—name, one that simply restates in the language of chemistry the creed that Alcoholics Anonymous members have declared for generations: "I am powerless over alcohol." To understand alcoholism (rather than alcohol) as a human problem—to appreciate its deadly grip on discipline, self-respect, integrity, hope, family ties—means acknowledging that human behavior exists at a level analytically independent of the behavior of molecules and atoms. Knowing that an alcoholic responds abnormally to a certain molecule can help us diagnose alcoholism, identify potential alcoholics, perhaps even develop an alcohol antagonist. It can't reveal what drives one susceptible person to a life on skid row and another to a life of willed sobriety.

Many of those studying sex differences, the Roses believe, reduce human behavior to reactions of molecules and genes, or to the interactions of computer parts, or to the actions of evolution. "Anthropologists and evolutionary biologists proceed in parallel fashion," notes Richard Alexander, a scholar of evolution. "First they study and compare variations (usually among cultures and species, respectively) and their probable significance or adaptive value." In which species or cultures, for example, do fathers devote time and care to infants? "Then they search for connections between the adaptive significance and the immediate (physiological, ontogenetic) mechanisms responsible for the variations." What kind of work life, for example, goes with which kind of care? Which bind fathers close to their offspring or keep them distant?

At the crucial next step, though, that of explaining these relationships, "the two kinds of investigators differ. . . . Whenever they are unable to resolve the question of connections between adaptive significance and immediate mechanisms for particular behaviors (cultural patterns), social scientists may often assume that no such connections exist while biologists usually continue to assume that they do."[8] If you can't exactly put your finger on why a behavior happens, you can assume one of two things: either that biology, genetics, and neurology can explain it, or that they can't. At this stage of our knowledge, the choice is a matter of taste or temperament rather than of scientific proof.

Scientists, of course, understand that published research findings are meant to be questioned. Because lay readers and journalists may not, a scientist's professional opinion becomes a fact, "hard news," a statement about objective reality. Indeed, it even has "ethical overtones, claiming to provide rules for the proper conduct of human society. . . . Science, a social product, becomes both the goal and method of all society," the Roses believe.[9]

Physicist Thomas Kuhn recalls his amazement when this idea first dawned on him. Preparing a physics course for nonscientists, he began to read the history of science. "To my complete surprise," he recalls, "that exposure to out-of-date scientific theory and practice radically undermined some of my basic conceptions about the nature of science and the reasons for its special success."[10] The catalog of antiquated notions—the physics of the monad, the chemistry of making gold from gross elements, the biology of the homunculus—forced a startling conclusion about the everyday conduct of ordinary investigations—what he calls "normal science." It was not the unbridled search for truth he had been educated to revere, but "a strenuous and devoted attempt to force nature into the conceptual boxes supplied by professional education."[11]

Scientists aren't lazy, dull, or intellectually dishonest. They merely plan and carry out their work according to the current consensus about what reality is like. This consensus—what Kuhn calls a paradigm—takes time to assemble and endures for years. It serves the very useful purpose of letting investigators know which questions are important and how to go about answering them.

But knowledge accumulates, and an existing paradigm may have to stretch, even burst, to accommodate all the new facts. Eventually someone suggests a new interpretation that fits both the old understandings and the new data, and research breaks into new areas. We recognize such "paradigm shifts" as epoch-making advances—the sort of revolutions associated with Newton, Copernicus, Darwin, Pasteur, and Einstein.

But these singular moments have little to do with daily life in the laboratory. Kuhn believes:

> No part of the aim of normal science is to call forth new sorts of phenomena; indeed, those that will not fit the boxes are often not seen at all. Nor do scientists normally aim to invent new theories, and they are often intolerant of those invented by others. Instead, normal-scientific research is directed to the articulation of those phenomena and theories that the paradigm already supplies.[12]

But, peering over from the physical sciences to his colleagues in the social sciences, Kuhn saw something deeply puzzling:

> Particularly I was struck by the number and extent of the overt disagreement between social scientists about the na-

ture of legitimate problems and methods. Both history and acquaintance made me doubt that practitioners of the natural sciences possess firmer or more permanent answers to such questions than their colleagues in the social sciences. Yet somehow, the practice of astronomy, physics, chemistry, or biology normally fails to evoke the controversies over fundamentals that today often seem endemic among, say, psychologists or sociologists.[13]

For natural scientists, unused to debate on basic definitions, the contentiousness of social scientists may utterly discredit their findings. "The biological scientist who turns to social science data is generally unimpressed by the explanatory power of the theories he encounters," observe psychologists John Archer and Barbara Lloyd. "Thus the anthropologist's view that differences in behavior reflect different positions in the social structure, or the sociologist's interpretation of similar behavioral data as reflecting group pressures or power relationships, may be ignored."[14]

Perhaps the social sciences, younger by three centuries or more than the natural sciences, are simply awaiting the somewhat tardy Newton or Lavoisier who will provide the paradigm that transforms them into "real" sciences? Perhaps, indeed, the future has already arrived in the form of E. O. Wilson and the sociobiologists? Wilson's new formulation of human motivation and necessity has certainly occasioned both the ecstatic acceptance and the bitter rejection that, according to Kuhn, precede a paradigm shift.

But they also greeted theories now long discredited. Lysenko's inheritance of acquired characteristics, the four-part typology of races, and the four humors all had eminent supporters as well as persistent detractors. But famous doctors also refused to wash their hands for a generation after the germ theory appeared. Galileo went to prison as a subversive. Einstein was luckier, but possibly because early in his career he proposed an astronomical experiment that corroborated his views.

The scientific method was never designed to meditate on first causes or evaluate basic axioms. Indeed, it most efficiently tackles the kind of problem that Kuhn terms a puzzle, a problem with a solution inside the existing paradigm that can be found according to accepted rules: "The scientific enterprise as a whole does from time to time prove useful, open up new territory, display order, and test long-accepted belief," he writes. "Nevertheless, *the individual* engaged on a normal research problem *is almost never doing any one of those things*" [emphasis in original]. Our researcher showing toys to infants, for example, isn't elaborating a new theory of maleness or femaleness. He only wants to clear up a small point in the accepted paradigm, which says that inborn sex differences influence behavior and that current sampling techniques can overcome the confounding effects of culture:

> What then challenges him is the conviction that, if only he is skillful enough, he will succeed in solving a puzzle that no one before has solved or solved so well. Many of the greatest scientific minds have devoted all of their professional attention to demanding puzzles of this sort. On most occasions any particular field of specialization offers nothing else to do, a fact that makes it no less fascinating to the proper sort of addict.[15]

You may think we've wandered far from the question that heads this chapter, but really, we've never left the immediate neighborhood. We can't know what constitutes a difference between men and women until we agree how to do fair comparisons. And for now, the various sciences studying gender play by very different rules.

They don't agree on what culture and learning mean in human life. Is culture a collection of discrete habits and customs that we can study individually—as, for example, some sociobiologists consider polygamy or the incest taboo comparable to the dance of the honeybees? Or is culture a web of meanings that binds habits and customs into a single seamless whole? Does it matter that one society occasionally resorts to polygamy to keep dowered property from being split among sisters' husbands, whereas another continually exploits it to cement political alliances among patrilineages?

Is culture, in other words, merely another, more elaborate form of animal behavior that does not in itself bias research results? Or is culture the ground of human consciousness, so pervasive that no observer can be both human and wholly objective? Ironically, the most abstract of the natural sciences, physics, has lately recognized limits to the human ability to define and describe. Two generations ago physicists began dealing with phenomena beyond the power of human measurement to wholly encompass. They accept that fact in the Heisenberg uncertainty principle.

Some deep students of sexual differences see a similar uncertainty in the data on the acts and motives of human males and females. If, as they argue, a human can observe reality only from within a particular cultural system, then Western observers peer out through a set of male-dominant, materialist assumptions. For a question as basic as gender, they believe, the ordinary sort of cross-cultural headcounts won't do. Comparing ourselves to some other male-dominant society provides no more information on our species' "natural" predilections than comparing two land-living animals informs us about the needs of sea creatures. Only comparisons between truly contrasting cultures—ourselves with an egalitarian society, for example—can give us a clear view.

But only if those data are themselves free of bias. But the anthropologists who gathered them also came from our own society and carried our biases, like blinders, into the field. The anthropologists may not have fully realized all the assumptions they made: that women contribute little of significance to high culture or spirituality; that power flows through formal organizations; that activity divides between public and private spheres; that formal deference equals real subordination; or that the world of men's activities truly represents the society.

Some sex differences obviously fall within the purview of hard sciences. Elbows, pelvises, knees, and facial hair everywhere differ by physiology, not by social role. But what of behaviors and abilities—mother love or mathematical skill? How can we be sure we're measuring real, inborn differences and not the effects of a lifetime of learning?

Can these most interesting questions even yield to scientific analysis? At least one neuroscientist, Ruth Bleier, argues that they can't —for the simple reason that they're not scientific questions at all, but philosophical and political issues in prestigious disguise.

Perhaps, for the moment, they'll have to remain social science questions. It's not because the social sciences are best equipped to answer them; obviously, answers will emerge only from the combined efforts of many disciplines. But researchers haven't yet agreed on the most basic definitions of what they're studying. What constitutes a difference, alas, depends mostly on whom we ask.

5

How Do We Know a Difference When We See One?

In 1940, the chairman of psychology at the University of Königsberg, Germany, published a warning. Evolutionary theory, he wrote in a respected scientific journal, revealed a grave threat to the human species' continued vigor; civilized living had so eased natural selection that harmful mutations had spread alarmingly. Ideally, of course, "our species-specific sensitivity to the beauty and ugliness of members of our species" should protect us from "the symptoms of degeneration, caused by domestication, which threaten our race." But this natural defense had failed, and "in some instances . . . we find not only a lack of this selectivity . . . but even a reversal to being attracted by symptoms of degeneracy." Thus, "socially inferior human material" could "penetrate and finally annihilate the healthy nation."

Luckily, though, one hope still remained:

> The selection for toughness, heroism, social utility . . . must be accomplished by some human institution if mankind, in default of selective factors, is not to be ruined by domestication-induced degeneracy. The racial idea as the basis of our state has already accomplished much in this respect. . . . We must—and should—rely on the healthy feelings of our best and charge them with the selection which will determine the prosperity or decay of our people.[1]

Many supposedly reputable thinkers disgraced themselves and their sciences during those dark times. Why, after all these years, single out this particular example of racist ranting in the guise of research? Because it still makes a telling point a world war and nearly five decades later. A crackbrained ideologue is exactly what its author was not; in 1973, for his contributions to the new science of animal behavior, Konrad Lorenz shared the Nobel Prize in physiology and medicine. His theory of inborn, fixed, action patterns has achieved substantial, but not unanimous, acceptance.

And this long-ago embarrassment illustrates an up-to-date truth. Scientists don't merely uncover facts about Homo sapiens. They fit them in among the other large ideas of their time. In wartime Germany, of course, the idea that behavior springs from inborn causes matched the views held—in rather harsher form—by the ruling Nazi elite. Of course, those German-speaking scholars who saw learning as the major shaper of behavior didn't publish in their homelands' scientific journals in those years. The lucky ones spoke from refuges in Britain and America.

In many eras, in many countries, opposing social interests have rallied to the banners of nature and nurture. Slaveowners in the nineteenth century, Nazis and nativists in our own, have argued that biological law decrees social custom—the righteous belief of entrenched, but threatened, privilege. Immigrants, minorities, the dispossessed of every race and nation, have always insisted that social arrangements explain social outcomes. The advantage has passed back and forth many times, with nurture ascendent in progressive times and nature in reactionary ones.

For the past two generations, though, from the Nazi period on, nurture theories generally dominated American academic thinking on behavior, which in most areas had a decidedly liberal cast. Those of Lorenz's colleagues who favored environment over heredity fled the central European universities—until then the world's leaders. Their presence on American and British faculties, along with the worldwide revulsion at Nazi atrocities, strongly reinforced a scholarly consensus lasting from the 1930s until the 1970s: inborn-tendency theories (when applied to racial groups) were benighted and probably dangerous claptrap.

Mere decades earlier, of course, scientific and political leaders had proclaimed and legislated the innate inferiority of non-Nordic stocks. For a good thirty years at mid-century, though, making such a statement in public constituted a scientific scandal. When, in the mid-1960s, the anthropologist Carleton Coon suggested—on the basis of blameless, purely paleontological evidence and drawing no modern implications whatsoever—that racial divergence might be older and racial differences therefore possibly greater than previously believed, his discipline exploded in a violent and protracted debate about the morality of giving any support at all to the notion that racial groups might systematically differ in anything but appearance. But gradually, as they always do, things changed. The refugee generation retired, their students—like all students—rebelled against received opinion, and the memory of the wartime horrors faded. New biological discoveries came to light. And the triumphant advances of formerly subservient groups put increasing pressure on settled social convention. Suddenly, it seemed to many, beneath the racist nonsense, there might have been some truth in those old theories after all. Almost unnoticed, during the 1970s biological determinism began to regain intellectual respectability and influence.

Theories of behavior seem particularly prone to these swings of scientific fashion; indeed, the enterprise of theory-making may well invite them. The scientific model demands precise measurement and strict definition, but human life—the phenomenon under study —proceeds in a cloud of ambiguity. Drawing conclusions requires cutting fog into neat pieces. "The distinction between biological and experiential causes is generally ambiguous enough to allow room for interpretations based more on the scientist's theoretical perspective than on the data itself," observes psychologist Jacquelynne Parsons, editor of a well-regarded book on sex differences.[2]

So what accounts for a given scientist's conclusions? If Parsons is right, the notions that researchers bring to the study in the first place play a major role. Scientific fashion is not wholly unlike the march of dress design: a silhouette can look dashing one season, preposterous a few years later, and hopelessly dowdy for a generation or so. Then, suddenly, it is back as the last word in adventurous elegance—like the pleated trousers, long, full skirts, and cinched waists that today's middle-aged people wryly recall from their own youths. The fortunes of ideas are no less expandable than shoulders, no more stable than hemlines.

But it was the bicycle and trolley car, not a simple change in taste, that doomed the floor-length skirt; technology helps set the ruling style. And today's current version of nature theorizing—the notion that steroids prime the human nervous system for certain behavioral tendencies—didn't arise out of thin air. The radio-immunoassay technique developed in the late 1960s, in part by Rosalind Yalow (who apparently overcame the promptings of estrogen long enough to accomplish this Nobel Prize–winning work), first permitted scientists to measure body hormones, and, not incidentally, to track steroids to the brain. A few years later, bioengineering had focused attention on the specific actions of particular genes. *Et voilà!* The fashionable ensemble of hormonal (and ultimately genetic) influence on behavior swept the smart set.

At any given moment, certain dress shapes and necktie widths look "right," and certain ideas seem to make perfect sense. Hardly anyone, though, may know how we all found them out or why we all believe them. Some years ago, psychologist Larry Reynolds decided to track one of those ideas down. He went looking for the evidence proving that women discriminate color more finely than men. The notion certainly made sense on first hearing; cognitive theory suggested that interests and attitudes could influence processes of perception. All Reynolds' colleagues agreed that a lifetime of attention to cloth and cosmetics ought to give women an edge, but no one knew the exact whereabouts of the supporting data. So Reynolds first asked Otto Klineberg for references to the studies mentioned (without documentation) in his standard text *Social Psychology.*

Klineberg, unable to name a specific source, passed Reynolds on to Anne Anastasi, whose acclaimed *Differential Psychology* also stated the fact. Disappointed again, Reynolds vainly searched such authoritative volumes as Alfred Lindesmith and Anselm Strauss's *Social Psychology* and Robert Bierstedt's *Social Order* for support of the claim that they, too, repeated. Lindesmith admitted that he couldn't pinpoint the source because "we may have regarded [it] as self-evidently true—which, of course, it may not be."[3] Bierstedt referred Reynolds to Amram Scheinfeld's *Women and Men,* which at last yielded a solid lead: a study by Ruth Staples showing a better female "color response." In the original paper, though, Staples had compared color preference, not discrimination, in infants, not adults.

An exasperated Reynolds now undertook to search the literature himself. He turned up several papers that refuted female superiority in color discrimination, but none that demonstrated it. Finally, though, he hit pay dirt: a research review by R. W. Pickford, who concluded that, except for the color-blind, men discriminate colors as well as women. Pickford did allow that "women may be more expert in the use of subtle colour names and they may be more interested in colours than men, owing to tradition and social influences"; at any rate, few men who knew ecru from eggshell or taupe from mauve advertised the fact. But most emphatically, women "are not fundamentally better at judging colour likenesses and differences than men."[4]

Of course, no modern person would dream of donning a bustle; every age also has ideas that informed persons would not dream of believing. In the late nineteenth century, for example, a trio of books propounding apparently outlandish theories of behavior fell into instant obscurity. But had they received the "attention they now appear to have merited," writes animal behavior authority J. H. Crook, "the history of ideas concerning the nature of animal societies and their relation to human ones might have been very different."[5] But in the last quarter of the last century, the new gospel of social Darwinism taught unbroken social progress from the dumb beasts, through the lesser branches of humankind, to the physical, cultural, spiritual, and intellectual perfection of the northern European bourgeoisie. Members of each species reflected in their brains, bodies, and behaviors their entire group's standing. Ontogeny recapitulated phylogeny.

A little-known and unfashionable thinker, A. Spinosa, chose the inauspicious year of 1878 to publish *Des Sociétés Animales,* now regarded as an ignored classic. Examining the ecology of animal life at many levels, he found no relationship between social organization and taxonomy—no "progress" of society from the "lower" forms of life to the "higher." A species' method of getting food, not its place on the ladder of physical evolution, predicted its way of life. Meat- and fish-eaters in sparse environments, for example, whether insects or mammals, fiercely defended their territories—not because they were closer to "evolved" notions of property, but (shades of Sanday) to beat out competitors for needed calories. Their cousins in more bountiful surroundings, again regardless of evolutionary standing, had no need to meticulously mark and defend boundaries when they could simply take what they needed from nature's ample supplies. The ways animals live, Spinosa concluded, arise not from traits of individuals but from relationships within and among groups.

Eighteen years later the immediately forgotten Raphael Petrucci added his voice to the meager chorus of dissent from the ruling Darwinian orthodoxy. His two major works on animal social organization came to Spinosa's conclusion: social structure relates to environment, not to organic evolution. He found no connection between intellect and social complexity; the dim-witted bumblebee lives in an insect metropolis whereas the dolphin, with an intelligence possibly rivaling our own, prowls the sea in small bands.

A major American school of animal studies now considers these ideas self-evident. But when they first appeared, almost nobody listened. Industrialization had lately torn apart the social fabric of Europe, heaping new wealth on certain groups—mainly capital-owning urbanites—and pauperizing others formerly secure—especially the great mass of penniless workers ripped from the safety of feudal agrarian tradition. What could better suit the temper of the times than a scientific doctrine relating social reward to the inherent worth or "fitness" of the individual or (in racialist interpretations) of the group? The savage struggle for livelihood in "dark satanic mills," pestilential slums, and filthy rural hovels reflected not injustice but nature's basic reality: each individual and species rose to the level that its innate qualities merited, and the fortunate could not be blamed for their great fortunes. Changes in social arrangements might palliate, but could never alter, the iron rule that some deserved to prosper and others to disappear. That most "evolved" of creatures, the Caucasian gentleman, crowned creation; the suffering of the lower orders simply contributed to the ceaseless improvement of the breed. Where poverty and hardship had once served to purge the soul of sin on the way to its eternal reward, they now purged the species of inferior traits on its way to eternal progress.

The ideas that everyone simply knows do ultimately come from somewhere: from the institutions charged with discovering what is true. In our own time, these consist mainly of university departments with "-ology" in their titles. They, in turn, grew out of departments of philosophy and natural history, and those, from ancient university faculties of religion in Britain and the Continent. And they, in the very beginning, arose from medieval establishments where communities of divines systematically pondered their creed.

It has been more than eight hundred years since women held real power in institutions forming intellectual opinion. The significance of this fact will soon become clear. For now, we must simply note that as recently as the turn of this century, distinguished institutions denied scholarly credentials even to those few women able to earn them through irregular channels. Mary Whiton, a student at Harvard's ladies' annex in the 1890s, couldn't enter the university's regular graduate program, then limited to men. She did work of such brilliance, though, that the great psychologist William James regularly journeyed from the Yard to Radcliffe expressly to teach her.

Under his guidance, she completed all the requirements of a stellar Ph.D.; the university twice refused to grant it, even when a national roll call of leading psychologists, including Yerkes, Woodworth, and Thorndike, added their petitions to James's. Later as Mary Whiton Calkins, a professor at Wellesley College—still without her doctorate—she published studies casting serious doubt on the ruling psychological dogmas about women.

Before our own time, we have to go all the way back to the days between the fall of Rome and the rise of feudalism to find learned ladies working and studying at major intellectual centers—some of the few that illuminated those dark centuries. The collapse of Roman law in northern Europe meant, among other things, the revival of Germanic tribal custom, and with it, women's traditional right to inherit and own property in their own name. In a time when title included not only land but inhabitants, female owners could dispense local justice, collect local taxes, and operate as independent personages.

This period, not coincidentally, saw the rise of great dual religious houses, the twin monasteries for men and women where the arts of learning and civilization flickered through the surrounding chaos. Female religious functioned not only as servants to male scholarship and piety but as intellectual figures in their own right. The dual abbey at Whitby, in Britain, founded and headed by the seventh-century aristocrat now known as St. Hilda, offered shelter and patronage to Caedmon, a lay brother and the first British poet we know by name. The Synod of Whitby, which established religious uniformity in Britain, met at Hilda's religious house. She joined in the deliberations (but her views did not prevail). Three centuries later at the monastery of Gandersheim in Germany, another nun, Rotswitha, revived the theater arts—dormant since Roman days—with her Latin dramas and poems. Yet another contemporary nun, Hildegard of Bingen, produced important treatises on medicine and nature.

But the influence of learned women religious began to wane, along with the temporal power of women generally. Feudalism, which tied land tenure and political authority to fealty and military service, permitted women only a subsidiary place. (As Sanday observed, martial values push men to the fore and women to the rear.) By the twelfth century, church reforms had also reduced females' religious possibilities; the Mass, a male monopoly, became a major vehicle of spirituality, and central authority, also exclusively male, a major principle of organization. This in turn implied less power for lay patrons, often aristocratic ladies, and more interest in celibacy, which, together with a renascent distrust of sex, doomed the formerly prestigious double monasteries. Male monastic orders grew into major centers of spirituality; female orders shrank into academically trivial girls' finishing schools.

Earlier nuns had prepared able women for the scholarly discussions of their day, invariably held in Latin. Twelfth-century convents no longer even taught the language of serious intellectual endeavor. Training for scholarship had moved to the universities, which completely excluded women.

Barred from the credentials of scholarship, no European or American woman, and none of the insights from her experience or study, received a hearing equal to that accorded men. When, in the nineteenth century, the young Beatrix Potter, to take only one example, proposed an original (and, as events proved, a correct) hypothesis on the nature of lichens, no biologist of standing listened to a privately educated woman, even in the age of the gentleman amateur. Stung by this rejection, Potter abandoned her independent scientific work and for the rest of her life applied her extraordinary gifts as a field naturalist to children's books (the first of which she printed privately, for want of a commercial publisher).

In every age, of course, some women pursued serious studies, but nearly always, like Potter, in the privacy of the home, through the leisure of wealth, and at the sufferance of fathers or husbands. Ladies' education culminated not in intellectual skills, but in ornamental attainments: speaking modern foreign languages (but rarely Latin or Greek), playing a suitably modest musical instrument, singing in tune, doing fancy needlework, sketching in watercolors or pastels, stepping to the fashionable dances, reading novels and poetry, conversing amusingly but preferably not wittily or brilliantly.

Though barred from intellectual life, however, European and American women of the lesser ranks still played an important, if often informal, role in the economy and community. A farmer's, artisan's, or workingman's wife, though unequal in law, was her husband's full economic partner. In our day, the household functions as a unit of consumption. Then it was the basic unit of production, and in this work women played a vital part. To call a woman a good wife was not to compliment her disposition, but to recognize her mastery of varied and demanding crafts: the arts of baking, cooking, food preservation, weaving, tailoring, laundering, decorative needlework, candlemaking, gardening, small animal husbandry, home nursing, child care, elementary pharmacy, and midwifery all fell within a competent housewife's province. Her husband, ignorant of these specialties, and unable to provide a replacement, depended on her to supply his daily wants. She assured her daughters' future security by passing on these skills. Any well-trained adult woman contributed importantly to the household; even those who did not marry, but lived all their lives as depen-

dents of fathers or brothers, carried the name of their work: spin-
sters (their male counterparts, bachelors, are known to us for their
work in watching other people's cows, or *bacca*). So completely did
European males depend on female textile work that the distaff, a
central tool of that craft, came to stand for an entire sex.

Apart from her own work, a woman helped her husband in his,
planting and harvesting, or in the artisan labor that went on in a
shop attached to the home. Or, in the very poorest households, she
might hire out as a washerwoman, wetnurse, or part-time servant to
more prosperous neighbors.

Indeed, she defined herself as wife and worker much more than
as mother. Except among the prosperous, childhood was short, and
everywhere, chancy. Few of a woman's many babies lived to adulthood; cherishing them each as unique individuals made a poor risk.
Nor did her endless duties and pregnancies leave her much time to
worry about psychic development in the half dozen years before
work also claimed the youngster.

Beginning in early nineteenth-century Britain, though, and later
in Europe and America, work—and woman's relationship to it—
underwent perhaps the greatest change since the Chaldeans (or
perhaps the Maya or Chinese) first learned to plant and harvest.
The industrial revolution moved production out of the home and
into mills and factories. Workers left the home too, to earn their
livings by trading their labor for an hourly or piecework wage.
Married women, however, burdened with their many duties, remained behind; in general males and single females answered the
factory whistle.

This meant a drastic loss of female power at home, and all the
more so because spinning and weaving were the first handcrafts that
decisively moved to the mill. The cloth that had formerly been a
home product now became a consumer good bought for cash.
Homespun had been every efficient housewife's pride; now it was
the stigma of the family too poor for the fashionable yardgoods
pouring off the power looms.

Woman's function shrank. She no longer worked alongside her
husband; she could contribute to his livelihood only by providing
respite for the next day's work. Indeed, companies that employed
married men now counted on the services of two workers for a

single wage: the employee himself and the wife whose unpaid domestic labor freed his full attention for the job. And in the increasingly pervasive cash economy, unpaid labor, producing no purchasing power, ceased to be "real" work.

As women's sphere of activity contracted, so did their influence. By the 1840s, in the social circles first affected by these changes, a new notion of woman's place and womans' nature began to rise. The so-called "Cult of True Womanhood" or "Theory of the Two Spheres" spread among the respectable urban classes. Through it, woman's new exile from productive work became not a restriction of her activities but an elevation of her efforts into a more rarefied, and uniquely suitable, sphere. Suddenly everyone knew that the miracle of industrialization, far from confining women in the home, freed them to follow their authentic nature.

Domesticity now expressed the essence of womanhood, a uniquely feminine calling of nurturance, esthetics, and spirituality. Only recently the debased daughter of Eve responsible for the fall of morally superior man, woman now became the "angel of the house," the cultivator of life's finer (because economically unproductive) values. Her man waged the daily struggle for survival in the noisy jungle of business; his spirit found its only refuge in the calm, upright, moral home that she provided. Gone was the bustling goodwife of earlier days—Abigail Adams running her farm in John's years-long patriotic absences. A wife's special duty now lay in becoming as womanly, in this special sense, as possible.

She most decidedly did not wish to become womanly in an older sense. The Industrial Revolution was only one of the vast upheavals that shook European and North American society in the nineteenth century. As sanitation and health care gradually improved, the northern nations also achieved a demographic revolution, shifting from a pattern of high birth and death rates to much lower ones. A middle-class woman in 1900 would bear only half as many children as her great-grandmother, and see more of them live to adulthood; the higher her class, the smaller her family. Indeed, the precipitate drop in native "old stock" births, as compared with the maddening fecundity of the new immigrants flooding the United States, contributed importantly to bans on abortion. The "better element" loudly feared that abortion—obtained mainly by respectable wives before 1880—would hasten the "race suicide" of the old WASP elite.

But economics spoke louder still. Urban industrial life transforms children from cheap, docile farm labor into clamoring, hungry mouths. Urban prosperity requires urban skills, and they require schooling, apprenticeship, capital. A merchant, professional, industrialist, or independent artisan can often assure the futures of a limited number of reasonably capable sons; a worker often can't provide even that. Good sense dictates cutting the family's size to a number that won't overwhelm its ability to offer a decent start in life. The demographic transition has occurred in countries throughout the world, usually within a generation or two of industrialization. The very first time it happened, in Britain and America a century and more ago, husbands and wives managed to drastically rein in their fertility without any reliable technology short of dangerous abortions.

Instead of pills, loops, creams, and diaphragms, they used the more demanding method that psychologist Ruth Lewin has termed "psychic birth control." Sex became something that nice people—and nice women in particular—didn't do if they could at all avoid it. This is not to say that married couples did not practice sensuality, because the evidence is clear that they did. (Even Queen Victoria, whose name will forever symbolize this era's ethos, bore her beloved husband nine children. But then, she had no worries about their future careers.) The reigning ideology of the time, however, held that women ("true" women, at least) had only the weakest of sex drives. So weak, in fact, was the truly refined woman's desire that disgust at the "baser" aspects of coitus could easily overwhelm it. A wife owed her husband intercourse, getting in return the elevated joys of motherhood. A considerate husband controlled his animal impulses (or took them elsewhere) so as to impose on his wife as little as possible.

By the middle of the century, enlightened medical opinion saw female sexual desire as an aberration, perhaps even an illness, to be "cured" by the latest scientific methods. A doctor in Berlin, the Boston of its day, hit upon clitoridectomy as the specific for excessive passion, performing his first in 1858. (This man of science probably didn't know that his breakthrough duplicated the common practice of North Africa, which sought the same end differently phrased. There the operation did not restore woman's true nature, but permanently suppressed it.) Up-to-date medicos in France and Britain (including a future president of the Medical Society of London) followed suit, as did some Americans until as late as 1937.

Male sexuality, of course, also held medical and psychiatric dangers. "Self-abuse" by either sex led to physical, mental, and spiritual consequences too appalling for nice people to dwell upon. But female masturbation occasioned even more fear and revulsion than male, because it more radically violated their "true" disposition and therefore implied a more severe illness.

Frightened by eroticism, inexperienced in sensuality, ignorant of her own physiology, and repelled by the mechanics of physical love, the gently reared bride did the least necessary to satisfy her husband's appetites. At its extremes, the Victorians' prudery reached heights that would have convulsed their lusty grandparents in bawdy laughter.

As the age of social science dawned, however, the new naturalistic observers of human behavior took their own time's excesses as the highest, most "evolved" expression of human nature. Woman was naturally delicate, moral, spiritual, asexual, and passive. Man was naturally robust, corrupt, carnal, sexual, and aggressive. (This was also a great age for ideal typologies; sweeping statements about the common traits of whole categories struck the learned as sensible scientific statements.) The protection of female sensibility guarded the family in two ways: it kept her pure, and her example purified him. (That such delicate beings gave birth without anesthetic perplexed none of the savants.) "By Freud's day," Lewin observes, "activity was synonymous with masculinity and passivity with femininity."[6]

Like his scientific colleagues, the sage of Vienna considered these traits inherent in, and logically derived from, the very states of being male or female. Still, they weren't biologically ingrained in the crudest modern sense; they arose from the early and necessary struggles between little boys and girls and their parents. (When anthropologist Bronislaw Malinowski showed that matrilineal Pacific parents inspired quite different struggles, orthodox psychoanalysis simply ignored him.) By rooting sex differences in lived—but inevitable—experience, the Freudians saved them from the intellectual stigma that later overtook other supposedly inherent behavioral differences. All men, therefore, might be created equal; but woman still—and inescapably—remained women.

The sex organs themselves expressed this dichotomy of intention. The active, aggressive, thrusting penis deposited the even more active, aggressive, thrusting sperm into the inert receptacle of the vagina. There, through the energy inherent in maleness, the sperm surged forward, racing each other for the ovum in the first trial heat of the coming struggle for survival. The egg, meanwhile, drifted in maiden modesty, awaiting a champion to claim her and permit her to fulfill the promise of her femininity. We now understand how the female organs set up powerful currents that draw the sperm forward, how the vaginal mucous changes at mid-cycle to a consistency that eases the sperms' way, how the ovum travels toward the uterus under impulsion of fallopian contractions. The Victorians not only didn't know these facts; they might well not even have believed them had they been discovered and reported.

Woman's moral and spiritual superiority, however, unsuited her for leadership. She lacked the male qualities of analysis and judgment. Her ethical instinct might have bested his, but, alas, it sprang from emotion, not intellect; therefore, the new scientists of the psyche taught, it did not meet the demands of abstract justice, but merely of personal mercy. The very source of her spirituality thus robbed her of intellect. It was as if, opined a prominent gynecologist in 1875, "the Almighty, in creating the female sex, had taken the uterus and built a woman around it."[7]

With her whole being concentrated on her uterus, woman simply lacked the sufficient life force to also grow an adequate brain. Freud's concept of limited libido or life force perfectly expresses the Victorian view of finite human powers. Dedicating life force to one organ, be it brain or uterus, automatically cut the supply to other, competing organs. Thus, a woman's intellectual pursuits put at risk the health (and even the existence) of future children. Higher education for women, therefore, threatened future childbearing, but not because it allows other interests to develop; it seemed to cause actual physical atrophy of their reproductive organs. The great American psychologist Stanley G. Hall—who had this nation's first Ph.D. in the field, founded its first department, and brought Freud on his only visit to these shores—once defended the notion that any excess energy devoted to her brain affected a woman's fertility. The very survival of the "better sort" meant keeping girls from advanced education! "How odd," remarked John Stewart Mill in 1867, "that those who consider marriage and motherhood to be woman's only natural state nevertheless act as though women would at once abandon those states if given the slightest opportunity to do so."[8]

As in our own day, the ideas current among the educated classes formed the bedrock of scientific thinking about behavior. Atop the ancient religious beliefs about female inferiority now lay a new stratum of scientific dogma about woman's special nature. Indeed, women's decidedly lackluster academic performance helped fit the entire notion of true womanhood into the reigning evolutionary theory. In the first place, women mature physically sooner than men. With a faith as sacred to them as $E = mc^2$ is to ourselves, scientists believed that "ontogeny recapitulates phylogeny"; each individual's development reenacts that of his or her entire type. By reaching full maturity sooner, women reveal that their evolution had been shorter, and therefore less extensive, than men's.

But even more pregnant was the fact that men stood at both the zenith and the nadir of intellectual endeavor. Many more males than females filled the asylums for the feebleminded and insane. Male ability appeared to cover a wider range than female; in evolutionary terms, it was argued, this meant that males were more variable (in other traits as well—height, strength, specific talents, and so forth). Because evolutionary changes arose from variations, it followed (somehow) that men provided better material for evolution to work on, were the cutting edge of organic progress. At their best, therefore, they were more evolved.

How half a species could stand higher on the evolutionary ladder than the other half (especially if both halves were needed to reproduce) was not a question that commanded much attention in the heyday of unilinear evolutionary theory. According to the prevailing view, evolution consisted not of alterations wrought by constant adjustment to changing environments, but of a single ladder toward perfection. The various primitive peoples inhabiting Europe's overseas empires (and the Indians inhabiting an ever-smaller portion of the United States) represented, to the enlightened bearers of the White Man's Burden, pure, frozen specimens of previous evolutionary stages. Rather than recognizing that the forces of selection work continuously on all living populations, that all groups and species live in a dynamic relationship with their environments, nineteenth-century science saw evolution as something that fitted the lesser breeds to the demands of their archaic habitats and then abandoned them as it moved on to more progressive locales.

Woman could therefore easily represent, to both scientist and layman, a different, and permanently inferior, form of human. What defined manhood were the traits distinguishing it from the fairer, or weaker, but certainly the other, sex. Indeed, we can't exaggerate the otherness of the female sex in the scientific thought of the nineteenth century. Had they but known the word, men could have defined their maleness as an existential state, the result of their will and intention to be wholly and exclusively men, to act in a manly fashion, to strive with every fiber of their being against the dread and humiliating fall toward womanhood.

Any advance of women into male territory, whether educational, political, social—or most horrifying of all, sexual—cut the distance separating the genders and the buffer separating male self-esteem from the threatening other. As men increasingly spent their lives in citified and sissified offices and stores, anxiety about maleness grew. Can it be an accident that scouting, a movement devoted to training boys for manhood (and, incidentally, allowing their fathers to practice the uplifting, manly arts of roughing it) arose in the years that suffragettes thronged the streets and "working girls" appeared behind counters and typewriters?

In these same years arose the new science of psychological measurement (which, in its modern form, provides much of the data for present-day sex differences theorizing). Not surprisingly, it incorporated the era's ruling notions. Early in the twentieth century, though, a small band of determined women had succeeded where Calkins had failed, and wrested Ph.D.s from major American universities. They took up the work of refuting these errors, but rarely from academic posts commensurate with their credentials or research results. The husband of one such pioneer, Leta Stetter Hollingworth, and himself an eminent professor of psychology, said later of his wife's often fruitless quest for grants to support her ground-breaking research, "No one will ever know what she might have accomplished for human welfare . . . if some of the sponsorship freely poured out on many a scholarly dullard had been made available for her own projects."[9]

Nonetheless, these women helped the growth of environmental influence theories. Lewis Terman, a leading theorist who opposed Leta Hollingworth on many issues concerning sex differences, wrote of her career: "comparable productivity by a man would have led to the presidency of the American Psychological Association or even to membership in the National Academy of Sciences. . . . This . . . is a reflection on the voting habits of male psychologists."[10]

From her teaching post at Wellesley, Calkins did battle on the crucial issue of male variability. Joseph Jastrow, a former student of Hall's teaching at the University of Wisconsin, had twenty-five students of each sex list 100 words as quickly as possible. He pronounced the women's efforts both less variable and less abstract than the men's, and drawn from "the peculiar field of women's household instincts."[11] With the help of a student, Cordelia Nevers, Calkins twice failed to replicate Jastrow's results. She found Wellesley women's word lists more abstract than Wisconsin men's, even when judged by Jastrow's arbitrary standards. For his part, he resorted to an argument frequently used to discredit the attainments of "unnaturally" accomplished women, finding them "less natural and unreflective."[12]

But Leta Hollingworth gave variability the coup de grace. As chief of psychology at Bellevue Hospital, she understood the mechanics of asylum admissions. Her careful studies showed no differences between male and female mental abilities. More men ended up in institutions, she concluded, because they led less sheltered lives and got into more dramatic trouble:

The subjective notion as to what constitutes intelligent behavior is different in the case of girls from what it is in boys. A female with a mental age of six years has as good a chance to survive inconspicuously in the educational, social, and economic milieu of New York as a male with a mental age of ten years.[13]

Mentally defective men, she argued, came to the hospital when the stresses of earning a living overcame them; mentally defective women, only when their male support died or the police arrested them as prostitutes. "There seems to be no occupation which supports feebleminded men as well as housework and prostitution support feebleminded women."[14] As to the dearth of women at the high end of the achievement spectrum, she succinctly labeled housework "a field where eminence is impossible."[15]

But something more convincing than women scholars finally ended the debate about female intellectual inferiority. In the early decades of this century, the new IQ tests, then at the cutting edge of psychology, kept turning up a startling result. Girls repeatedly, almost systematically, scored higher than boys. Somehow, though, the test-makers didn't pursue conclusions about evolution or the nature of the sexes. They simply remade their scales, so that male and female scores came out roughly the same. And the interest of sex differences researchers quietly passed elsewhere.

But the notion that male and female mentalities differed in some basic way didn't fade or even flicker. It merely shifted from the intellectual to the emotional sphere. In the 1930s, Lewis Terman and Catherine Miles produced the first systematic modern statement of the idea that was to rule psychology for almost two generations: "Masculinity and femininity are important aspects of human personality. They are not to be thought of as lending to it merely a superficial coloring and flavor; rather they are one of a small number of cores around which the structure of personality gradually takes shape."[16]

The difference may not be strictly biological in origin; it may, as Freud thought, arise from experiences that each sex necessarily undergoes. Still, it precedes mere custom. Terman and Miles wrote: "The M-F dichotomy, in various patterns, has existed throughout history, and is still firmly established in our mores." Trouble comes from ignoring it, as modern society encourages the unwary to do. "In a considerable fraction of the population it is the source of many acute difficulties in the individual's social and psychological adjustment."

At the core of each gender, Terman and Miles believed, stood an ideal model of masculinity and femininity; how closely an individual's personality resembled it, largely determined his or her psychological health. To help the mass of Americans assess and improve their adjustment (then psychology's universally recognized goal), Terman and Miles devised the first of many pencil-and-paper tests of masculinity and femininity. Since the triumph of the IQ test, translated for America as the Stanford-Binet Intelligence Scale, machine-graded multiple-choice inventories had become major tools of psychological research and treatment.

To the task of assembling the Attitude Interest Analysis Survey (AIAS), Terman brought impressive credentials, especially his work twenty years earlier adapting the French Binet test for American use. That instrument (originally designed to screen out feeble-minded schoolchildren) had become *the* operational definition of intelligence—until then an extremely complex and elusive concept. Terman set out to also distill masculinity and femininity to a similar, simple number.

The Stanford-Binet produces a score by comparing a child's answers on a list of factual and interpretive questions with those typical of his or her age. IQ is a true arithmetic quotient; you divide an individual's test score by the average score of his or her contemporaries. A child who gets more right than average, scores high (above 100, which is "normal"), one who gets fewer, scores low. Intelligence thus *becomes* the ability to divine the answers that test-writers decide are correct.

Much later we learned, of course, that IQ scores correlate somewhat better with cultural experience than with native gifts. Studies of human ability have lately revealed a far more complex and nuanced picture than the Stanford-Binet's crude strokes can capture. Intelligence isn't a single trait, like height, but a single name applied haphazardly to a cluster of aptitudes. But nothing has broken the IQ's hold on the American imagination.

Still, this reification of intelligence serves at least one good purpose. It shows us again, as we saw in the last chapter, a pervasive bias of science: if scientists are objective students of the real world, then the fact that they study something makes *it* objective reality. Thus, the attention of psychologists transforms a capacity to answer questions into the measurable phenomenon of intelligence. The proof of a phenomenon's existence becomes its ability to engage the interest of a scientist, regardless, as we shall see, of whether anyone can isolate, describe, or even define it.

To find their model of masculinity and femininity, Terman and Miles returned to the school room, specifically, to a group of elementary, junior high, and high school students who answered long lists of miscellaneous questions on facts, attitudes, moral beliefs, aspirations, and preferences. On some, boys and girls, on average, gave different responses. These became the body of the M-F instrument.

Strangely, though, this approach exactly contradicts the Stanford-Binet; there, to minimize sex differences, the test-makers removed items that strongly distinguished boys from girls. In the AIAS, however, the ideas, knowledge, and prejudices of school children become the definition of appropriate sexual identification. Selecting a "masculine" answer gave a subject M points, a "feminine" one gave F points. To arrive at the all-important MF index, the psychologist subtracted the F total from the M total. With piquant but probably unintentional symbolism, Terman and Miles made masculinity a positive numerical value and femininity a negative one.

Some of the items were, to put it politely, idiosyncratic. "On test 3, Information," psychologist Miriam Lewin observes, "the girls received Masculinity points if they knew too much. To get Femininity points girls should believe that Goliath was killed by Cain, that the earth turns once on its axis in about 12 hours, that tides are caused by ocean currents, that Belgium was an ally of Germany in World War I [this in 1936!], that TNT, not FOB, is a shipping term, etc."[17] Girls proved more easily disgusted, more fastidious, more emotional, especially about injustice and dishonesty—but not about interruptions. Boys revealed more iconoclasm, mercenariness, and independence. Girls disliked "baldheaded men" but liked "washing dishes"; boys disliked "tall" or "mannish women," especially "those cleverer than you are."[18]

"The masculine person is fearless, dislikes school, and is bad," Lewin writes. "The feminine person is timid, obedient, and good. These items measured superiority and subordination. . . . They tell us a lot about training girls to know their place and about boys' struggle to resist the socialization attempts of those good Victorian women, his teachers and his mother."[19] And again, we see an "abstract" male sense of justice, and a situational and emotional female sense of pity. A student of Terman's carried the work even further, using a comparison of ninety-eight high school boys and seventy-seven homosexual males, some engaged in prostitution, to make a test for "inversion."

Once made, the tests proved hard to validate, a failing of no great concern to their developers. Adolescent boys and girls scored more strongly masculine or feminine than adult, sexually active, men and women. Lawyers got higher M scores than policemen, architects than carpenters, realtors than firemen. Grocers, perhaps because they know a lot about food, made a sorry showing. Educated women, of course, got high (that is, low) F scores, despite being wives and mothers.

But America was gearing up to process millions of citizens through huge wartime bureaucracies and needed easy ways to sort the acceptable from the unacceptable. The Minnesota Multiphasic Personality Inventory (MMPI) became perhaps the nation's most widely used screening device, scoring countless students, recruits, applicants, and psychological patients over several decades. First published in 1943, it included an M-F scale, originally included as an experiment but soon incorporated into the test proper.

M-F scores, and the related interest in symptoms of "inversion" (homosexual tendencies) formed only a part of the MMPI's ambitious intention, so the male-female items received even shorter shrift than from Terman and Miles. Those pioneers had at least constructed the scale from the answers of real males and real females. But the MMPI, in a genuinely spectacular display of theoretical befuddlement, chose its femininity questions not from grown women, or adolescent girls, or even pigtailed elementary students. It used *thirteen male homosexuals*, whose responses it contrasted with those of fifty-three heterosexual male soldiers.

This astounding blunder, this extravaganza of naiveté, more

clearly than any theoretical statement, lays bare the assumptions behind M-F research. Masculinity and femininity are the two extremes of a single dimension; in a very real sense, they are opposites. If a person is not "masculine," the only other thing he or she can be is feminine. A numerical M-F score therefore represents a certain point along a fixed continuum. The test further assumes that the tested honestly disclose their inner natures through short answers, and that those natures exist in a timeless limbo free of social influences. Indeed, it reveals in the starkest possible form psychology's bias toward "context stripping," the insistence that inherent personal traits, not social, cultural, or political influences, account for behavior.

And traits, perhaps because they are easy to name and measure, loom very large in this sort of psychological discussion. Bunches of them, bound up by the odd compulsion or drive, cluster together to form the psyche and personality. Traits are real, unchanging, enduring, nontransferable. Like chicken pox and pregnancy, they have symptoms easily spotted by the trained observer.

And like eye color, they don't change. The femininity of a ten-year-old girl resembles in its essence that of a young bride, a thirty-year-old mother, a forty-year-old spinster, a fifty-year-old nun, a sixty-year-old grandmother, a prostitute, a widow, even a male homosexual of twenty-eight or forty-seven. The masculinity of a ten-year-old boy differs not at all from an adolescent's, a husband's, a divorced father's, a grandfather's, a confirmed bachelor's, a celibate priest's, a life prisoner's, or, presumably, a female homosexual's. The experience of gender and the behavior that manifests it likewise form constants. Men and women would presumably express their sexuality in just the same way regardless of whether they lived in Victorian times, the jazz age, the desperation of economic depression, the frantic fatalism of war, or the self-indulgence of a prosperous peace. All that differentiates them is the amount and proportion of the two traits that each possesses. The belief that personality is a finely woven web of meanings, that it grows through a concrete encounter with history, that it changes over a lifetime of personal and social change, never produces a numerical measure of anything.

Terman's first detailed statement of the remarkable theory of trait permanence coincided—not coincidentally—with the severest test to the breadwinner role—and thus to nineteenth-century masculinity—ever experienced by the American people. In classic M-F theory, men who had masculinity when they had jobs, farms, businesses, community standing, and self-respect couldn't lose it in bread lines and Hoovervilles. Nor could the women who once depended on them lose their femininity by waiting tables, picking fruit, washing clothes, or selling their jewelry or their bodies to feed their children. Masculinity and femininity remained as fixed and immutable as their eye color.

Margaret Mead had published *Sex and Temperament in Three Primitive Societies,* her exploration of sex role in the New Guinea tribes, mere months before. Terman simply dismissed "the present-day bias of the cultural anthropologists" against his views.[20] Mead decisively won over her own colleagues, but the psychologists—far more influential in the lives of ordinary Americans—stood staunchly with Terman.

At the core of M-F femininity stood the necessity of motherhood. Since the mid-nineteenth century, of course, scientific interest in a mother's influence on her children had grown as her other roles shrank. Psychic nurturance became woman's highest calling, her goal in life, and ultimately, her reason for being. But femininity and maternity were really side issues. The real interest centered on masculinity—and how to defend, preserve, and foster it. (Indeed, the core of childrearing advice concerned how to rear properly masculine boys.)

By the 1950s, the dominant Freudian theorists even began to uncover "unconscious" masculine or feminine leanings or yearnings that could complicate someone's psychic life. Anomalous test results—of individuals whose scores didn't match their gender—now indicated the "cross-sex identification" of persons who unknowingly longed to belong to the other sex. Particularly worrisome were the newly large numbers of fatherless boys—sons of dead soldiers or divorced parents—at risk because they lacked father figures. And black youths, social commentators opined, lived in even greater peril because of the disorganized social conditions that surrounded their growing up. Indeed, they consistently tested less masculine than comparable whites. (In fact, the most masculine males and the most feminine females always belonged to the white working class. Could the black tradition of female self-reliance, or the sharp sexual separation of blue-collar life, or the more literate interests of middle-class men possibly play a role? Testing experts certainly didn't seem to think so.)

But, suggests historian of psychology Joseph Pleck, tongue firmly in cheek, the difference between white and black men could represent something other than deficient black masculinity: the long overlooked trait of "negritude." Inasmuch as white women "answer these items more like black males than white males, white females are thus higher than white males in negritude and thus have racial identity conflicts."[21]

Black men and white women did, of course, share something important, but it's not excess femininity or high negritude or confused ideas about who they are; it's the experience of social subordination and the need to trim their behavior to the wishes of white men.

But the experts' worry was all unnecessary; there's not even any evidence that unambiguous M or F scores correlate with success or happiness. The traits' purest exemplars do not, in their factories and kitchens, embody the richest possibilities of American life. Indeed, there's good evidence that the man who fixated on a locker-room notion of masculinity, or the woman frozen in the adoring dependence of her high school days, can muster fewer resources for the long years after the last homecoming game and senior prom.

Still, M-F rallied once more before finally expiring. Talcott Parsons, who ruled sociology in the 1950s and 1960s, saw immutable reality in lives of the new Levittowns. Males and females naturally divided the family's work, he said, the former being its ambassador in the outside world, the latter the cultivator of its inner life; the one naturally "instrumental," the other "expressive." So for a while, the tests reported scores on a scale called I-E.

By the 1970s, though, the time had clearly come to decant this very old wine into some rather new bottles. A newer generation of psychologists, many of them female, had begun to suspect that the difficulties in measuring M and F were not technical but conceptual. Just as physics nearly a century ago had struggled and failed to chart currents in the ether, so psychology futilely grappled to find the outlines of masculinity and femininity. By the time Michael Jackson had ascended to the Beatles' and the Rolling Stones' old throne, psychological measurement had a new byword: androgeny. And science once again accommodated the newly changed facts of life.

What does this sorry century of thinking show us? Mainly this: those who find differences are usually looking for them. But also this: scientific theories about behavior seem strikingly impervious to contrary evidence. One researcher in the heyday of I-E testing rejected over a third of his sample households because neither spouse clearly dominated; Parsonian functionalism insisted that normal families had dominant partners.

For a century and more, psychology has studied male and female not in their own terms, but as actors in an ideal household. Man, rather than woman (or both), stood as the model of humanity; where she differed, she deviated. She existed to reflect and serve him, not to pursue her own ends in her own way.

A century of theory and testing may not have turned up real differences, but real differences do exist. In the next section, we'll try to find out what they are.

III

WHAT ARE MALES AND FEMALES LIKE?

6

Different Bodies?

A glorious fall day in the woods: a few leaves still cling to branches above a forest floor newly paved in red and gold. Jim and Paul, playing hooky, are out in search of arrowheads and adventure. They get their wish suddenly, when Paul ducks off the trail to relieve himself. Stepping behind a largish bush that has shed its leaves, he carefully finds a place invisible from the footpath. He studies the ground all the while; there's no telling where an arrowhead might turn up. A handsome rock streaked with pink lies under a shrub. He crouches to pocket it, reaching through the branches, and something square and shiny catches his eye. Funny place to leave a belt buckle. Then he sees the white-gray thing lying next to it. . . .

"Jim!" he shrieks, bolt upright.

His friend bounds through the brush to his side. "What the . . . ?" His gaze follows Paul's trembling finger. "Omigod!" The boys instinctively grab hands and flee. Paul reaches home with his own belt still unbuckled.

The anthropologist that the police summoned from the university needs only a couple of minutes for a preliminary opinion. "In descending order of certainty," he says, "Male, white, probably early twenties." The missing persons detective is already checking his lists. A close look at the skeleton in the lab confirms all three surmises; the belt buckle, together with dental records, produce a positive identity by nightfall: a young man who several years before had succumbed to deep depression, carried a bottle of sleeping pills into the woods, and lain under a secluded bush to die.

Bones are simply that certain. Stripped of flesh, muscle, and connecting tissue, a skeleton proclaims its gender in at least four places: the pelvis, the skull, and to a lesser extent, the elbows and knees.

The pelvis, which in our quadrupedal ancestors and cousins hinges the horizontal spine to the vertical hind legs, serves additional functions for us. Tipped upward and spread open, it forms the bottom of an abdominal bowl holding our internal organs. It also provides places of attachment for the powerful trunk and thigh muscles supporting our upright posture and bipedal gait.

In all female mammals, of course, the pelvis also girds the birth canal. But in human females, the bony structure that must bear the whole weight of the upper body, anchor the thigh and trunk muscles, and securely support the upright, load-bearing spine, needs to incorporate an opening wide enough for the enormous fetal head. Opposing selective forces have carved the distinctive shape of the human female pelvis, making it one of the most crucial factors in our species' evolution. Selection for strong walking promotes a sturdy, solid girdle of bones, with plenty of broad planes for muscle attachments but not too wide overall—something rather like what males have. But selection favoring sound, fast, and subtle thinking promotes a wide birth canal, to permit as large a head as possible to pass safely through.

The compromise that evolution has struck—the widest pelvis of any primate relative to size, but one still permitting a reasonably efficient attachment of upper leg bones and muscles and a reasonably serviceable knee—is the single, absolute limiting factor on the size of the infant brain. Before modern surgery, women with undersized pelvises and babies with oversized heads were simply "selected out" by evolution, together and in great pain. Primates can cling to their traveling mothers just hours out of the womb, sheep and deer run with the herd by their first nightfall, canines walk within weeks and hunt within a season, mammals of all kinds reproduce within a year or two. But our babies are born—and remain for years—utterly helpless. The extended human childhood (extended further still in prosperous societies) does, of course, provide time to teach the vast amount of information a human adult needs. But still, we organize our societies as we do in large part because women must both walk upright and give birth.

The wider pelvis means that female thighs descend at a somewhat sharper angle, producing both a distinctive female gait and a slightly less stable female knee. Male and female elbows also articulate at slightly different angles, though the meaning of this—whether to clear the wide pelvis, more efficiently throw spears, or more effectively cuddle babies—is not known. The male skull is also somewhat more massive.

An even more striking difference between male and female skeletons—or, more exactly, between numbers of them—is their size. On average, in populations that have been studied, men stand 10 percent taller than women; as scientists usually phrase this, women reach 85–90 percent of male height. How we describe the difference is more than a matter of semantics; which sex—if either—we take as the ground plan of humanity has important implications for theories about why we grew the way we did. Generations of scientific habit have taken the male body as the human standard—despite the fact that he develops from a process "extra" to the one producing women. Recently, however, scientists have begun to suggest that a female standard makes more sense—for analytical rather than ideological reasons. The male body may incorporate features added onto the standard model fairly late in our evolutionary career. But in fact, neither sex truly represents an example of "pure" human evolution, because each has always been subject to selective pressures that didn't affect the other.

The taller male skeleton is not simply a stretch-model female. The greater height comes mainly from longer long bones. A man's trunk forms a smaller proportion of his total height than does a woman's; he has longer arms and legs, both absolutely and in relation to the rest of his body. His lower legs and forearms—the so-called distal portions of his limbs—are longer, his hands and feet larger. His entire skeleton has what anthropologist Grover Krantz terms a "peripheral emphasis." Hers, conversely, and probably to prepare for the great and unbalancing weight it is built to carry, has a "central tendency."[1]

Clothing these distinctive bones are even more distinctive mantles of muscle and fat. The very constituents composing them occur in different proportions. At "ideal" weight—or at least at the weight that we seem naturally to maintain—and at every age after puberty, she carries considerably more fat than he does. Indeed, a woman as lean as a well-fed, athletic young man couldn't function as woman at all.

With its markedly uneven arrangement in the breasts, over the hips, thighs, and buttocks, this fat gives her her distinctive form, but we don't need sexuality to explain most of it. Mammals generally tend to carry fat toward the body's center and in the proximal (toward the body) portions of the limbs—the arrangement that interferes least with mobility. Fat feet, ankles, and calfs would waste energy for the same reason that, on the playground seesaw, we put the heavier person close to the fulcrum and the lighter person farther away to balance them; it's harder to lever up a weight placed far from the fulcrum than a similar weight placed closer. So an overweight man also accumulates flab near the middle in his thighs, buttocks, and upper arms. But female fat obviously owes its layout to something other than mechanical engineering. Large breasts produce milk no more efficiently than small ones. Ample padding adds nothing to the hips' ability to let a baby pass safely through. These particular deposits may well have some unclearly understood relationship to the evolution of sexual attractiveness.

But the profoundest difference between male and female bodies (apart from their gonads) has received the least attention. It underlies—indeed, it explains—some of the other great differences, but its own cause and meaning remain mysterious. We speak of the two-year gap between the ages when female and male puberty begin, which surely accounts for the height difference. Males grow taller mainly because they grow longer—for a longer total period of time, that is. Average male and female height differs not at all until girls go into their adolescent growth spurt, the final burst before their bones freeze at adult size about the time when pregnancy becomes possible. A girl has essentially reached her adult height at age sixteen; she is within millimeters of the tallest she will ever be. But a boy destined to be tall, is still growing, though slowly, in his twentieth year or beyond.

Girls are taller than boys only once in their lives—during the junior high awkwardness, when sixth-grade classes seem to include boys aged ten and girls approaching sixteen. This moment is deceptive, though. The girls shoot up suddenly at about age eleven, but the now smaller boys continue to grow slowly but steadily. When, at about thirteen, they take their own growth spurt, they start from a higher base, so they add more absolute inches to achieve the same percentage increase. And they continue to grow after that, not approaching their full adult height until about eighteen.

The big question is why. Such a big discrepancy between creatures that grow at the same rate for most of their lives obviously has a profound meaning. And logic argues that it has to do with evolution favoring the traits of people who leave lots of descendents.

Our ancestors' short lifespan must have limited the number of children any woman could bear, so the advantage lay in getting an early start—just about as soon, in fact, as their pelvises could accommodate an infant head. But time presses less heavily on the prolific male; he needn't devote nine months plus more months of nursing to every single child. For him, an early start is less crucial.

But the size discrepancy merely underlines the really basic one: a girl has stopped growing before she can conceive, but a boy usually has not. After menarche come a year or two of adolescent infertility —during which, coincidentally or not, girls reach full size. But boys can produce viable sperm while still growing.

There's no mystery about why. As mammals, women nourish their young for almost a year—and often longer—entirely from their own bodies. They "eat for two" the whole time they're pregnant or nursing. But their own young body also needed large quantities of high-quality nourishment. Were a young mother's growing bones and muscles competing with her baby's for calcium, protein, iron, and calories, neither would thrive on the food supplies that normally sustained our ancestors (or that sustain many of our contemporaries today). So the very hormones that make reproduction possible prevent potential conflict by ordering the growing ends of her bones to fuse.

Thus, the real question isn't why the female stops growing, but why the male continues. There are two possibilities. First, males may continue growing simply because they don't stop; simply, that is, because no evolutionary and hormonal imperative forces the bones to freeze at the moment of reproductive maturity. Evolution may have favored the early freezing of female bones, but left the male growth-stopping mechanism less perfectly developed.

But, on the other hand, male growth may continue because height *in itself* provides some advantage; the selective point may not be a more efficient female but a larger male. Or both theories may be true. A female who can feed her young and a large male might both have selective advantages. But a very important theoretical distinction separates the two possibilities. The idea that men are larger has attracted intense ideological energy, when the main evolutionary point may be that women are smaller—precisely as small as they can be and still function as mothers.

A great theoretical weight hangs on this question—as heavy as the load that once hung on the notion of greater male variability. Modern evolutionary theory has developed a modern version of sexual selection theory, based, of course, on the modern reading of human prehistory—and that often incorporates a rather peculiar notion of the lives our distant ancestors lived.

Protohumans emerged into humanity, it now appears, on African savannahs, where they survived on a combination of plant and animal foods. Their way of life accounts for at least 90 percent of our species' career as humans. Exactly how they obtained these foods, therefore, and what their methods mean for human prosperity, is the crux of human sexual selection.

A popular theory known as Man-the-Hunter argues that our ancestors got their animal calories by catching and killing wild game. The males, alone or in groups, outsmarted or overpowered wily and dangerous animals, felling them with spears, knives, arrows, or clubs. Those conspicuously successful at procuring protein on the hoof naturally had the pick of the women, and probably many more women than stay-at-homes or also-rans. And chances were that these desirable mates had physical traits that made them good hunters: stamina, strength, aggressiveness, perhaps size.

An uneven distribution of female favors led inevitably to an explosive result: fighting. Not content to watch others monopolize the women, disappointed suitors attacked their rivals, or perhaps banded together to kidnap women from neighboring groups. So the best fighters could also get a disproportionate share of the reproductive action. Big and strong men would thus leave more descendents than puny, weak ones. The genes for size and strength would become more prevalent in succeeding generations, and the corresponding traits more widespread among males (who were not subject to the countervailing forces working on women). Indeed, women and their parents would begin selecting suitors for the mere promise that they would prove good hunters and fighters; they would begin to prefer large men. The mating market would resemble the beach in the old Charles Atlas ads: the 97-pound weakling, scorned and humiliated, would watch the muscle men get the girls.

Weighing against this theory, though, is an inconvenient fact: Homo sapiens is not a true tournament species. Human infancy and childhood is so demanding that fathers must "invest" fairly substantially if their children are to survive. We are really a pairbonding species ("imperfectly so,"[2] observes anthropologist Melvin Konner, but as we shall see later on, most living systems are somewhat imperfect). So, many less than perfect male specimens get the chance to reproduce. The tendency toward large size and strength that we saw in the elephant seals doesn't get full expression. (In fact, the size difference between male and female humans is much smaller than that among many other primates and other mammals.)

Notwithstanding these realities, Man-the-Hunter theorists continue to write books in which our ancestors enact a stone-age version of a boy's Wild West fantasy. Violent, venturesome men and helpless, homebody women live with the constant threat of attack by human and animal predators. And the proof of this theory is always with us, proponents argue. Men are larger and stronger—and most markedly in the arms, shoulders, and chest, the parts of the body most necessary to swinging clubs and throwing spears.

But is it true that men *are* everywhere larger and stronger than women? It certainly seems so among ourselves; but we Americans —the best-fed hominids ever, living with a sharp division of labor by sex—hardly represent a random sample of the human condition. Could our spectacularly abundant diet and our particular way of dividing the chores skew the results?

We know for sure that nutrition influences height. Millions of American family albums attest it: stunted immigrant parents and grandparents beam up at their native-born, vitamin-stuffed progeny. But we also know that bad nutrition influences male height more than female. Poorly-fed men and women differ in height less than we do. A tall frame may seem an unqualified advantage to salaried professors living close to supermarkets, but it becomes markedly less desirable when every added inch ups the number of calories needed to survive on a chancy or meager diet. That male height is indeed more variable than female—that is to say, that it is more susceptible to environmental influence—seems to imply that it matters less to success in reproduction. Within the limits of available nutrition, notes biologist Katherine Ralls, "a bigger mother is often a better mother; that is, larger females may produce a greater number of surviving offspring."[3]

But the fact that underfed people differ less than we do doesn't disprove a general male predisposition toward height. It merely suggests that the predisposition can't arise from an overwhelming or universal selective pressure *among humans.* It may even have arisen—like our fingernails, appendix, coccyx, and other bodily souvenirs—from selective pressures on distant ancestors who lived in conditions very different from anything Homo sapiens ever experienced. Useless but harmless traits do seem to linger for a very long time. Our close primate cousins show size dimorphism greater than ours—in some cases much greater. (They also have fingernails, a legacy from the claws of the tiny, nocturnal, tree-dwelling founders of the primate line.) And we really don't know how much our ancient ancestors differed. Paleontologists working with incomplete skeletons customarily call the larger ones male and the smaller ones female.

If the question of height clouds over on close inspection, that of strength nearly vanishes. The plain fact is that we have no idea whether men are "naturally" stronger than women. In modern Western culture they generally are. But modern Western culture hardly provides the sexes with identical opportunities for physical conditioning. The American man's shoulder girdle is twice as strong as the American woman's; a boyhood swinging baseball bats and throwing forward passes may account for some of his advantage. But the difference between his legs and hers—which may have danced, swum, or pedaled a bike—is much smaller. Observes Elizabeth Ferris, a scholar of sport, "The problems found when making comparison between male and female physiologic parameters in response to exercise are reminiscent of those encountered in comparing blacks and whites with respect to intelligence."[4]

Until the early 1970s, men's sporting superiority was a foregone conclusion. But then women began to participate in sports formerly foreclosed, and to get coaching and training like that traditionally available to men. Female performance in strenuous sports such as running and swimming improved suddenly and much more sharply than male. Between 1963 and 1978, the best female marathon time fell from 3:50 hours to 2:50 hours, the male from about 2:20 to 2:10. At these rates of improvement—and no one knows how long they can be sustained—women will overtake men in speed swimming by the year 2056, in cycling by 2011, and in marathon running by the 1990s.[5] Women surpassed men in Channel swimming decades ago.

Until puberty, boys and girls in Western societies show no difference in strength, stamina, coordination, or other components of athletic potential. (Boys in our culture generally show greater *interest* in sports.) Between ten and twelve, however, girls become less active and fall behind in strength. The gap widens with each passing year until boys peak as sportsmen in their late teens and early twenties. For most men, though, graduation marks the end of the athletic career and the beginning of declining strength. Indeed, between twenty-five and thirty most men, now devoting their time to work rather than play, become less and less strong (except, of course, the minority of Americans doing physical labor). Ferris suggests that both male and female declines have more to do with cultural scheduling than with inherent physiological differences. The female physiology responds to training much like the male. In one ten-week conditioning program, nonathletic women increased their strength by 35 to 50 percent; they differed from men mainly in the fact that they experienced no great increase in muscle bulk. Ferris believes that a small, talented slice of both sexes possess the "high athletic potential" of champions. The males and females of this elite differ from each other less than either of them do from the common run of their own sex.

And, indeed, where culture has created natural experiments, women grow as strong as men in at least certain respects. In Burundi the female head is a significant mode of transport and women can carry substantially greater loads than men. "Yet men generally win physical battles with their wives, apparently because they are more agile."[6]

The memory of hard labor may be so painful, or the lure of mythology so strong, that a generation or two have erased from American recollection the endless, backbreaking toil that was the housewife or chambermaid's lot well into this century—and still is in much of the world. The old counting rhyme told the tale: washing day, ironing day—day after day of heavy labor. She drew and carried all the water—at more than two pounds a quart—that the family used. She hefted bushels of wet clothes in and out of great, steaming tubs. She wielded ten-pound flatirons, further weighted with coals, hour after hour. She carried her baby to and from the fields, and sowed or harvested—often with it strapped to her back. In times of hardship, she guided or even pulled the plow. We have good evidence from biblical times, if not earlier, that drinking water, wood, and goods for market came and went on the heads of women. Children weighing fifty pounds or more traveled long distances on their backs. When Rachel captivated Jacob while drawing water for the flock, and on the nineteenth-century farm, or in the Third World today, the difference between male and female strength may well have been smaller than it is in postindustrial America.

If the strength differential is exaggerated, then what of the theory behind it? Foraging societies, with a few conspicuous exceptions, don't live from the hunting of men. Plant food gathered by women provides the steady, reliable daily diet, and well more than half the calories consumed.

Women forage alone or in small groups, generally out of the sight of, and often at considerable distance from, their base camp. So foraging bands depend on their survival on the safe passage of women over long, undefended distances. Is it really reasonable to suppose that unescorted women and children face routine danger from neighboring men? Can it be that male competition, fighting, and violence really figure so conspicuously in daily life?

Richard Leakey for one, doesn't think so. "The most extraordinary feature of our ancestors' behavior is that they brought this food back to their campsites to share with others in the group. This cooperation and sharing was the basis of our success as a species."[7] As Sanday's observations confirm, modern-day foragers, depending as they do on the vital food contributions of both sexes, live in egalitarian, not male-dominant, societies. With nearly every woman alone on the plains carrying both someone's child and several people's dinner, "normal" violence against women—the kind that Western societies see as "natural"—becomes an intolerable threat to group survival.

And what of the hunters, chasing down game while the women crouch in the dust picking berries? Leakey suggests that the entire notion of the club-swinging caveman killer is a wishful fantasy:

> It's been assumed that we always killed to get our meat, and that the basis of our success was man the hunter. Yet our ancestors were amongst the slowest animals on the savannah, and had only the crudest of weapons. There were far more formidable hunters seeking meat then as now. It's probable that it was the leftovers from these kills that fed our ancestors. We know from the success of modern-day scavengers in Africa that there is always plenty of meat left over. It's a myth that it was hunting that made us human.[8]

But it's no myth that modern-day foragers hunt, or that they bring down animals large enough to provision week-long feasts. But they achieve this not by poor imitations of those truly efficient brutes, the big cats or wild dogs. Instead, they do what comes naturally—and best—to human beings. On the Kalahari desert, in the Amazon jungle, in the Congo forest, modern-day hunters kill not with brawn but with brainpower. A man, or even a group of men, have no hope of beating or slashing to death a major catch— let's say a giraffe or an antelope. The animal has all the advantages, in tremendous size, great speed, deadly hoofs, pointed horns. And even if men armed with clubs or knives could win this fight, the blood and gore would attract far more dangerous predators who could easily harvest the portion known with good reason as the lion's share.

But a single well-aimed arrow or spear, dipped in a well-selected poison, tips the battle conclusively toward the humans. Exploiting his genuinely unique adaptation of intelligence and memory, the hunter applies an extensive knowledge of natural poisons and a profound understanding of projectile trajectories to the challenge of injecting a lethal dose into his prey. Once the arrow or spear hits its mark, the hunt becomes simply a matter of tracking and outwaiting the dying beast. "Simply," of course, doesn't imply that these tasks require no skill. The animal may cover many miles, retreat high onto branches or deep into burrows before the inevitable overtakes it. The men must follow diligently, for success depends on being there first when it dies. (Only the men, of all the competing predators, enjoy the advantage of knowing that death is imminent.) They might have to run for days, or dislodge large corpses from treetops, or reason out where a mortally ill creature might head for comfort, but they almost never have to hack, slash, or batter wild animals to death. Hunting, as practiced by modern foragers, is not an exercise in violence, but a discipline of patience, judgment, knowledge, skill, calculated boldness, and perseverance.

And, alas, of frequent disappointment. Anthropologist Napoleon Chagnon, whose descriptions of the Yanamamo of South America figure prominently in sociobiological interpretations of human behavior, has often accompanied tribal hunters:

> Hunting depends as much on luck as it does on skill and is not a very reliable way to supply nourishment. I have gone on five-day hunting trips with the Yanamamo in areas that had not been hunted for decades, and had we not brought cultivated foods along, we would have been extremely hungry at the end of this time—we did not collect even enough meat to feed ourselves. On other trips, we often managed to collect enough game in one day to feed the entire village.[9]

But even if the successful hunt isn't a regularity of Yanamamo life, another element of the Wild West theory is: unremitting male violence. Chagnon's engaging description of this tribe, subtitled "The Fierce People," presents them as the world's nastiest, most belligerent group. They fight with their neighbors and among themselves, and over everything: thefts, imagined slights, traditional rivalries, land tenure, women. They fight dirty, viciously, gleefully, inflicting grave wounds. And with this fighting goes a particularly overbearing form of male dominance; men not only beat up on each other, singly and in groups, but they routinely beat up on their wives. Even if hunting with poisoned arrows may not favor height and muscles, this endless, everyday mayhem does.

But, whatever the Yanamamo do proves nothing about the early conditions of Homo sapiens. Despite influential claims that they somehow typify hunting peoples, in fact they don't. Their lives differ markedly from those of the !Kung, for example, and also, very probably, from those of our early ancestors. In the first place, they practice a rather unsophisticated horticulture, so they're not even pure foragers. Secondly, their South American jungle, despite its apparent lushness, provides far less food suitable for humans than the more temperate African savannah. It's "much less productive and reliable than one would imagine," Chagnon writes. "The most abundant foods, palm fruits, are seasonal—a group of people could only rely on them for a few months of the year, during which time some eighty group members would have to forage over a wide area to obtain sufficient palm fruits to keep everyone well fed."[10] In any case, their habit of random violence against women rules out the gathering trips most efficiently undertaken singly or in small groups. We don't know which came first, the fighting or the farming.

Authors of less-known works on the Yanamamo came to very different conclusions from Chagnon's. Sheldon Davis reports that "for nearly a century, it appears as if the Yanamamo were forced to retreat defensively into their present territory between the Orinoco and Marauia rivers. To the south, they were attacked by Brazilian rubber collectors and settlers. To the north, they fought off the expanding cattle frontier of Venezuela and the more acculturated and rifle-bearing Makiritare tribe."[11]

These conditions—unstable food supply and encroaching enemy —ought to sound familiar; they're Sanday's basic description of the outer-directed, male-dominant society. Indeed, Sheldon Davis, anticipating Sanday's more general conclusions, suggested that "It is . . . more than probable that a fierce territorial struggle contributed to the development of the sexist warrior complex which Chagnon described."[12] A more isolated group of highland Yanamamo, living on land of no value to outsiders, is a much less violent, more egalitarian people. Just because a group is "primitive" doesn't mean it has no history.

So if the Wild West theory can't account for the differences between male and female bodies, what can? The sociobiologists have part of the story right: our ancestors faced fierce selective pressures, and the bodies they bequeathed us reflect them. A dimorphism far larger and more dependable than height or strength proves it: a grown woman carries twice as much body fat as a man. In a day when the marathon provides the metaphor for fashion and barely pubescent models grace lingerie ads—when bony angles symbolize chic—it's easy to forget that feminine allure used to depend on what were known as "curves." A century ago women struggled to match the ample elegance of Lilian Russell, the paragon of style. A generation ago Marilyn Monroe ruled the silver screen and the only modeling assignment open to Cheryl Teigs would have been "before" in a food-supplement ad. "Where she's narrow, she's as narrow as an arrow," sang Rodgers and Hammerstein's randy sailors through thousands of performances, "but she's broad where a broad should be bro-o-o-ad." Even that cheery vulgarism has passed from the language as women battle their body's basic inclination to stockpile excess calories.

Regardless of fashion and fitness, no woman can function as a woman without that supply. Rose Frisch of Harvard, the chief student of female fat, found that girls of eighteen carried, on the average, sixteen kilograms (over thirty-five pounds) of stored fat—one hundred forty thousand calories, in other words, or enough to "carry a fetus to term and three months lactation as an infant."[13] In the worst possible nutritional case, when the mother can barely keep herself alive, pregnancy will take fifty thousand of them, and ninety days of nursing, at a thousand calories a day, will consume the rest.

The female body lays in its provisions beforehand for a very good reason: the child's birth weight—an excellent predictor of its ability to survive—relates directly to the mother's weight before the conception. At puberty the girl's bean-pole figure blossoms into the womanly shape that so enraptured the men of "South Pacific." She puts on height, her pelvis broadens, but perhaps most noticeably, she lays down conspicuous and substantial deposits of fat. Adrenal androgens in both sexes trigger the first growth of adult body hair (which probably, according to some recent thinking, help spread sexual aromas produced between the legs and under the arms). But it's the estrogens, also involved in bone maturation, that signal that most female of fat deposits, the breast.

Indeed, a woman can't menstruate unless and until her body contains certain absolute and relative quantities of fat and lean. Girl athletes—swimmers, runners, gymnasts who begin competitive training before menarche—lag months, even years, behind their less active age-mates. "Each year of premenarche training delayed menarche by five months," Frisch found in a study of college runners and swimmers.[14] The girl demanded by professional ballet companies—a long-legged, flat-chested wraith who can flutter weightlessly *en pointe*—has retained, through the intense energy drain of her training, the contours of a prepubescent child. Late-maturing girls grow longer limbs than early maturers; a "coltish" body quite literally keeps the outline of immaturity. Significantly, young ballerinas experience normal onset of body hair—related to androgen and unrelated to estrogen and fat—but very late development of breasts, and even later menarche.

The most sedentary of children—the blind, for example—menstruate earliest. And any woman whose fat supply drops too low—marathon runners, drought victims, concentration camp inmates—simply stops menstruating until it is restored. These physiological precautions made very good sense in our distant ancestors' lives. The modern !Kung San of the Kalahari, even in the best of times, weight 80 percent of what Americans do at the same height. During the dry season, they even lose 6 percent of that. The women cease menstruating until they can eat adequately again, producing what we might call a "New York blackout effect": a peak in births nine months after their highest weight.[15]

Age at menarche clearly ties femaleness to fat. For a hundred years, it has been dropping about three or four months a decade, clearly mirroring the advance of nutritional and health conditions. In the U.S. today, an average girl has her first period at twelve years, 6 months—at least three, and perhaps four, years before the wealthiest, best-fed British girl of high Victorian times. In those days, when upper-class girls began to menstruate when they were from fifteen and a half to sixteen and a half, and became fully fertile a year or two later, a social debut at eighteen announced physiological reality. Parents anxious about pure bloodlines launched their daughters on the marriage market the moment they could fulfill the dynastic duty of aristocratic wives. But working-class girls, with their poorer diets, menstruated six months to a year later, and fully half of wives under forty-five suffered "female complaints," amenorrhea prominent among them.[16]

The Duchess of Windsor thought that a woman can't be too thin or too rich, but only the rich can *afford* to be thin. We Americans no longer die young in childbed or of cholera or typhoid or TB; we live long enough for fat to choke our elderly arteries. So we don't see body fat as our grandparents did, promising life, health, and prosperity. For millennia, though, the ability to plump up in times of plenty safeguarded our survival.

Storage and expenditure of fat is not, as diet theorists used to believe, a simple matter of adding or subtracting calories. Research now plainly shows that this income and outgo follows a regimen as rigorous as a well-run business. The underfed body hoards fat like a miser, as dieters ruefully discover, and a high-fat or carbohydrate splurge results immediately in extra pounds. This spells frustration to our sedentary, citified selves. But to our distant ancestors foraging on the savannah, it made perfect evolutionary sense.

They often went for days, weeks, or even months without any excess food. Sometimes they suffered real deficiencies. Only those who spent their fat grudgingly survived the bad times or maintained the supply needed for childbearing. Once in a while, of course, seasons of bounty provided huge, delicious concentrations of calories. Obviously, only those who used the bonanzas to build up their fat supplies got through the next—literally—lean period.

We all descend from distant common ancestors on the African plains. The great majority of Americans, though, descend from closer ancestors with even more pressing needs to lay down fat quickly and spend it slowly. Migratory foragers like the earliest humans can tolerate only smallish seasonal variations in food supply; technologically simple and regularly on the move, they can't store or carry much uneaten food. But settled cultivators—the peasant forebears of most Americans—can and must. Their survival hangs on one or two chancy harvests a year; they live with a risk and reality of hunger much greater than foragers face. If you depend on a few staple crops, a spell of bad weather or an insect pest can spell catastrophe. A single potato disease caused hundreds of thousands of Irish deaths by starvation and countless thousands more from diseases that emaciated bodies couldn't resist. Irish history changed course forever, and one quarter of Americans claim Irish ancestry, because a single type of plant failed to grow (and the English government refused to provide a substitute).

So it follows that if stored fat is essential to human life everywhere, it is particularly essential to peoples living with highly seasonal climates and periodic crop failures. And thus, as body composition studies show, Caucasians of both sexes, who have for centuries lived by agriculture in northerly, seasonal climes, tend to carry more fat than do persons of other races. (Eskimos, of course, carry even more.) Even in a state of Olympic training, a Caucasian athlete will carry more fat than will a black or Oriental competitor.

Men are not only less fat than women; they are also more lean. If a she carries twice as much fat as he does, he carries one and a half times as much muscle and bone. Does this mean, as some theorists have suggested, that "men got food like carnivores, women like herbivores"?[17] In the very crude sense that foraging males run after fast-moving food while foraging women walk to stationary food, perhaps it does. But the plain fact is that we know nothing of our early ancestors' body composition. We have no samples of their fat or muscles, only an incomplete scattering of their bones. They might have been fatter, or leaner, or more or less dimorphic than modern humans. Perhaps a more muscular man can shoot or throw more truly, or carry back more food to camp, or run longer distances. It is certainly true that present-day long-distance runners tend toward a slight, not a muscle-bound build, but then so do long-distance walkers.

Indeed, from the standpoint of the work he must do, a farmer can make better use of size and strength than a hunter can. Controlling draft animals, guiding the plow, swinging the scythe, hauling the sheaves all benefit from a very muscular body. A strong farmer's family might eat better, and so better survive plagues and epidemics than a weaker neighbor's.

But there's another possibility we've overlooked, one that parallels our discussion of height. Maybe male selection hasn't been favoring more muscle but *less fat*. Adipose tissue—plain body flab—as well as the specialized fatty tissues like bone marrow, serve other chemical functions besides storing calories. They aromatize androgens to estrogens (perhaps explaining why plumper girls menstruate early and plumper older women suffer less osteoporosis, a condition retarded by estrogen). The same process occurs in men; we don't know its extent, or the effect of excess estrogen on the biochemistry of reproductive maleness. But mightn't selection for leanness really mask selection for less estrogen-producing tissue?

The edifice of reasoning about fat and lean, though, stands on a shaky foundation: the theory of sexual selection. The basic notion makes good sense, but scientific consensus goes no further than that. Much of the theorizing involves animals with quite spectacular dimorphisms: antlers and peacock tails, for example. Obviously species so far out on their particular evolutionary limbs have histories very different from ours, with our much more modest differences. And most theorists assume that the secondary characteristics differentiating the sexes must in some way relate to fitness, or the ability to leave large numbers of offspring. Perhaps they have practical effects: massive antlers permit one more effectively to bash rivals for female attention. Or they might function as advertisements: massive antlers indicate the ability to grow sound bone, an important advantage to ungulates whose young must stand on their own strong legs the very day they're born.

But these theories, tempting though they may be, remain conjectures. And two recent findings throw the whole business into question. In the mountain streams of British Columbia, biologist Mart Gross made a striking discovery: a sexually *tri*morphic species. The coho salmon don't have three sexes, but three distinct ways of being normal. The females come in only one version, but the males, surprisingly enough, come in two. The large, red hooknoses with their curved snouts, long seemed the norm of coho masculinity. These tournament battlers seemed to embody all the usual pressures toward size and aggressiveness. On the sidelines of these struggles, though, lurked other, smaller, silver males, which matured in a third less time and grew to a tenth the size. These so-called jacks long seemed random freaks condemned to sneak among the rocks in the forlorn hope of persuading a few females to mate. But Gross found that the jacks are as normal—and as fully masculine—as the hooknoses. The species has evolved not one but two male strategies, almost equally successful in getting genes into the next generation.

Even this species can fit under the umbrella of sexual selection if battling out in the open and darting furtively among the rocks both result in matings by males who father fit descendents. But do the traits that favor copulation—fighting skill or cagy darting—actually relate to the ultimate survival of young? Do the traits that attract females represent "truth in advertising" about the genetic package they tout?

One of the very few persons who tried to find out thinks not. Biologist Christine Boake tested the sex appeal and staying power of red flour beetles. The males attract mates with special perfumes, or pheromones, some of them markedly more alluring than others. Boake mated both glamor boys and also-rans to randomly chosen females, and then measured the offsprings' growth rates. She reasoned that quick development related to early maturity and hence larger numbers of offspring. She also counted the number of grandchildren each male produced.

To her surprise, the perfume ad proved to be genetic hogwash. She found no relationship between attractiveness and "good genes" conducing to large numbers of healthy offspring, nor did the "sexier" fathers, who in normal circumstances would find more, and more willing, mates, produce fitter offspring.[18] This single case, of course, doesn't mean that sexual selection might not go along with superior fitness in other species, including ourselves. But it disproves the universal assertion that success in procreation equals superior survival potential. From now on claims about the evolutionary meaning of sex differences will have to be examined case by case.

Keep this proviso in mind as we trace our human past through our present glands and hormones and minds. We've already found differences, and substantial ones, between male and female bodies. But those that we can identify with assurance don't seem to bespeak generations of bashing enemies and slashing beasts in the African wilds. Rather, they seem adaptations to a long pregnancy and a longer childhood dependency. It may not be the economy of "gaining copulations" that have made men and women different, but the demands of carrying that big-headed, expensive baby—the costliest in the animal kingdom—to term and on through childhood. The demands of this most central of human tasks account for important physical differences: her earlier maturity and resultingly somewhat smaller stature, her greater supply of fat and his of lean. Are there other differences as well, more subtle but perhaps farther reaching? This is what we will try to find out next.

7

Different Sexuality?

You know this scene by heart:

He, masterly and irresistible—perhaps a fighter pilot or a matador—strides into the frame. She, hesitant and irresolute, waits on a porch swing or beside a rose bower. He approaches, standing a bit closer than for normal conversation. She tries to retreat, but the swing's arm or a trellis pole bars the way. Now he touches her gently, without permission or apology. He tips her chin upward (he is always taller than she) to lock her wavering eyes into his constant, confident gaze. Now a tremulo on the soundtrack, and the strings begin their swell toward crescendo. Strong arms pull her toward him. Her palms now tentatively graze his chest.

"Oh John! . . ." she breathes.

"Oh Mary!"

Then, as the violins melt to climax, her arms steal around his neck. Her murmur dissolves in the kiss.

Through hundreds of tingly moments in the velvet moviehouse dark, through thousands of shivery pages, through countless reveries, we have all lived that moment. Hollywood didn't invent the scene, but merely perfected it; no one can invent the essence of a thousand million dreams. No director contrived the basic elements: John's insistence, Mary's demur, his passion, her surrender, his possession, her relinquishment. The victory, the triumph, in the natural course of events, is his. He "takes" her, he "has" her, she "gives" herself to him. We know that this is how nature meant it to be.

But, then, what can we make of another equally human fantasy? If the Kaulong of Papua–New Guinea made movies, an island Hollywood would grind out endless variations of this:

"Mary" chooses a couple of long, firm palm fronds and goes looking for "John." She finds him alone in a forest clearing, just returning from his work. She approaches confidently. He stops, shifts his weight self-consciously, glances over his shoulder. She takes another step toward him, smiling. He steps back, wavers, steps back again, torn between attraction and fear. She continues to advance, the frond at the shoulder now, ready to strike. He shifts his weight as if about to run. She swings the frond and strikes him. He staggers a bit from that blow and the next, and shifts his weight, but does not turn or flee. She smiles happily into his face, and he smiles back. By choosing not to escape, he has given his consent.

And there, for Kaulong romantics, is *la différence.* Retold around a stone hearth or dreamed in a hammock, the scene distills the elements of their sexual fantasy: male terror of lust, the inevitable female overture, his deeply ingrained abhorrence at fighting back against a female. For the Kaulong, the power of female sexuality is literally awful, its delights masking the constant threat of death. Women pollute, spiritually and physically; for a man, then, satisfying physical desire entails risk of contamination, illness, and death. And in the end, it means the duty to die with one's spouse. So desire, brought on by female advances, is something to be resisted manfully, sometimes for a man's entire life.

In the space between these scenes, the Kaulong's and ours, we set out on the thorniest path of all: finding our species' true sexual nature. Which fantasy, if either, represents it? What part of male and female sex drive is purely natural, what part mainly cultural?

Obviously, of course, sex, like hunger, thirst, and fatigue, arises from the body's signals and needs. But like them, it also wears many confusing disguises. We eat at cookouts and state dinners, we drink from GI canteens and champagne flute glasses, we sleep in foxholes and under damask canopies. And the human sex drive goes spooning on the porch swing and cruising through leather bars. Eating, drinking, and sleeping, of course, are programed in the genes; but eating with chopsticks, drinking from snifters, and sleeping between sheets most certainly are not. Copulation must be programed too, but what about courtship? Can we unmask the genetic message behind the varied customs? Do we have it right, or do the Kaulong? Or does human nature have the latitude for both, a difference far wider than that separating fish forks from blubber knives?

For generations, thinkers have failed to agree on what drives men and women into each other's arms and loins, but that hasn't prevented theorists from holding their opinions as tightly as any lover in the night. Trying to find out what is actually *known* about human sexuality will be the toughest challenge we've faced so far. We'll have to go very far afield, back to the prehistoric savannah, into the treetops of present-day jungles, into bedrooms and discos, to try to find out. We'll have to trace some tricky theories back to their axioms and out to their conclusions. And before we can even begin, we have to face some facts that may well make the whole enterprise impossible.

First is the fact that we have no unbiased reports about what happens during sexual encounters. How can we tell who attracted whom, and why? Should we consider that he "scored"? Or that she "landed" him? Or that both "performed"? Every human society recognizes sexuality's explosive possibilities and fences them into the everyday rituals of courtship and consummation—the tempest of creation in the teapot of manners.

But even more important is our own culture's thoroughgoing confusion about what a sexual event *means*. For Westerners, anyway, and Masters and Johnson notwithstanding, it's only rarely a straightforward affair of hormones and orifices. The Christian tradition, grafting Greek mind-body duality onto Hebrew notions of purity and separation, made sexuality central to the drama of sin and salvation, a metaphor for the natural evil that only Christ can expunge. At the core of the Christian worldview is a mystery even more confounding than the Trinity: a Creator who assigned the exalted task of transmitting life to the debased mechanism of the human loins. The imperative of physical creation forever courts the danger of spiritual destruction. True spirituality—victory over eternal death—requires victory over sexuality, the mechanism of continued life. And it was promised through a Savior without carnal sin born of a Mother without carnal knowledge.

These problems have long conspired to complicate scientific consideration. The birth of modern biology coincided with the frantic prudery of the Victorian age. The theory of evolution itself more easily toppled Genesis than a science of sexuality shook polite convention. Freud's and Havelock Ellis's suggestions that modern analytical techniques might throw some light on our sexual nature startled and horrified their contemporaries. So did Kinsey's mid-twentieth-century application of modern survey techniques, and, some years later, Masters and Johnson's application of modern physiological measures.

The end result is that, though a great deal has been thought and written, very little is truly known about sexuality, if by "known" we mean widely accepted and firmly replicated. And even more frustrating, the interesting questions are the hardest to research: they have to do with motives rather than motions. What distinguishes our species is not what we do, but why and how we do it. We may be the only mammal species that copulates face to face. We are certainly one of very few primate species that lacks estrus—the limited season of female receptivity or "heat"—and we are probably one of the equally few that experience female orgasm. But much more significantly, we are also the only one that engages in duels of honor, that relishes erotic art, that distinguishes legitimate from illegitimate offspring, that possesses the *Kama Sutra*. What we really want to understand is not the act we share with hamsters and kangaroos. The true mystery is not that we copulate, but that we build the Taj Mahal to celebrate the fact.

What do we know about the strictly animal part? We have early, quite fragmentary evidence that the sexual centers in male and female brains are physically different. We also know that different levels of the sex hormones affect arousal; athletes taking steroids report increased libido. But do different clusters of cells and different levels of hormones imply inherently masculine and feminine ways of feeling and responding to desire?

Our two best scientific bets in recent decades, Kinsey's questionnaires and Masters and Johnson's electrodes, give opposite answers. Indiana's master pollster found great divergences between the sexual experiences and drives of men and women, but the St. Louis technologists concluded that "attempts to answer the . . . question 'What do men and women do in response to effective sexual stimulation?' have emphasized the *similarities, not the differences,* in the anatomy and physiology of sexual response."[1] (Emphasis original).

And neither position, alas, is theoretically pristine. Critic Paul Robinson observes:

> [Kinsey] clearly gave in too readily to the proposition that the differences he discovered between male and female sexual behavior were biologically determined. . . . And it is an enormous tribute to the power of sexual prejudice that this most consistent critic of Western sexual values, the scourge of Reinhold Niebuhr and Lionel Trilling alike, should have articulated a theory of male-female sexual differences that, for all its sophistication, tended to confirm popular opinion.[2]

If the Kinsey group may have biased their results in favor of accepted ideas, Masters and Johnson may have biased theirs against. They only used female research subjects who had achieved orgasm, thus assuming as proven one of the most hotly contested gender issues: whether women are normally orgasmic.

So physiology and demography don't provide an answer, but an increasingly influential group of researchers thinks that evolution can. "With respect to sexuality," writes anthropologist Donald Symons, one of the most highly regarded of this school, "there is a female human nature and a male human nature, and these natures are extraordinarily different, though the differences are to some extent masked by the compromises heterosexual relations entail, and by moral injunctions."[3] Thus far at least, both we and the Kaulong may be right: *la différence* surely runs more deeply than differences in anatomy. And it does so for reasons we can recognize: "Men and women differ in their sexual natures because throughout the immensely long hunting and gathering phase of human evolutionary history the sexual desires and dispositions that were adaptive for either sex were for the other tickets to reproductive oblivion."[4]

We're going to look into Symons's ideas in some detail, because he represents a school of thought gaining ascendency in many university departments. But first, we have to understand some modern evolutionary thinking on the subject of fitness. In the classic theory of evolution, you will recall, it was a qualitative characteristic: possession of the traits needed to survive life's perils. Modern theory has made it quantitative: an individual's relative fitness is the number of descendents he or she adds to the total of living creatures. Scientists with computers have come to view evolution as change in gene frequencies rather than change in living populations, so they began to judge an individual's fitness by how many of his or her genes get passed to the next generation. A short-lived parent of many offspring would have a greater evolutionary impact than a long-lived parent of few. Fecundity, rather than mere survival, marked the "fittest."

If natural selection depends on who has many offspring, not who lives or dies, then selection "is evolutionarily (genetically) significant whenever differences in performance owing to genetic differences correlated with differences in reproductive success," argues biologist Richard Alexander.[5] Reproductive differences between the sexes, obviously resulting from genetics and just as obviously affecting numbers of offspring, seemed the very type case of this principle. Genes now seemed to count for more, theoretically at least, than the individuals who carried them. Or, as theorist Richard Barash puts it, "insofar as a behavior reflects some component of gene action, individuals will tend to behave so as to maximize their fitness."[6] Those who fail to do so seem doomed to an ever-dwindling share of future generations.

Now, lower animals, including those we descend from, obviously do not weigh the pros and cons of their actions—but only act as though they do through the impetus of their inborn drives. These drives, of course, represent brain wiring and hormones—and indeed, in a number of rodent and bird species, scientists have found specific connections between neurological events or hormone infusions and animal behaviors.

If this theory is right—if differential reproductive success does drive evolution—then reproductive behavior must sit in the driver's seat. Reproductive strategy must define a species' whole nature; in Alexander's words, "We are programmed to use all our efforts, and in fact, to use our lives, in reproduction."[7]

What does this mean to us humans? For Symons, the key is that a woman can produce only about one child a year, and then only between menarche and menopause. But a man can theoretically produce hundreds or even thousands—one for every time he can convince a fertile woman to copulate. Philandering ought to pay a man handsome reproductive dividends, Symons reasons. A womanizer can love 'em and leave large numbers of progeny, whereas the faithful family man limits himself to his wife's reproductive capacity; he might even raise some of the philanderers' children as his own. In each generation, therefore, a larger proportion of the boys will descend from men with a wandering eye. And it follows (from the assumption that courtship customs are under genetic control) that over many, many generations, these tendencies will become a masculine approach to sexuality.

Specifically, Symons argues, a taste for variety is built into the male psyche, probably even into male neurology. Male barnyard livestock show the "Coolidge effect"; they tire of copulating with one female, but perk up immediately if offered another. A visually-oriented species like Homo sapiens, Symons adds, would naturally develop a built-in tendency to arousal at the mere sight of a potentially fertile woman. He believes that men can make a rough judgment of fertility by looking for the traits they value: principally youth, as indicated by firm, unwrinkled flesh, and a shapely physique composed of good-sized breasts and hips. (This despite the fact that a proven reproductive bet probably resembles a hausfrau more closely than a movie starlet; she sports the distended breasts and ample, dimpled fat of repeated, recent pregnancies. Renoir and Rubens celebrated her. Slenderness, though highly prized by Berkeley professors, probably didn't presage fecundity on the African savannah. Nor did the well-turned ankle or the shapely nape, despite their power to drive Edwardian or Japanese men into fits of erotic rapture.)

Evidence of this peculiarly male propensity for visual stimulation comes from the male taste for pornographic pictures:

> Pornotopia [the sexual never-never land of the girlie magazines and X-rated films] is and always has been a male fantasy realm; easy, anonymous, impersonal, unencumbered sex with an endless succession of lustful, beautiful, orgasmic women reflects basic male wishes. Pornography has changed so little in the last century compared with other aspects of social life and relations between men and women because pornotopia lies closer to the genes than behavior does.[8]

Lying close to female genes, this school of thought argues, is something rather different. Women must go for quality, not quantity, which they achieve by selecting the fittest possible fathers for their children. Here Symons slips a bit back toward the old sense of fitness—traits conducive to survival. He thinks that women, unlike female red flour beetles, judge potential partners according to their prospects as providers.

So, if every man continually desires every fertile woman (except perhaps his own wife, who bores him) and every woman wants the most desirable men, then women must spend lots of time fending off suits from genetic (economic?) also-rans. The better her choice, the better are her children's genes and the better, presumably, their own chances of reproducing, especially in competition with the offspring of less selective mothers. In each generation, therefore, the proportion of persnickety women's children should rise. Choosy mother's genes will (if genes control such things) produce choosy daughters, and eventually, choosiness will spread to womanhood at large. Stringing a man along while sizing him up, holding out long enough to increase his interest without trying his patience, all the subtle wiles of making a man pay handsomely in time, affection, flowers, candy, furnished flats, wedding rings, and fidelity ought to "lie close" to female genes, Symons thinks.

Once she's found a suitably fit mate, a woman's reproductive interest dictates holding on to him, both to father future children and to help support existing ones. Thus, Symons believes, women lack sexual wanderlust, the innate taste for variety. "Women do not generally seem to experience a pervasive, autonomous desire for men to whom they are not married," he writes, ignoring demography; in primitive societies, women marry so close to puberty that just about every act of adultery involves two adulterers. "A woman is most likely to experience desire for extramarital sex when she perceives another man as somehow superior to her husband or when she is in some way dissatisfied with her marriage."[9] Men, of course, also seek women who are, by their unfamiliarity, "superior to their wives." Nor does Symons name the women he queried to reach his conclusions.

But Symons enthusiastically concurs with Kinsey, who did query American women. "There seems to be no question but that the human male would be promiscuous in his choice of sexual partners throughout the whole of his life *if there were no social restrictions.* . . . The human female is much less interested in a variety of partners" (emphasis added).[10] But neither writer permits women the benefit of the same doubt they provide men: sexual expression free of "social restrictions." For them, men's sexuality exists independently of the social consequences of copulation; women's evidently cannot. Tolstoy's Vronsky didn't lose his child and hurl himself under a train; only Anna lost her whole social world in a moment of passion.

Still, Symons sees the female strategy producing a very distinctive creature. The mere sight of the opposite sex doesn't arouse her. A man must woo her while she weighs his potential net worth. If he responds to "innate rules" favoring youth and shapeliness, she seeks high status. And unlike him, she has no genetic reason for resenting his roving; impregnating another woman, after all, doesn't keep him from also servicing her. But his very genes make him jealous of his nonpregnant women; other men can, after all, fool him into raising their child as his own and thereby reduce his fitness. Thus, Symons reasons:

> Selection favored men who kept mistresses, changed wives, and obtained additional wives when these activities increased their own inclusive fitness, regardless of the effects on the fitness of the women involved. . . . I suggest that selection has favored the female capacity to learn to distinguish (not necessarily cognitively) threatening from

nonthreatening adultery, and to experience jealousy in proportion to that perceived threat.

Unfortunately, Symons leaves unexplored the exact nature of this fascinating but heretofore unremarked phenomenon, the feminine capacity for noncognitive (or perhaps extracognitive) discrimination.

Once having chosen among her eager suitors, Symons believes, a woman acts differently even in the heat of passion. Her temperature rises more slowly and never as high as his. Even hotting her up a bit takes work. But then, the survival of the species depends on his orgasm, but nothing except her pleasure depends on hers. In point of fact, he doesn't even need her active cooperation, and can strike a blow for fitness even if she ardently resists. Why women climax at all puzzles Symons. After all, they vary more in sexual response because selection doesn't drive them toward a single goal, as in men. In this new, improved twentieth-century version of evolutionary theory, variability marks female sexuality as *less* central than male to the main purposes of our species.

Besides orgasm, women possess the even more perplexing ability to climax apart from sexual intercourse (unlike men, who must ejaculate), and to climax repeatedly or continuously. And they lack the male "refractory period" following orgasm, when sexual arousal can't occur. They even possess a special organ, the clitoris, lacking any known function except registering sexual excitement.

For Symons, this self-tied Gordian knot merits no more than a single, deft swipe of evolutionary theory's terrible, swift sword. "The female orgasm may be a by-product of mammalian bisexual potential: orgasm may be possible for female mammals because it is adaptive for males. . . . Multiple orgasms may be an incidental effect of their inability to ejaculate."[11] Thus, in a species with every sexual trait fine-tuned by eons of natural selection, with esthetic preferences and courtship habits honed to the purposes of fitness, with social arrangements commanded by the needs of its genes—in this superbly engineered reproductive organization, Symons sees the most elemental feature of mature female sexual experience, a reaction engulfing the entire body in a particularly female neurological conflagration, as nothing more than a by-product of masculinity, the true engine of species survival. Males, Symons had previously noted, are programed to discard wives and mistresses "regardless of the effect on the women's fitness." Orgasm, however, because it does not fit into a scheme meeting male needs, apparently meets no needs at all.

Still and all, these two very different creatures need each other to carry out the purpose they were built for. Joining forces means compromise; each mate trims nature's tendencies to the other's taste. To give just one example, Symons suggests "that heterosexual men would be as likely to have sex most often with strangers, to participate in anonymous orgies in public baths, or to stop off in public restrooms for five minutes of fellatio on the way home from work if women were interested in these activities, but women are not interested."[12]

But some men, unconstrained by female tastes, are interested. Frequent sex with strangers in anonymous public places was—until AIDS—a staple of the gay male subculture. It contrasted sharply with lesbians' long-standing, often not very physical, liaisons. Does each gender, when free of the other's preferences, simply revert to type? Without the female fixations on caution and intimacy, Symons believes, men again become the voracious hunters who prowled the African plains. Without the male need for copulation and variety, women become the patient nurturers who waited at the camp fire for their return.

Gay men value looks, he argues, not because they're "effeminate, but simply because they face the same problem that heterosexual women face: they wish to be sexually attractive to males, and males assess sexual attractiveness primarily on the basis of physical appearance."[13] Lesbians, presumably, often ignore looks, because they want to attract women, who (even in the absence of any possibility of conception) evaluate lovers socially, not physically.

But Symons fails to track this very provocative idea to its logical conclusion: Can persons who violate the most basic tenet of fitness theory really express the true nature of sexuality? Far "closer to the genes" than interest in youth and appearance, or concern for social standing and personality, must lie the simple need to feel attraction to the sex that permits reproduction. Natural selection can't possibly favor homosexual desires. If genes influence sexual behavior, and if a man's or woman's wiring is so awry that it defeats conception, then it can't represent any other "normal' evolutionary tendency.

Anyway, there are other equally simple and equally elegant explanations. Male homosexuals may value appearance because they highly value anonymity; American culture still forces many into double lives to protect careers. Anonymity drastically cuts the risk of disclosure, blackmail, or disgrace. Having no other basis for choice makes appearance paramount. And the desire for promiscuous "scoring" mimics the heterosexual culture, except that it meets no resistance from women trained from childhood to be "good girls." Lesbians, on the other hand, in casting off the dominance of male-oriented sexuality, may well discard its most onerous requirement—the need to appear young and "feminine." But they retain the heterosexual culture's unease with female sexual advances, and they don't have to deal with men trained from childhood to "make out."

Symons's theory, for all its illogic, is only a moderate version of a widely held view. Some theorists see genetic influence under, and in, every bed: in the incest taboo, in polygamy, in women's tendency to marry older, richer, more powerful men.

Underlying all this is a single, essential idea: *we act to maximize fitness*. Elegant, intuitively logical, and above all, absolutely essential to the entire school of reasoning, it has a wide appeal both in and out of science. "At the moment there is something of a bandwagon in natural history for inventing functional explanations of behavior," observe zoologists J. B. Krebs and N. B. Davis, of Oxford and Cambridge, respectively.[14] Despite the growing popularity of modern behavioral Darwinism, however, "we do not want to leave the impression that [its] ideas . . . are completely accepted by all evolutionary biologists. Far from it, even our basic assumptions are very much in dispute in the literature."[15] And none is more basic, or more hotly disputed, than this notion of fitness.

"We are programmed to use all our efforts, and in fact to use our lives, in reproduction," declares Richard Alexander, one of the strong defenders.[16] All this fussing about fitness may seem a detour from our discusion of sexuality, but seemingly innocuous assumptions have led to intellectual—and social and political—conclusions so vast that honesty requires us to follow this line to its end. Like Horton on his egg, Alexander meant what he said and said what he meant: that people are faithful 100 percent to their inborn natures, which force us to bend all our efforts to making the largest possible number of babies. But do we really act with such storybook singlemindedness? "Obviously individuals maximize something," writes the anthropologist Frank Livingstone, "or they think that the choices they make are in some way the best for them. They don't minimize. But, in striking contrast to other animals, we maximize in terms of the ideology and values of our cultural environment."[17] We use all our efforts, he believes, indeed our whole lives, in making ourselves the sort of person that our culture tells us we ought to be:

> No animal behavior is comparable to "It is a far, far better thing I do than I have ever done. . . ." E. O. Wilson [the leading sociobiologist] has pointed out that "human beings are absurdly easy to indoctrinate." Culture, through the symbolic codification of rules and customs, is the major indoctrinator.

Often, of course, culture presses us to "be fruitful and multiply," but sometimes people see just the opposite as their "far, far better thing." In 1849, for example, a Georgia doctor noted something that "all country practitioners are aware of"—to wit, "the frequent complaints about the unnatural tendency of the African female to destroy her offspring [by abortion]. . . . Whole families of women . . . fail to have any children."[18] Even more unnatural, of course, was the fate awaiting these children: lives as chattel slaves. By refusing to breed field hands for the planters, the women maximized all that they possessed, which was simply the will to resist. Another doctor, addressing the medical society of Rutherford County, Tennessee, reported on slave-quarter birth control: "They take [camphor] just before or after menstruation in quantities sufficient to produce a little nervousness."[19]

This technique worked less well than that used on another Tennessee plantation. A Nashville medical journal noted that "four to six slave women of the proper age to breed" had produced only two live births in a quarter century.[20] Miscarriage in the first trimester struck every time, even in women newly purchased. This singular coincidence arose, of course, from the medical knowledge of an elderly slave woman.

Even in situations far less desperate than slave plantations, women have attempted abortion or, failing that, infanticide, throughout history and around the world. A third of all American pregnancies now end in elective abortion. Who aborts and why neatly demonstrates Livingstone's idea. Middle-class white Americans most typically abort a first pregnancy in the late teens or early twenties to safeguard their future options. Poor black women, who have no options, abort third or fourth or later pregnancies to safeguard the precarious life chances of their existing children. Each woman thus "maximizes in terms of values."

But it turns out that our ancient ancestors probably never had the leeway for the single-minded womanizing that Symons's theory requires. From the dawn of time until a generation or two ago, nearly everyone spent their entire life within sight and earshot of close kin. Cruising for one-night stands makes sense in a world of singles bars, but not when everyone within three days' walk is a relative. "In a population of between three and five hundred people, after six generations or so there are only third cousins or closer to marry," observes population theorist Robin Fox. And five or six hundred people are more than a forager undisturbed by civilization may see in a lifetime. As late as the nineteenth century, an amorous rural Englishman, living in a landscape vastly more populous than his foraging forebears, had to satisfy his yen within five miles of home—"the distance a man could comfortably walk twice on his day off—his roaming area by daylight. . . . The bicycle [introduced at mid-century] extended the radius to twenty-five miles. This was a big shake-up."[21]

Even granting that a footloose hunter might encounter a compliant gatherer in some secluded glade—and further granting the unlikely condition that both were alone—she still would belong to one of the neighboring bands bound to his by countless generations of cooperation and intermarriage. In small, face-to-face communities, where, in Evelyn Waugh's words, "unlettered men have long memories," there are simply no strangers available for anonymous one-night stands.

Australian aborigines, possessors of perhaps the world's most primitive technology, divide their entire social universe into eight or twelve interlocking classes of kinfolk. They mentally manipulate matrices that anthropologists must represent in three dimensions. Everyone falls into the category of permitted or forbidden mate. Everyone is the sister, or niece, or aunt, or classificatory sister-in-law or second cousin once removed to someone who knows you. And so, unable to jet off to a distant academic convention, enroll in a computerized dating service, or even check out the offerings on neon-lit city streets, most men for nearly all of human history have had to choose between maximizing their reproductive potential and keeping their good name.

Most, it seems clear, must have taken the long view when it came to bashing females into submission. Indeed, this "decent respect for the opinions of mankind" was what drastically enhanced their fitness. Simple societies lack studio condominiums and frozen dinners; ostracism means the equally simple certainty of painful death —from starvation, from thirst, from attack by predators in the night. That's why hospitality to the wayfaring stranger is a virtue observed in demanding environments around the world. A man alone has very little hope of providing all the necessities of life in a world without pack animals and trading posts; he cannot simultaneously hunt, gather firewood, carry water, collect plant food, and guard the supplies cached at camp. He cannot, therefore, regularly outrage his fellows (who in egalitarian foraging societies include women) and expect to live long enough to leave many descendents.

And, in fact, it's not clear that men anywhere act to maximize their reproductive fitness either, if other considerations—perhaps something as evolutionarily trivial as maintaining a middle-class standard of living—weigh against it. In 1985 Richard Alexander, born in 1929, had two children. E. O. Wilson, born the same year, had one. And Donald Symons, divorced as he entered his forties, had none.

Even if, for the sake of argument, we grant that the forces Symons suggests did drive early humans, there still remains real doubt that they would—or could—have produced the result he deduces. Harvard biologist Philip Darlington writes:

> Every generation of evolutionists has its blind spots, as any good history of biology shows. The blind spot of this generation . . . seems to me to be failing to see and understand simple fundamental principles—and especially the principle of natural selection, which is most fundamental of all—before expounding sophisticated complexities. . . . Almost all writers on evolution use natural selection, but hardly anyone tells us what it is or how it works.[22]

Defining it as alterations in gene frequencies "is not a definition of selection but a statement of its result. It . . . hides the details and costs of selection in a black box." In a series of articles remarkable for their passion, he pries the black box open.

A generation of mathematical theorists, growing up with the best nutrition, sanitation, and medical care in human history, has forgotten a basic fact: " 'Differential reproduction' depends very little on the different reproductive capabilities of different individuals; . . . most individuals of most species are selectively eliminated before they have lived long enough to reproduce."[23] The wastage in most species has always been and remains gigantic; an instant ago in evolutionary time, industrialization spared a lucky minority of humankind (who have since eliminated scores of millions of their own kind through mechanized slaughter). Not until a hundred years ago did even three-quarters of English women live to the mean age of childbearing. A hundred years before that, just before the American Revolution, two out of three girls died childless.[24] And in some poor countries today, half the children still die in their first year.

Early death is now and has ever been the fate of most creatures born, hatched, spawned, and sprouted on this planet. They die from disease, predation, starvation, cold, heat, and accident. Those who most often give their lives in the cause of fitness are women perishing in childbirth. In frontier times, twice as many American Indian women between fifteen and twenty died (usually delivering a first child) than did their men—who were warriors. Selection for a man's ability to conceive a baby has been mild compared with selection for a woman's ability to bear it. Darlington marvels:

> That natural selection is "only" differential reproduction and that nature is really not red in tooth and claw—I do not see how any observant field naturalist can believe it. And much more important, this definition, which ignores the nonreproductive events that mainly determine the direction and costs of natural selection, has allowed complexities and costs to be forgotten and unrealistic conclusions to be reached about the rapidity of selective processes and the perfection of adaptations.[25]

Selection, after all, is merely another name for what Shakespeare more insightfully called "the slings and arrows of outrageous fortune." It favors persons who can simultaneously resist infection, digest the foods available to them, get adequate oxygen, suppress the tendency of certain genes to turn their cells cancerous, maintain proper body temperature, staunch bleeding from cuts, keep on reasonable terms with their fellows, stay out of the path of speeding cars, and otherwise get from one day to the next. Multiple genes influence each of these processes; selection can clearly maximize one set of traits only in mathematical models.

Indeed, selection for some traits sometimes works at cross-purposes to selection for others. Frank Livingstone began his career with an elegant demonstration of evolution in spite of itself: the recessive gene that, in a double dose, produces deadly sickle-cell anemia protects against malaria when it appears singly. Selection works both for and against this gene, favoring solos and eliminating pairs. We live in a real world of countless selective pressures, of constantly changing conditions, of sheer, dumb luck, and not in the computer-program world of three or four carefully balanced factors. "It is pure metaphor . . . to describe numbers of chromosomes, patterns of fertility, migrations, and religious institutions as 'adaptations,' " says Richard Lewontin, a Harvard population geneticist who has emerged as a leading critic of modern biological determinism.[26]

Of course, a very great selective advantage can produce rapid evolution. The first of our ancestors to find that standing, however unsteadily, on his or her own two feet left hands free for tools and weapons and parcels had a considerable jump on competitors. They must have watched in amazement, supporting themselves, gorilla-like on their knuckles, as he or she carried home big loads of food or knocked fruit out of trees with sticks or snatched a child from harm's way or tossed a rock at a passing animal. Imagine the demand for a mate with such astonishing talents! But, Darlington observes, no matter how central this discovery became to our fate as humans, the "secondary details are still imperfect several hundred thousand generations later."[27] Our free hands have reshaped the world and our sturdy feet have walked every part of it. But we're still primates perched rather unsteadily on our hind legs; bad feet plague and bad backs cripple many of us. Our primate hearts struggle, and sometimes fail, to pump blood brainward, against gravity. Even more generations separate us from the first ancestress who bore her young live through the vagina. And still this process, utterly central to the survival of every mammal line, continually claims lives.

Darlington insists:

> Selection does increase the quantities of advantageous genes in a population, but this does not mean that individuals act to "maximize representation of their genes in the next generation." They act to maximize successful offspring—individuals—in continuing, adaptable lineages. Increase of gene quantities is the result of this process; it is not selectively advantageous in itself.[28]

Indeed, sex and gender won the selective struggle against cloning exactly because they permit diversity. It's illogical to argue that selection would also favor transmitting large numbers of identical genes for traits not immediately concerned with survival.

If the forces that made us human don't explain our sexuality, perhaps the answer lies even further back in our primate past. Clearly, we owe much to the germ plasm of those distant ancestors. We have full-color, three-dimensional vision and wrap-around binaural hearing because they lived in trees. We have long, independently moving fingers because they swung from branches. We walk upright because they came out of the forest onto the grasslands. Over eons we have bent their capacities to human uses, turning them into reading, the symphony, brain surgery, flamenco. But we also have fingernails because they had claws and coccyxes because they had tails. What part of our sexual inheritance serves purposes specific to humankind and what part is nothing more than selective excess baggage? How many motives, in other words, can dance on the head of a gene? And where can we look to find out?

Here the plot thickens, rather like a fog. No living primate is our ancestor, or stands any closer to our common ancestor than we do. We have spent millions of years developing our humanness; they have spent the same eons developing the special traits of baboonness or gorillaness or monkeyness. Most of them, in fact, have had considerably shorter generations and thus much more chance to shuffle their genes.

Among our close cousins, the great apes, and our more distant kin, the monkeys, we find lives that suit nearly any fantasy possible about the "real" nature of human sexuality. Some species live idylls of homey monogamy; others fulfill the dearest wishes of the Wild West enthusiasts. This variety, of course, will surprise no one who has ever attended a family reunion, even if it does rather complicate the search for illustrative cases and the probable path of our descent. If, over the wedding hors d'oeuvres, the branch of the family in the plumbing business finds little in common with their second cousins the classics professors, what can we expect to learn about ourselves across the vast abyss that separates us from our primate kin?

According to the sociobiologically inclined theorists, a great deal. They solve the problem of choosing by discerning general primate traits that they believe run through all the family's branches, just as curly hair or a tendency to asthma can tie us to unknown cousins a continent away. The more vocal, numerous, and influential school, of course, sides with Symons. Sarah Blaffer Hrdy, who calls herself both a sociobiologist and a feminist, is prominent among those who have rethought the primate past from the female standpoint.

She agrees with Symons and company that different selective pressures have molded the two sexes, but strongly disagrees about their nature and results. Female evolution, she believes, focuses no less sharply than does male; earlier theories markedly overestimated the degree of variation in female sex drive. This mistake followed inevitably from a previous one: failing to notice that women actually bear and rear widely varying numbers of children. One study of !Kung bushwomen found, for example, that after eleven years the most fertile woman had five children and the least fertile had none. Indeed, half the women had no children at all, and another 5 percent would have no grandchildren. The theoretical difference between the most and least successful mother is smaller than that between the most and least successful father, but the difference among women's reproductive success, Hrdy argues, permits harsher selection favoring the successful mothers' traits. And those traits add up to scheming, manipulative, competitive Scarlett, not to sweet, passive Melanie.

Several African studies concur. Monogamous wives produce somewhat more children than polygamously married co-wives, except for a single, telling exception. The senior co-wives appear, in one study at least, more fertile than the rest—perhaps because they eat more and work less than their more oppressed juniors.[29] And, Hrdy admits in a footnote, several other factors could account for this result. Still, she maintains, "If true, this is one of the rare examples in the ethnographic literature which fits patterns emerging for females in other species of primates: differential use of resources and differential fertility according to rank."[30]

Rank, and its corollary, dominance, figure very prominently indeed in much of the thinking about apes' sex lives and our own. All good things, it seems, come to primates who push their fellows around. For males, the position of "alpha" may mean the chance to increase (new-style) fitness by beating out rivals for female favors. It might even mean license to kill other fathers' babies. For females, high rank means increasing one's own and one's children's fitness (in both senses) by getting a bigger share of the scarce resources needed to survive.

Richard Wrangham watched vervet monkeys try to weather a drought. "Mortality" among the females "was . . . rank-related."[31] Highly-placed females—those who could cow their social inferiors—hogged the scanty water in the tree-holes on the group's territory. Males managed to raid nearby territories for drink, but the neighbors carefully kept out female interlopers. The lower-ranking females simply died of thirst.

But female rank, though closely related to survival, attracts little theoretical attention. What really fascinates evolutionary theorists is act two of the Wild West fantasy, when our hero finishes fighting on the range and returns home to beat off rivals for the womenfolk. In a scene played out in countless movie houses, our hero, with full and awful pomp, enforces his right to sexual access. The denouement is swift and terrible to see, with the loser borne to Boot Hill by men who mutter under their breath and solemnly shake their heads.

Rank and dominance first appeared in animal research with the observations of poultry that added "pecking order" to the language. As behavioral biologists began looking closely at primates, a series of interlocking observations emerged. Many (but certainly not all) species live in groups apparently organized around the leading male ("alpha") and his female consorts. Certain belligerent and aggressive individuals won subservience from others. And often, a single male enjoyed exclusive access to a group of females, a form of organization generally called the harem. It all seemed to add up to a clear case of sexual selection for dominance in males and submission in females.

But three potentially faulty assumptions short-circuit the arithmetic. First, and perhaps most basic, is the notion, that "any behavior that improves the chance of survival . . . will be favored by natural selection."[32] Hrdy accepts this without demur, but ignores the old question of how genes encode complex behaviors. Even more damaging, though, she offers the exception that severely tests her own rule. It's worth following a complicated argument to make a crucial point.

Relatively few primates live in permanent pairs. Three that do—the Mantawei langur and simakobu monkey of the coastal islands of Sumatra, and de Brazza's monkey of Africa—"appear to have adopted monogamous mating systems . . . during historical times," she states.[33] Within the last several hundred or thousand years, in other words, these creatures have completely reorganized their lives to outsmart the world's wiliest and most persistent predator, Homo sapiens. They hit upon an effective combination of stealth and deceit. When they spot hunters, both sexes scuttle for cover in the treetops and sit motionless until the danger passes. But when hunters spot them first, the male rushes noisily forward, offering himself as a screaming, leaping, arm-waving decoy while the female spirits the young to safety.

The plan works because the female can count on a trusty, vigilant, nearby mate. In his devotion to her young, indubitably carrying half his own genes, he is everything that fitness theory could ask. But in another important respect he violates the sexual selection doctrine. "In de Brazza's and simakobu monkeys . . . males remain substantially larger than females. These are among the very few exceptions to the rule that among monogamous species, males and females are approximately the same size."[34]

It's this very discrepancy, of course, that suggests a recent change. But solving the puzzle of when merely unmasks the deeper one of how. Hrdy provides no detail. She simply notes that a "shift to small family units [monogamy, in short] has . . . arisen." But if natural selection dictates mating habits through gene frequencies, then so radical a change couldn't happen quickly enough, no matter what the pressures on the species.

Under the old, tournament system suggested by the size discrepancy, almost everyone had polygamous parents; no other pattern assured fitness. But selection can choose only among traits already present; it can't call needed variations into being. So there had to be *some* faithful male homebodies around before selection for monogamy became severe. The problem is that this implies substantial variation in mating patterns, which are utterly central to the species' entire way of life. It also implies that human beings hunted these species almost to extinction (killing all but the rare monogamists) before the change took place. And it's hard to understand how individuals who offered themselves as decoys survived to reproduce in sufficiently large numbers to repopulate the species. But nothing else explains how the genes of the scattered eccentrics came to predominate.

But what if certain individuals didn't actually practice monogamy in the old days, but still had the capacity to practice it when circumstances changed? Well, recognizing change and acting accordingly comes very close to a definition of learning. Somehow, some monkeys found a trick that saved their young from hunters. They used it again and again, and taught it—perhaps the way signing chimps pass on their human-taught vocabularies—to their offspring. If this is what really happened, then the monkeys carry genes for quick thinking, not for pair bonding. And that, rather than an inherent tendency to fidelity, is what selection selected.

We have good evidence, apart from the signing chimps, that wild primates can learn new tricks. One fastidious band of Japanese macaques took to washing the sand off their dinner of sweet potatoes. Nine years after the first animal washed the first yam, all of them under the age of twelve had the habit. Primate expert Thelma Rowell notes that these innovations spread by what, in humans, we'd call word of mouth, along the predictable paths of individuals who spend a lot of time together.[35]

So what happens to the theory of genetically-programed mating? Well, if primates—and macaques are far from the most intelligent—can learn and teach table manners, they might do the same for other branches of etiquette, including courtship. Indeed, the whole matter of male dominance comes into clearer focus if we view it as a system of manners rather than a trait of individuals. Dominance, like courtesy, Rowell observes, exists not within but between individuals. "The outcome of an approach-retreat interaction must, when you think about it, ultimately be decided by the behavior of the potential retreater—you can't chase an animal which won't flee."[36] The dominant male owes his position to the other males who let him dominate. (Do they carry genes for subservience?)

The fact is that we really don't know very much about primate social life; no insider has ever given us the lowdown on the daily round in a baboon band or monkey harem. All we have are the jottings of uninvited eavesdroppers, whose titles in departments of primatology don't make them social intimates of the animals they doggedly observe. "In the year that Jonathan Pollack spent in Madagascar observing *Indri indri* [one of the class of small tree dwellers known as prosimian—or premonkey—primates], he did not observe a single completed copulation."[37] Hrdy concludes from this failure that *indri* mates very little. Having slogged though the same steamy, hilly forests, having pulled the same leeches from her own flesh, she clearly admires Pollack's persistence in the cause of data collection. But, despite his exemplary devotion, we can profitably consider another possibility: maybe Pollack simply missed the action, like the child who looked at his brother and then asked his mother in amazement, "You mean you and Dad did that *twice?*" Bigger than *indri,* and clumsier, and earthbound, and a foreigner, Pollack made a much easier object of study than the small creatures scampering and calling in the trees above his head.

Rowell finds many primatologists too quick to draw large conclusions:

> Instead of describing the interactions observed, students have written in terms of subjective concepts such as "leadership," "dominance," "protection," "relaxed" or "intense societies," "friendliness," and "aggressiveness" without these qualities ever being defined in terms of the behavior that was observed. . . . [The eminent primatologist] Zuckerman suggested that the temperament and sex of the observer might well be important filters in determining, for example, the amount of agonistic (aggressive and fearful) behavior that was reported.

In other words, if you go looking for dominant males or submissive females, you're likely to find them. And you may even let your own labels mislead you. Primatologists have tended to call any group of females that live together and mate with a single male a "harem." This word, trailing memories of veiled concubines and eunuchs standing guard over the arcaded seraglio, seems to tell us something more—intended or not—about the relationships among the animals that compose it. But no khalif or vizier would recognize the "harem" among the patas monkeys. Here the group focuses not on male appetites but on female relationships. Living together over the long term, a cluster of mothers, sisters, and daughters tolerate a male on their periphery for the services he provides: copulation, lookout, and decoy. For his part, he doesn't threaten them, or much of anyone else, for that matter.

But an Oriental potentate would feel right at home in the harem of the hamadryas monkey. The male attracts females to the group, and their interest centers on him rather than each other—except when they shower attention on a new infant and its mother. For his part, he holds rarely disputed sway, herding the youngsters along and rounding them up when they stray.

So words can shape what we see. What primatologists observe in the trees and clearings, Rowell believes, depends in good measure on what they think they're looking at. And many, over many years, have thought they were looking at the inner workings of undisturbed primate groups. But she draws a vital distinction between "wild" animals—those completely "undisturbed" (except, of course, for the nearby presence of an observer) or who take "very small amounts of bait" from humans—and "free-ranging" animals who, though unconfined by cages, are "fed almost all their food by people." American workers, she believes, are particularly lax about this distinction, "commonly [using] free-ranging for all animals not in cages."[38]

But the piper still gets paid, and all too often, Rowell believes, researchers unwittingly alter the melody by putting out food to attract study animals. It's easier, of course, for humans to provide food on the ground than in the treetops. Arboreal groups generally remain undisturbed, but much of the data on ground-living species comes from groups systematically fed—and thus lured away from their more arduous foraging life.

Thus, "it seems quite possible that many of the characteristics . . . thought to be associated with coming out of the trees and into open country might in fact be related to artificial feeding."[39] Male baboons and macaques taking scientists' food seem more aggressive and belligerent—and hierarchical—than those who find it on their own. Do they fight because of their nature as males, or because of the free—but limited—refreshments? Influential ideas about sexuality rest on the notion of the dominant alpha male at the center of the group's concentric rings as it comes out of the woods. Around him range the females and their infants, the higher ranks closer to the position of power. The less dominant, immature males ring the outer fringes. Baboons, Japanese macaques, and rhesus monkeys have all been reported moving thus arrayed—but only, Rowell notes, in troops that have come to expect food drops from humans.

Fully wild baboon troops follow a very different marching order. In Ishasha in East Africa, wild baboons moved through the forest in the formation favored by school outings and scout troops: a long, nearly single file, with adults in the lead, followed by juveniles, with more adults sweeping the rear for stragglers. The leaders did not "dominate" the others into following; they had no way to compel numbers of them onto a certain path. Instead of high aggression, the males showed much "politeness" and "conciliation." A feeding test on wild monkeys produced the rings; observations of undisturbed foragers did not. As Sanday predicted, limited resources produce competitive masculinity; ample resources do not.

But if struggles among males don't account for primate social structure, what does? "In fact," believes primatologist Irwin Bernstein, "the alpha male's position is generally associated with a particular social role, the control animal role, which consists primarily of buffering the group against various sources of disruption and disturbance."[40] Perhaps, he suggests, alpha is the group's best politician, not its fiercest fighter. This primate Lyndon Johnson, wheeling and dealing in the corridors of power, may owe his preeminence to the support of the "central hierarchy," an inner circle of male and female influentials who guide the group's destiny. "A male does not carry his rank with him" [from group to group], Bernstein notes, "but acquires it in each troop he joins, and the correlation between rank and seniority may therefore reflect the ability of a male to gain acceptance into a troop."[41]

The charm and polish that boosts a male up the social ladder (or tree trunk) might also account for his appeal with the ladies. Neither rank nor competition, it turns out, reliably predict what actually happens when mating season arrives. Male chimpanzees "amicably shared copulation, apparently without reference to rank; among ring-tailed lemurs the normal rank order of males in the group was completely changed during the brief mating period, and a normally low-ranking male won fights and performed the majority of copulations seen; the males reverted to their original ranking when the season ended."[42]

The missing element in the models emphasizing male dominance is female choice. Alpha finds it no easier than Jonathan Pollack did to keep track of many different animals among the forest trees.

Hamadryas males mate exclusively with their harems, but the females remain true only in their own fashion. One study of birds, with far less brainpower than primates, found a level of adultery and cuckoldry that simply astounded researchers. Establishing paternity through cell protein studies revealed many more extracurricular liaisons than even the most vigilant observers suspected. Some mothers switched eggs in nests cleverly enough to fool not only professors of animal behavior, but even other birds.

So female choice is more than a metaphor; it may well be a physical fact that every human male carries with him. Indeed, man's most prized emblem of manhood, the supposed instrument of his dominion, might well have arisen to defend against female inconstancy. "Relative to most apes, man has a long penis and large testes for his body size," writes biologist Leslie K. Johnson.[43] Why should evolution have expended the effort to enlarge it? Presumably because reasonably powerful selective pressures favored size. But what pressures? Not the ones beloved of the Wild West theorists. "Given that sperm are motile for seven to nine days in the female tract," Johnson placidly notes, "and that females may copulate with two or more males during the space of a week, it becomes possible for sperm competition to influence the evolution of human sexual attributes."

He means quite literally the competition between different men's sperm in the body of the women they have both—or all—mated with. The winner-take-all dash for the ovum may indeed favor the man who deposits his sperm deepest, and thus closest to the prize. The more lengthily endowed man—who gave his entries a head start over his less sizeable rivals—quite possibly leaves more descendents.

So the adolescent boy's worst fear may come true—in the rational discourse of scientific journals, not the rantings of ideologues. Size may well relate to reproductive potential—but only if —and a theoretically enormous "if" it is—our ancestors' sperm competed not on the field of battle *but within the woman's body.* The theory makes no sense unless women commonly took more than one mate. A male with sole access needn't worry about depth; he wins regardless of which sperm takes the prize.

Males of many species have evolved ways of getting the better of a rival's sperm. A dog locks inside his mate (becomes "uptight") to prevent leakage. Insects blitz eggs with spermicides. Spiders reel in webs to keep perfumes from spreading. In none of these species does the female passively accept a single mate, and in none can the male assure himself sole access.

So primate males perhaps needed blandishments more subtle than "dominance." Rhesus females seek out males that don't threaten them; lady baboons favor those that maintain "special relationships." Indeed, believes primatologist Barbara Smuts:

> There is increasing evidence that a male baboon's behavior and, ultimately, his reproductive success, are greatly influenced by his social (not just sexual) relationships with females. The same appears to be true in macaques, chimpanzees, and probably many other nonhuman primate species that live in multimale groups.[44]

Attention to these relationships, she suggests, can help solve "puzzles that have troubled primatologists for years," such as why rank in the group simply doesn't predict sexual behavior.

So the successful male may not be passing down genes for dominance and belligerence, but for social adeptness and acumen. Indeed, some have suggested that even successful aggression depends on the ability to choose the right fights to walk away from. "Traditionally at this point," Rowell muses, "a reviewer proclaims that further work is required—it is indeed in progress. But I suggest that we now have enough studies to be able to say that there are unlikely to be generalizations relating to habitat and grouping that will hold for all primates."[45] Or even necessarily for all members of a single species in all circumstances.

In one group of zoo-dwelling baboons, for example, the first-generation males—those born before captivity—"herded" the females in the manner of their fathers. The second generation, however, in a pattern familiar from another context entirely, had begun to lose the old ways. These zoo-born males made very inept herders, tolerating such disarray that finally "one of the original old females chased and punished quarreling females in the way a male would have done in the wild."[46]

That bossy dowager clearly shares something with humans of both sexes: the determination to keep things the way they ought to be. Where her "ought" comes from, we can't say; perhaps some need for decorum lies close to baboon genes. For ourselves, though, a "cultural template"—that sense of order learned in a particular human time and place—is, for now at least, the likelier explanation. A Swedish researcher, pondering the nature of the sex drive, has come up with some very convincing evidence for this conjecture. But then, Bo Lewin had the good sense to query some world-class experts whose ideas had previously been ignored.

What originally piqued his curiosity was a long-established fact that, to put it mildly, "has been in need of explanation": Why have girls, despite their two-year lead at puberty, "tended to have their first intercourse at a later age than boys?"[47] In terms of physical maturity, this means a lag of three to four years, sometimes even more. Any other discrepancy of this size—one sex lagging three to four years in learning to talk or walk, or even in learning to ride bikes—would have long ago generated its own research industry.

The parental investment theory, of course, finds nothing to explain, and neither did psychoanalysis, Kinsey, or most other observers. It struck no one as peculiar that pubescent boys, like Prince Charming, leap into action while equally pubescent girls, like Sleeping Beauty, wait for the right kiss to awaken them. The really big mystery—why evolution should have selected for an early female puberty so that girls could then take no advantage of it—appeared not mysterious in the least.

But in the mid-1970s Lewin's experts, a sample of Swedish teenagers, suddenly disclosed "a 'new' [and quite unexpected] sex difference."[48] To wit: among youths between twelve and seventeen with coital experience—among young persons, in other words, born since the Pill made twenty thousand generations of coyness obsolete—more girls than boys had had intercourse, and they had started younger.

Shortly afterward, a West German research group asked similar questions and got even more startling answers—especially when you compare them with what young Germans had said a mere fifteen years before. In 1966, men and women born between 1936 and 1946—who had come of age in the era of the condom, the diaphragm, and the dread of "reputation"—had followed the formerly "natural" pattern: boys had first coitus younger and masturbated more. Most girls' initiation came at the hands of an experienced man or boy.

By 1981, though, Germans born between 1951 and 1961—children not out of puberty when the sexual revolution burst on the world—gave the same answer Lewin had heard in Sweden. Age at first coitus had dropped for both sexes, but now girls systematically started about a year younger than boys, much closer to the same stage of physical maturity. At a given age, girls now had experience of more partners. The sexes had similar—small—numbers of lovers at any one time, but girls had more intercourse outside their steady relationship. They also had as much homosexual experience as boys and masturbated almost as often. And perhaps most striking, the age of girls' first masturbation had dropped, too—particularly important because it now constituted the first sexual experience for at least two-thirds. On seven indicators of sexual activity, the boys now outranked the girls only in monthly frequency of masturbation —hardly a sign of promiscuity or dominance. The 1981 results, their startled compilers announced, had simply "inverted" those of 1966.[49]

Fifteen years of social change, in other words, had overturned millennia of "human nature." In the space of less than a generation —but the first generation that offered females the freedom from consequences long enjoyed by males—girls growing up in the sexual laissez-faire of northern Europe had developed habits and appetites paralleling what boys have done for ages. And much of their sexual activity depended on their own initiative, not that of men. So Lewin's mystery really needed no explanation. In northern Europe at least, boys will be boys, and—given social permission—girls will be girls.

Ironically, though, it's the new state of affairs that the researchers felt constrained to explain. Fortunately, they did not have to look beyond the nearest high school, finding the answer not in selective pressures or gene frequencies but in that basic institution of teenage life—going steady. Most Swedish girls lost their virginity to a steady beau—who, in keeping with long-standing European tradition—is somewhat older than she. Most boys, though, didn't make love first with a steady. But at high school age fewer boys than girls have steadies to begin with. An eighteen- or twenty-year-old beau can provide a great deal of status, security, and emotional support to a not-very-confident sixteen-year-old girl. The fourteen- or fifteen-year-olds who will go steady with her male classmates cannot. So in Germany at least, the old double standard is gone. By 1981, sexual attitudes had become more permissive than ever, and young women's even more permissive than young men's. The new pattern held for rich and poor, devout and unbelieving, though churchgoers took rather longer to get started.

And so, for youngsters born into an atmosphere of sexual freedom and suggestion with few precedents in human history, *la différence* appears more a matter of timing than of essence. These young people, growing up under conditions new to the Western world, and perhaps to the human species, may have invented a new fantasy altogether.

So what, in the end, does distinguish male and female sexuality? Are the differences so much smaller than countless Western generations have thought? The short answer—indeed, the only complete answer now possible—is that we don't know and won't for the foreseeable future. Perhaps reliable birth control has finally freed female sexuality, for the first time in the memory of our species, from the risk of pregnancy. Or perhaps two decades of hedonism and sexual frenzy have imposed drastic new pressures toward libertinism that distort women's actions but not their underlying natures.

Or perhaps human beings have no single "true" sexual nature apart from the culture that surrounds them, any more than we have a "true" native language or style of eating. The experience of our species provides no basis for deciding among these possibilities.

Nor do we get much help from those great technicians of arousal, Masters and Johnson. Their painstaking investigations—the largest recent body of information on the mechanics of sexuality—consistently emphasize the similarities rather than the differences between male and female sexual response. Indeed, in their women subjects (who, admittedly, are a biased sample) they find a capacity for excitement, a level of appetite, that equals or even exceeds men's. Desire follows a similar trajectory toward consummation, with the sole exception that men, because of the mechanics of ejaculation, never feel the sustained or rapid-fire orgasms common to many women. Standing Symons on his head, they come close to suggesting that the requirements of maleness short-circuit an arc of energy that reaches its full expression in female neurology. Ejaculation relieves physical tension, but can't recur without a new supply of semen. So it has a discrete beginning and necessary end. Female orgasm does not.

Simple plumbing, not basic wiring, may account for something else, they believe; the penis itself may incline men to a certain brashness. Jan Morris, the literary transsexual, agrees. It's simply more prominent, physically and psychologically, than the clitoris. It states its needs more insistently. And it plays a second role, not shared with the clitoris, in urination. Boys very early become used to handling it; several times a day they casually experience sensations that the female anatomy generally requires to be purposeful. (Can the same sort of casual, and largely unacknowledged, stimulation account for the passionate attraction—rarely shared by boys— that girls near adolescence often feel toward horses?) Indeed, some researchers blame on the same cause the notably unladylike behavior of female rats exposed to early androgens. Perhaps their enlarged, almost phallic, clitorises give off the same pleasurable feeling that the normal penis does. Perhaps a simple, unsubtle desire for more of the same, rather than any complex hormone action on the brain, accounts for these females trying to do what males do.

So it seems that something simpler than genes may account for human action. And homosexuals, just as Symons suspected, are the exceptions that prove this rule. Philip Blumstein and Pepper Schwartz, in an extensive study about American couples, explore the immense power of "ought." They found that homosexual lovemaking does differ for the norm in the ways that Symons describes. But both the promiscuous men and the retiring women share a surprising problem: who makes the first move. Our culture gives that prerogative to men; only lately have women challenged masculine control over the terms of a relationship by asking for a date, proposing marriage, stealing a kiss. Women now in early middle age grew up thinking that calling a male classmate on the phone might mark them as a trifle "fast." Making a first sexual move still puts some women's self-respect in a certain jeopardy—even if her partner is another woman. It's this unease in the role of aggressor, of a person who openly wants sex, not any lack of desire, that explains lesbian couples' relatively chaste existence.

Gay men have the opposite problem. It's not the aggressor but the object of his desire who confronts the loss of face. The male habit of control can deteriorate into competition over who initiates and who refuses. Thus, getting started means breaking out of the mold of custom; it requires an even stronger habit of spontaneity. "In lesbian and gay male couples, it is the more emotionally expressive partner who initiates sex."[50] Because the couples themselves violate the symmetry of their own expectations, this most "masculine" role falls to the more "feminine" partner. For as surely as Western culture shackles "inconstancy" to "woman," it shackles "strong" to "silent," and both to manliness. Active homosexuals do not represent, as Symons believes, the pure quintessence of their sex's natural tendencies, but rather, distinctive alloys of their culture's roles.

This must be so because, on another point, Symons is more profoundly right than he realizes. As structured by the economy of childbearing in a male-dominated society, the very act of sexual intercourse carries opposed meanings for men and women. In a central metaphor of victory and defeat, he wins, scores, triumphs in possessing her; she must, in some sense, lose in permitting possession.

This metaphor colors our entire response to the fact of our own sexuality. For generations, American men have taught their sons to glory in their physical manhood as an expression of their social power, to cultivate their impulses, to broadcast their prowess. Women have taught their daughters to hide their active womanhood as a root of their vulnerability, to muffle their sensations, to husband their good name. What a boy could scatter heedlessly, a girl had to keep inviolate and then sell to the highest bidder. That's why studying erotic pictures—scrutinizing women powerless in their nakedness before any or all men—is a communal rite of boyhood. But women's erotic fantasies have hidden modestly in over-ripe romantic fiction, where dreams of ravishment allow the same freedom that men have known—to enjoy sex without responsibility.

And, completely contrary to Symons's prediction, Blumstein and Schwartz found women more, not less, possessive than men. As the less powerful partner, and the one who derives status and even livelihood from a sexual union, she loses far more than he does by losing him. This, not inborn calculations about her genes, accounts for her ability to tolerate his adultery and her wariness about practicing it herself.

And American society opens another great abyss between male and female sexuality: it denies men the right to express many emotions available to women. Touching without either sexual or aggressive intent unmans. Deprived of a woman's license to hug, caress, or embrace another adult, men must force affection, grief, tenderness, remorse, apology, forgiveness, into sexual disguise. Women, of course, learn finer gradations of feeling, if only because erotic and maternal love flow through the same breasts and vagina. So American men *need* sex more than women; for many "the act" provides the only way of expressing tenderness.

In any other field of science, of course, such radical discrepancies among experimental subjects, such asymmetrical experience, would fatally taint all comparisons. But then, any other field of science would strive to consider, rather than selectively ignore, the factors that might influence outcomes. We saw examples of such a factor at the head of this chapter, and only by treating it seriously can science begin to make sense of human sexuality. "In dreams," the poet said, "begin responsibilities," not in the requirements of evolutionary theory. In dreams, in fantasies, in images too deep ever to come to full consciousness, begin the human response to the fact of two sexes.

We are the species hard-wired for symbolism. We are the species that, eons ago, based our adaptation on trading ideas. Not until science begins treating that fact as seriously as it treats the actions of hormones will it begin to find the truth about human sexuality.

But sex, for all its complications, is only part of a larger question, one that overflows hormones and gonads to become personality. And that is where we will look next.

8

Different Personalities?

What's wrong with this scene?

An infant stirs, opens an eye, and smiles a great, pink, toothless smile into the grown-up face hovering above. As automatic as an echo, the adult smile beams back. Now gentle hands lift the child into the cradle of a crooked elbow. Hugging the baby close, the parent sits under a shady tree to watch the sun glide down to meet glowing water. Wordless moments pass, marked only by sighs and gurgles.

There's nothing wrong so far, except that perfection, as it so often does, attracts an admirer, who promptly destroys it.

Rougher hands now reach under the child's armpits and lift him from the safe embrace. He whimpers his dismay. The newcomer coos brightly, balancing the baby in one hand while the other pats the little bowl of the belly. The small face seems ready to crack into a howl, but the pats become tickles and the little squeaks of complaint become bursts, then whoops, of laughter.

Nothing's really wrong at all, you're probably saying, except that the father's boisterous affection snapped the tranquility shared by mother and child.

And that's what's wrong. The shining ocean is the western Pacific, seen from a beach of the Outer Fiji Islands. A father had watched it while cuddling his infant son. Then the father's sister happened by and, as is the habit of Fijian friends and relations—

perhaps because they lack the parents' intimacy with the child—
wanted to see him shout with laughter.

This chapter is not about childrearing. It's not about species survival, or parental investment, or sex roles. It's not about muscles or
wiring or cells. It's about the point where they all converge, where
general rules become particular incidents, where traits become motives. It's about how we feel the experience of being Homo sapiens
in a certain time and place and brain and body. In short, it's about
men's and women's emotions.

Emotion hasn't gotten the attention lavished on some other gender issues, but, like the modest ball bearings between machine
parts, it is crucial to the functioning of certain influential theories. It
buffers the intellectual space between two great, independently
moving masses of theory—the macrosystem of the species and the
microsystem of the individual consciousness. If, for example, hunting or suckling (or any other particular action) fill the species'
needs, it still won't happen unless millions of individuals separately
decide to chase fleeing antelopes or put children to the breast. But
how do strings of molecules in cell nuclei become hours of exertion
or years of devotion?

Those who believe the world runs with the economy of mathematical models often assume that personality is the switch that turns
on motivation. They see it lying deeper, "closer to the genes," than
culture, making men and women strongly and individually want to
behave as the species needs them to. The species can't count on
each person's calculating his or her own best interest; that might
conflict with the species' or the genes' interest—and rationality can
produce unpredictable decisions in unpredictable circumstances.
Only emotion, these theories assume, with its power to override
reason, is sufficiently simple, strong, and universal to translate general principles into specific, imperative, individual—but uniform—
commands. So males and females ought, in this view, to come
equipped with different emotional repertoires. But do they?

We don't have to look far for the source of those simultaneously
uniform and compelling feelings. Each of us carries it inside our
skull. Science may understand only part of the intricate molecular
minuet that is the nervous system in action, but it has penetrated far

enough to know for sure that brain chemicals and emotions move in tandem. Disordered feelings go with chemical and electrical disarray; the brain waves, urine, and blood of schizophrenics and manic depressives cry out as much. Confidence, serenity, pleasure, even hope, can pour from a bottle or crackle from an electrode. So it's reasonable to wonder whether human beings' original equipment includes hormones and brain chemicals that subtly and precisely engineer the psychic states needed for survival—the sustained aggressiveness of the hunter, the tender concern of the mother. What could be simpler and more elegant than an inborn tendency to those emotions that natural selection seems to favor in any case?

Biological determinists have embraced this idea as wholeheartedly as any hunter ever heaved a spear. John and Georgene Seward, psychologists and authors of a standard monograph on sex differences, forthrightly state the traditional view:

> What sex-specific characters are most likely to resist cultural change and thereby survive as biologically ingrained dispositions?
> The answer is: the stablest characters will be those required by the demands of mammalian (and specifically primate) reproduction, with the division of labor that it involves . . . impregnation by the sperm-bearing male; ovulation, gestation, and lactation by the egg-bearing female. . . . Generalizing these inclinations, we should expect males, more than females, to be active, dominant, aggressive, and competitive; while females, more than males, should be compliant, timid, nurturant, and affiliative.[1]

This puts it mildly. E. O. Wilson, flatly (and mistakenly) states, "In hunter-gatherer societies, men hunt and women stay at home. This strong bias persists in most agricultural and industrial societies and on that grounds alone, appears to have a genetic origin."[2] But even the Sewards, who hedge their conclusions, make several unexamined assumptions: first, that sex-specific "characters" exist and can, by "resist[ing] cultural change," become "biologically ingrained." Secondly, that the reproductive division of labor between male and female requires an aggressive male and a compliant, nurturant female. Finally, and most deeply buried, lies the idea that these tendencies precipitate—even produce—suitable personalities in individuals.

But does biology really precede emotion? Do neurons and proteins really *cause* joy or sorrow, anger or tenderness? A man runs—after a buffalo or a bus—and electrical signals jump his synapses, chemicals surge through his cells. But they don't *cause* the dash; they *are* the dash, seen at another level. And what about anger, fear, joy, grief? An emotion floods our consciousness, chemical messengers flood our bloodstream; but which—if either—came first? We can't tell; not even animal experiments give a straight answer. In male rhesus monkeys, fighting and high plasma testosterone go together, but when a rhesus faces defeat, the hormone level rapidly falls. This happens to many primates under stress, such as monkeys in nerve-wracking experiments and army recruits in basic training.[3]

If fear, dejection, and anxiety can precede (and perhaps even cause) hormone level changes, we can't give definite priority to either feelings or physiology. Poets and neurobiologists, it seems, may simply be using different languages to describe the same incidents. Like a many-headed Hindu god, human events have several faces. The felt emotion reveals one, strings of molecules and banks of equations reveal others. But no single one of a divinity's aspects, the Hindu philosophers know, reveals the whole essence; each simply makes it real to a particular sensibility. This kind of multilayered reality, does, of course, violate a cherished notion: that chemistry and physics, hormones and neurotransmitters, being "harder" than mere, unmeasurable sensation, are more basic, "closer to the genes," and thus ontologically and perhaps even temporally prior. But a multilayered reality more elegantly explains masses of otherwise contradictory empirical results.

Still, thinking like that of the Sewards has shaped the questions researchers usually ask about personality and gender. Many researchers simply assume inborn emotional differences between the sexes. What else can explain the spectacle of two generations of psychologists debating this serious methodological issue: Do frightened, anxious rats or relaxed, confident rats defecate more? If copious feces indicate inner peace, then males are more "fearless." But if they mean agitation, then males show more "fear." Possible methods of telling the difference have filled countless papers and conferences. But many fewer pages and hours have gone into the debate about what fear can mean to a creature without enough neurons to imagine a future, and why a rodent reaction merits the same name as a human being's certainty of impending risk.

This debate may throw little light on the inner lives of rodents, but it illuminates those of personality researchers. A now-classic 1970 study asked mental health workers, doctors, and social workers to choose words from a list to describe a well-adjusted man, woman, and generic adult. The healthy male and adult were independent, assertive, adventurous, competitive, and not overemotional, oversensitive, or easily influenced. Not so the healthy female; she showed many fewer traits leading to independent achievement and many more of those adding up to submission.

Like many studies, these confirm what we might call Jessie Bernard's corollary to Strathern's law: research will find men (and males of other species) superior in the traits that men in our highly individualistic, relatively fluid society most value. But this isn't a sexist plot, argue Ruth Hubbard and Marion Lowe. "When a difference is established between groups that have different positions in the social hierarchy, the attributes of the dominant group are the 'right ones' to have."[4] In twentieth-century America, hustling go-getters get ahead. But a century ago in Britain, a closed, hereditary aristocracy held sway. Conspicuous competitiveness was a failing of the grasping lower orders, particularly those "in trade." Real gentlemen strove to fit seamlessly into the social position attained effortlessly at birth. Obvious intelligence or ambition clearly had no place among the "best people."

Whatever natural selection has required of men, apart from the occasional copulation, remains controversial. What it has demanded of women is much more straightforward: bearing and suckling babies, and often supplying their other needs as well. Effective mothering is thus the linchpin of primate survival. But many find it unlikely that evolution would hang so great an outcome on the whim of the fickle sex. Mustn't it have taken out an insurance policy, in the form of a female instinct for nurturance?

Of course, in communities that send boys of three to school with male teachers, or that set six-year-olds to work beside their fathers in the fields, among the herds, on the hunt, or in the shop, or that admit boys of any age to the men's section of the synagogue or the porch of the men's house, this necessity may seem less obvious. In these societies men also see to children's needs while doing important, manly things. But in Europe and America, men of the classes who get their opinions published rarely see children during the workday; youngsters are only, as Longfellow put it, "a pause in the day's occupation."

A natural predilection to nurture logically has two main parts: superior ability in dealing with children and deeper satisfaction from those dealings. (This superiority of skill—one of the very few conceded to females—involves a domain that, as Bernard, Hubbard, and Lowe could easily have predicted, enjoys exceedingly low social status. Ladies of power and wealth have long managed to avoid the more elemental aspects of their "instinctive" work—those, such as feeding and hygiene, that really do insure the child's survival.)

Those well-to-do women must have worked mightily to overcome their powerful inborn desire to clean up tiny bowel movements and spoon pablum down unwilling little throats. Darwin placed maternal love among the "simple emotions" we share with animals. By the late nineteenth century, science had accepted the distinction between primary instincts—those arising out of natural selection—and secondary ones, involving higher mental processes such as reason and learning. Mother love, of course, fell among the former; but paternal affection, although it commanded many fewer pages of print, appeared to arise from a general tendency to help the weak and dependent (and this, of course, involved such higher notions as justice and obligation.) Freud also placed mothering at the center of the female character. The ability to grow a baby in her womb became woman's consolation for her inability to grow a penis on her groin.

The early twentieth-century behaviorists saw that maternal care plainly didn't spring full-blown from the nervous system, like breathing or sleep; it involved an element of learning, and thus rated promotion to the category of secondary instincts. But the underlying drive remained so strong that only advice from an expert in child development (as opposed to a woman experienced in raising children) could save mothers from the excesses of unguided instinct. Still, the concept of maternal instinct was socially necessary; it split reproduction from sexuality. Only motherhood, in fact, justified sex in a society that now viewed women as properly asexual.

But there remained a problem: nobody could say for sure what a human instinct was, at least not until Konrad Lorenz and others developed ethology. Lorenz saw instincts as "fixed action patterns" coded in the nervous system and waiting to be triggered by some element in the external world that acts as a "releaser." For example, the particular combination of features we recognize as "cute" might serve to release nurturance, Lorenz speculated. Large eyes set in a small face; a large, protuberant forehead; short limbs; a plump body with soft, round contours—these universal traits of mammalian and avian helplessness set in motion, he believed, the behavior that sees an otherwise useless and bothersome creature through its crucial period of dependence.

Anyone who has shouldered the exhausting, consuming burdens of child care can understand that baby cuteness might well pack real survival value. In the drafty darkness before a winter dawn, little except relief from crying and a toothless smile rewards the parent torn—again—from broken slumber. But anyone who reads a newspaper knows that this instinct—if instinct it be—is easily overcome.

Lorenz's argument seemed to hold more water when he wrote of baby ducks, which experience what he called a "critical period"—a moment of decisive possibility—right after hatching. They form an immediate, unbreakable attachment to the first moving object they see after poking out of the shell. Occasionally that was Lorenz, but fortunately for them, it's more often their mother. And following her slavishly clearly helps them outlive their fluffy, fragile babyhood.

As biodeterminism gained ground in psychology, the critical-period concept mated fertily with the dogma of maternal instinct, bringing forth, in the early 1970s, Klaus and Kennell's theory of automatic human attachment. For a short time after birth, they argued, hormones "prime" mother and child to "bond" to one another, especially if they share an interlude of close contact. The researchers claimed to discern emotional and cognitive benefits months and even years later. "Bonded" mothers seemed to pay closer attention, and bestow richer love and more constructive teaching; they adjusted quickly to their unfamiliar new job and dispensed skillful, sensitive, highly committed care. Presumably, their children sensed this deeper security and devotion. A quarter hour on mother's belly seemed a small price for such large rewards, and hospitals promptly added the option to their obstetrical offerings.

The idea helped strengthen the trend toward viewing childbirth as a natural female function, not a medical procedure, but it also strengthened the trend toward deterministic thought about mothering. "As in the early maternal instinct literature," writes psychologist Stephanie Shields, "the individual woman is simultaneously relieved of individual initiative because the processes, innate and invariant, are assumed outside her direct control, yet she is held culpable as the single figure ultimately responsible for the baby's well-being."[5]

No one has replicated Klaus and Kennell's specific results; close analysis suggests that sociology may explain them. But the central idea—long-term hormonal influence on human child care—continued to spread across the intellectual landscape. By 1983 it had penetrated so stout a bastion of doubt as the American Sociological Association. In her presidential address that year, the feminist Alice S. Rossi exhorted her colleagues to begin "rethinking the issue from an evolutionary perspective," specifically, from the biologist's gene-frequency, natural-selection point of view. She scorned orthodox sociobiology as naive, but rejected the sole hegemony of social forces just as strongly. "Organisms are not passive objects acted on by internal genetic forces, nor are they passive objects acted on by external environmental forces, as some social scientists claim."[6] In a flurry of italics, she made her central point: *Ignorance of biological processes may doom efforts at social change to failure because we misidentify*

*what the targets for change should be, and hence what our means should be
to attain the change we desire.''*[7]

Indeed, "the attributes of mothering and fathering are inherent
parts of sex differentiation that paves the way for reproduction."
With "parenting styles of men and women [built] upon underlying
features rooted in basic sexual dimorphism," fathers and mothers
can't give the same kind of care even if they try; "biological predispositions make certain things easier for one sex to learn than the
other."[8] Thus, "men bring their maleness to parenting, as women
bring their femaleness."[9] With reformers demanding nonsexist
rearing by both parents, Rossi concluded that care by men ought to
make the sexes *less* similar.

Then she tracked the different parenting styles through primate,
cross-cultural, and American studies, finding females of every race,
nation, and primate species showing more interest in infants, and
more tolerance for their needs. She acknowledged that "prior socialization no doubt presents difficulties to contemporary young
adults" trying novel divisions of parental labor, but she maintained
that "there is more involved than a need to unlearn old habits and
learn new ones specific to parenting. That the issue is not simply
past socialization running against current ideological commitment is
suggested by developments on Israeli kibbutzim in recent years."[10]
The second *sabra* generation's values have swung away from radical
equality and back toward traditional roles. Kibbutz parents want
more time with their children; kibbutz wives now even want larger
families.

With anthropologist Melford Spiro, Rossi sees the possibility of
"precultural sex differences."[11] She offers the "working hypothesis
that all sexually dimorphic characteristics contribute to the species'
function of reproduction, and hence have persisted as biological
predispositions across cultures and through historical time."[12]

But this working hypothesis rests on some possibly unworkable
assumptions. First, it takes for granted what it set out to investigate:
that male and female parenting are dimorphic enough to be subject
to differential selection. Secondly, it disregards Darlington's mis-
givings: in the face of capricious and multifarious selection, not all
traits contribute to reproduction.

And finally, it ignores a much simpler possibility. Israel lives on a permanent war footing. Foreseeing an endless, remorseless state of siege, Israelis may simply have followed Sanday's prediction and veered toward male dominance. What's more, traditionally-inclined Oriental and Orthodox Jews have wrested power from the East European secular socialists who founded the state. Their beliefs, along with the universal draft, press for a high birth rate; "In this country," says a rueful Jerusalem father of four, "you need two sons." Nor had kibbutz practice ever matched the egalitarianism of kibbutz theory. Women have always staffed the communal kitchens, laundries, and children's houses; men have always worked in the fields.

Still, despite Rossi's startling conversion to biology, she retains a sociologist's disciplined attention to the details of human lives. Of all the genetic-predilection theorists, she alone perceives that child care consists of skills, not mere attitudes and emotions. One of the few who has actually raised children, she grasps precisely how uninstinctively one first manipulates a diaper or brings up the bubble. She knows that a mother's "intuitive" knowledge of her baby's needs comes from months of close observation, not minutes of close bodily contact. So she leaves open a place for the empirical study of what mothers and fathers actually do. Only that, in the end, will produce the truth.

A husband and wife sit chatting over the remains of a late dinner. Their first baby sleeps fairly reliably now, and the woman had hoped that a meal immediately after the early evening feeding would give the couple several quiet hours alone. Now, an hour and a half later, as her husband refills her brandy glass, she leans contentedly back in her chair, relaxed for the first time all day.

A series of short cries from the nursery bring her bolt upright. "Damn!" her husband mutters.

She waves him silent, listening. "I think it'll be okay. He'll quiet down in a minute." Perched on the edge of her chair, she concentrates as the cries become softer, less frequent, and finally die away. She rises, checks on the baby, and returns smiling. She takes a sip of brandy. "I knew he was okay."

Another hour passes in leisurely talk. Again a cry interrupts—a bit shriller, a bit more sustained. She's on her feet and moving in seconds. "Something's wrong." Her husband rises and follows.

In the crib, the baby lies on his back, thrashing his arms and yelling steadily. He starts to roll over, but a leg, caught between the bars, stops him. The mother leans down and frees him. He rolls onto his stomach, and while she pats his back rhythmically, the cries subside. "I knew he needed something," she whispers. "Sounded the same to me," her husband whispers back.

A mysterious feminine power, like Symons's noncognitive perception? Research suggests a simpler answer: experience. One study found that mothers who take primary care of an infant can easily distinguish their own baby's (but not others') hunger, pain, and anger cries. Secondary caretaker mothers and fathers couldn't decipher any child's. And "decipher" is the right word: in long hours together, caretaker and child work out a system of signals. When skilled mechanics develop a similar wordless familiarity with an engine's drone, they rarely have to share credit with genes and natural selection.

A mechanic, of course, enjoys the status of an expert in an arcane and useful field of knowledge—something rarely ascribed to mothers. But if we accept the premise that anyone with major responsibility for a baby has a professional's specialized understanding of that child—and, to some extent, of children generally—a whole clutch of mysteries simply evaporates. Psychologist Phyllis Berman reviewed the literature to find out if females truly and consistently respond to children differently from males. She found a simple rule: people who had the most to do with babies showed the most interest in them. But most women seemed to *think* that their excitement should exceed men's, even when it really didn't.

A real maternal instinct ought to show itself, regardless of circumstances; people feel instinctive reactions like hunger and fatigue even when relieving them could cost their lives. But Berman found that adult reactions to babies varied with family status, not with hormones. In a sample ranging from unmarried, cohabiting couples to grandparents, responses ranged just as widely, paralleling subjects' "involvement with infants at particular stages of their lives." Mothers of infants responded most eagerly. Pregnant childless women—presumably in the grip of nesting hormones—acted no differently from other nonmothers. And new mothers still in hospitals, their systems awash in female chemistry, differed from their husbands only in that they smiled at the babies more; but women, Berman notes, generally smile more—it's the traditional defense of the subordinate. The sexes diverged significantly "only during the years of active caretaking, neither before caretaking nor after the children had left home." Male responses varied less, but the most responsive of all men were grandfathers. Could this reflect hormonal changes in later life? Probably not, because the effect related to family status, not to age.[13]

And in any case, what persons do might not reflect what they truly feel. Anne Frodi and Michael Lamb, a leading student of paternal behavior, suggest that though behavior may dissemble about motive, the classic tests of physiological excitement—diastolic blood pressure, skin conductance, and heart rate—probably don't. They measured all three in boys and girls aged eight to fourteen. Even during these sensitive years straddling puberty, they found no gender differences in responses to infant cries and smiles. A similar test on young parents produced similar results. But, the girls *acted* more excited; Frodi and Lamb speculate that this is because society expects them to.

Men and women seem to differ more in what they say than in what they actually do; self-report studies find the most consistent differences; and students at a Southern university reported a larger sex difference in responses than counterparts from the Northeast. But do self-reports represent true feelings, or just the desire to appear normal? There are data to support both conclusions. All we know for sure is that no one has shown a uniform male or female reaction.

Nor do young boys and girls treat babies any differently. Reactions only diverge in later childhood, and then mainly among those who actually help care for smaller children. Adolescence, when sex-role tension is as strong as it will ever be, sees significant differences in both behavior and self-report, but "the trend is not maintained . . . in college-age youth and adults."[14]

There's one telling exception: persons who become parents. The first birth moves most couples—regardless of their beliefs or inclinations—toward more traditional roles. As long as social expectations for the sexes remain so different—as long as "mothering" and "fathering" children mean such different things—history provides at least as elegant an explanation as do hormones. For men, the mere fact of siring provides a fulfillment of manhood. For most women, fulfillment still seems to lie in the many acts of mothering —the daily duties of caring for a child, rather than the single accomplishment of bearing it. Indeed, bearing without caring has long seemed so "unnatural" that an elaborate adoption bureaucracy developed early in this century to shield from disgrace young mothers who had to give their babies away. While women pursue the temporary "career" of motherhood, their interest in helpless young creatures remains high, "generalized," Berman believes, "from the gender-differentiated roles taken with their own young children."[15]

Still, we can't dismiss the claims of evolution so lightly. We're mammals in good standing, and haven't escaped a hundred thousand generations of selection. But selection for what? The most studied mammals do show a strong hormonal basis for maternal behavior. Nonpregnant female rats need a week or more with pups before they act like mothers, but those in late pregnancy start mothering much sooner, and new mothers begin right away. Even a virgin rat becomes maternal in less than a day if injected with a birthing female's blood. But mothers need pups to *maintain* motherliness; if the young disappear right after birth, nurturance does too, and doesn't return even if they do.

Our closer kin show similar hormonal influence. Experienced rhesus mothers, even those deprived of ovaries by menopause or surgery, will "mother" unfamiliar infants, but females without offspring will not. Thus, a single hormone trigger may "set" mothers for a lifetime. Still, in other primate cousins, habit, not hormones, prevails. "Marmoset fathers carry their first-born infants [generally twins] from birth unless they are being nursed," observe Lamb and Carl-Philip Hwang. "With later-borns, siblings and fathers share the child-care responsibility."[16]

Primates have almost as many styles of caring for their young as they do for conceiving them in the first place. In various species and circumstances, males assist at birth, defend, carry, clean, cuddle, sleep and play with the young, chew their food, and even, in cases of extreme need, "adopt" an orphan. But males also use youngsters more selfishly: as effective and convenient buffers in conflicts with other adults and, once in a while, when adult conflict has escalated beyond conciliation, even as food. The typical primate cannibal is an interloper ousting the established male in a group of females.

A single, by now familiar, conclusion emerges from the great mass of mammal field data: parents seem to meet, sometimes uncannily, their species' particular needs. Thus, each mother sheep bears a single very precocious lamb during the few springtime weeks when the meadows resound with the bleats of the newly born. Within hours of birth, the youngster can get about on its own shaky legs, poking a curious nose into the doings of the flock and perhaps even under the belly of someone else's mother. But each female unfailingly knows her own baby and it alone is allowed to feed from her udder. So every lamb moves with the flock under the watchful eye and solicitous care of a single adult female carrying an exclusive food supply—a more efficient plan for optimal survival rates in a migratory breed could hardly be devised. Mother rats, meanwhile, bear five to six litters a year, nursing each for a short time in a secluded nest. The tiny pups spend their largely immobile dependency with a dam who can't recognize them as individuals— and who never needs to. She would care for any pups who came her way, but in nature none but her own ever do. So she succeeds admirably using a cognitive approach precisely opposite that serving the persnickety ewe.

It *is* a central fact of evolution that each species seems preprogramed to be exactly the parents its youngsters need. But equally central, argue Lamb and Hwang, is the fact that preprogramed behavior is utterly stereotyped. The sheep and the rat have no leeway for novelty—no ability to take on a waif or round up a stray. But this rigidity wouldn't serve most primates, with our longer dependencies and complex behaviors; we seem programed for more flexible responses. And human parents face an additional task unprecedented in the animal world—transmitting the incomparable vastness of a human culture to each new member. Can we reasonably argue that any single, inborn plan meets the huge range of circumstances our species faces? At this moment, human parents— members of a single species—are preparing children to hunt with spears; to plow with water buffalo; to herd sheep; to transplant rice seedlings; to weave baskets and cloth; to carry loads on their heads; to operate manual transmissions; to balance check books; to run computers; and to speak any of a thousand different languages. What single, predetermined scheme could possibly serve mothers raising their children in an egalitarian forager band, or under a nomad's tent shared by co-wives, or in the courtyard of her peasant in-laws, or in a cabin on an Alaskan homestead, or in a houseboat or an igloo or a split-level on a quarter acre or an apartment on the eighteenth floor?

We can't say with any certainty how the thousands of generations of our foraging ancestors raised their children, but their modern counterparts take a highly pragmatic approach. They need to, because getting a forager's living takes both men and women away from home for long hours. Nursing babies ride on their mothers' backs or hips, but slightly older children, still too young to walk briskly under a heavy load or keep perfectly still while the hunter takes aim, simply stay in camp, loosely supervised by any responsible person whose work schedule permits: a yet older child, a woman resting from a foraging trip, or a man preparing for the next hunt. And quite early on, children begin earnest training in their trades, as apprentices to their parents. It takes years of disciplined practice and gentle instruction before the spear's trajectory unfailingly mimics the eye's, or the pattern of twigs on the dusty surface unfailingly reveals the choice, juicy roots beneath. If evolution has truly outfitted each species to be the parents its offspring will need, then it can only have equipped human parents for flexibility.

Michael Lamb concludes:

> It would be misleading to claim that the observable sex differences are "biologically determined." They are the joint product of biology and supplementary experiential pressures, and it is the experiential factor, if anything, that ensures large and observable rather than trivial sex differences in behavior. In the case of parental behavior, for example, we know that role reversal is readily accomplished, and with the exception of lactation, males are every bit as competent at parenting as females are. That so

few males assume a primary parenting role is testimony to the pervasiveness and power of social pressures rather than proof that biology is destiny.[17]

But isn't there another possibility? Even if a woman's hormones don't naturally guide her toward child care, couldn't a man's naturally guide him away from it? Even if estrogen, prolactin, and the like, didn't make for a distinctively feminine personality, mightn't androgens, long associated with aggression and high activity, be the key to a distinctively masculine personality?

But getting the answer means first divining what researchers mean by "aggression"—a task possibly even more demanding than discerning the meaning of "maternal instinct." In the name of measuring aggression, rats, human beings, and creatures in between have run mazes; leapt obstacles; fought with claws, teeth, hands; bashed one another with sticks; pulled electric switches; and filled out questionnaires. Each experiment may have a quite precise (but often nontransferable) operational definition: animal A is more aggressive if it attacks more often than its fellows, or wins more fights, or attacks more adversaries. In practice, for example, rat studies generally measure *fighting,* rather than any inherent, measurable abstract quality.

But researchers don't undertake costly, exacting studies merely to identify rodent bullies. No, the rats often stand in for a much more complex and interesting mammal with whom they share certain basic neurological features; the point is to learn about aggression, not about rats. So a transformation takes place, and definitions become distorted: "A particular and specific measure of one sort of aggressivity has been made synonymous with aggressivity in general," writes neuroscientist Ruth Bleier, who sees danger in this seemingly innocent step.[18] Animal aggression studies, for example, often detail such fine points of physical mayhem as "latency of initial attack [how long an animal waited before attacking], threat displays, the duration of fighting, and the outcome of fights," notes the British psychologist John Archer. But human aggression studies generally take a more refined approach, cataloguing "verbal aggression, teachers' ratings of impulsivity and assertiveness, laboratory experiments simulating administration of electric shocks, questionnaire and personality studies."[19]

Obviously, the term "aggressivity" means many different things to different people; "it is not value-free, objective, or uniquely defined, and when it is used with reference to people, it is not synonymous only with fighting behaviour."[20] If it were, of course, studying it would produce very little of interest; relatively few human beings of either sex spend significant amounts of time fighting. Hunters and gatherers, who live in widely scattered, highly cooperative bands, spend hardly any time at it at all. Among the !Kung San, front-runner for living group most like our distant ancestors, "preparation for fighting did not occupy the men in any way," report anthropologists Mary Maxwell and Melvin Konner, "and learning to fight was not considered an important skill for boys."[21]

So something else is at stake in aggressivity studies. "In primate research, the word has often been used synonymously with dominance," Bleier continues. "With respect to humans, . . . the inordinate amount of scientific and popular interest in a biological basis for sex differences in 'aggressivity' does not have to do with explaining why women so seldom fight in bars, but rather with explaining differences in achievement in the public world."[22] The quality that sets rats snarling at each other through the bars of their cages has been transformed, in a series of unexamined and possibly unconscious connections, into the one that animates corporate executives vying across their boardroom tables. Thus "invested with qualities . . . such as assertiveness, independence, intelligence, creativity, and imagination," it distills the essence of the "man's man"—and therefore of manhood itself—in a violent, competitive society. From battling rats through "killer apes," from "man the hunter" to the Superbowl, the "male" hormone testosterone (which, of course, also circulates in significant quantities in women's blood) seems to tie together the essential traits of masculinity.

But what we really know about "aggressivity" (even in the narrow sense of fighting) proves much more complicated. The notion of aggressivity as a single, unitary trait can't stand up to close analysis, nor can the fallacy that female mammals don't fight. "Chauvinistic assumptions about male dominance and superiority over females in competitive situations" often bias research, says psychologist

Bruce Svare.[23] But Patricia Ebert sees a less sinister cause: the common laboratory practice of caging several breeding females with a single male. This economical though artificial scheme naturally encourages "selection" against females inclined to fight with their fellows (which is fairly common in nature).

Only her sort of painstaking analysis, Ebert believes, can reveal the truth about animal aggression. Even simple mammals fight for several diverse reasons, and under the control of several equally diverse hormonal and neural pathways. The Wild West theory, of course, favors the image of massive reindeer or gigantic bull seals bashing each other for droit du seigneur. But an image much closer to mammal survival (and equally "close to the genes") is a clutch of vulnerable, defenseless pups or kits or cubs—defenseless, that is, except for the snarling dam crouched in attack position above them.

Male tournament jousters may form the popular image of fighting bravado—aggression as manly sport. But for fierceness and tenacity, for aggression as an unwelcome matter of life and death, nothing matches the enraged mother bear or dog or lion—or even rat—battling for her threatened young. And, ironically, the less she can depend on male protection—the more closely, in other words, her species resembles the Wild West ideal—the more completely she must depend on herself. Even beasts who top their local food chains, even the most ferocious predators, start out as small creatures too slow or weak or unskilled to evade all their wily enemies alone. And so, if selection chooses for minimal paternal help, it must simultaneously choose for maximal maternal pugnacity and guile.

Maternal aggression, like much else tied to species survival, may well come under hormonal and even genetic controls—but not the same ones that trigger other kinds of attacks. Ambushing dinner and attacking a species-mate follow different motives—and different neurological pathways. Fighting arises from many causes, but stalking prey, from only one: hunger; it is, in Ebert's infelicitous but precise phrase, "exclusively linked with ingestive behavior."[24]

This small fact suggests a big possibility. Animals don't confront conspecifics in the same way they attack prey; they certainly don't intimidate their intended dinner with elaborate charades of chest-puffing, teeth-gnashing, and threats. An effective predator simply sizes up the potential nourishment and goes straightforwardly for the kill. In a face-off with a peer, an animal wins if the adversary flees, but the flight of edible calories spells defeat. Despite the scattered reports of animal cannibalism, conspecifics don't form any species' steady diet.

The two forms of aggression, in other words, serve quite different adaptive functions, demand rather different abilities, and thus may well have arisen through different selective pressures; they don't constitute a single, generalized tendency to beat up on other creatures. Ebert continues:

> If one can extrapolate . . . to humans [following the problematic habit of theorists of all persuasions] it seems unreasonable to assume that such intraspecific aggression as homicide and violent assault are related to an evolutionary history involving hunting as a major food gathering activity. Therefore, if there is a genetic bias to intraspecific aggression in humans [and Ebert is not at all sure] it probably did not evolve as a result of predatory behaviors.[25]

Man the hunter, therefore, stalking game with the stealth demanded by his mediocre speed and very poor natural armaments, did not necessarily father man the barroom brawler, squaring off noisily against a well-matched fellow human.

And maternal aggression is the most distinctive aggression of all. Belligerent male rats size each other up for several minutes before joining battle. A nursing mother waits mere seconds, then attacks with such suddenness and ferocity that males and females alike often immediately submit. And, if necessary, mothers of many species will fight on to victory over recalcitrant males. Female fighting has another function, too: it forces neighbors to keep their distance and so helps distribute scarce food resources among mothers. Some kinds of female mice even defend home territories in the wild.

But circumstances can alter cases, even with apparently very stereotyped behavior. Groups of females can also cooperate in exploiting an "abundant, but localized, food source."[26] In rats, at least, maternal aggression has a hormonal component; the tendency to fight rises as pregnancy advances and remains during lactation.

So, can belligerent varmints teach us anything at all about our aggressive selves? The tie between testosterone and certain kinds of fighting seems clear, both in humans and many animals. Higher testosterone alone may explain some male fractiousness. Certain very violent criminals, who began raping or murdering in their teens, have shown elevated circulating testosterone; one study even related levels to the age at first arrest. Some rapists and sex criminals find relief from their violent compulsions, and the fantasies fueling them, in drugs that counteract androgens. But law-abiding men show no clear hormone patterns, even though athletes of both sexes who commit the lesser illegality of taking steroids often report increased anger and hostility. Very large changes in androgen levels might encourage men to violence, note psychiatrist Robert Rubin and associates, but variations in the normal range appear, in normal men at least, "to be strongly modulated by psychosocial factors."[27] That's jargon for the idea that most men, despite what their adrenals tell them, learn to let their consciences, or their moral values, or the threat of disgrace, or the simple fear of the slammer, be their guide.

But on the margins of respectable society, where some boys learn these lessons poorly, "testosterone might be an additional, endocrine factor placing some persons at risk to commit aggressive crimes."[28] We don't know, of course, just how much androgen and how little social control prime the criminal brain in the heated moment of action. Tests only come later, after months or years of police sirens, handcuffs, trials, guards, cells, prison routine. Couldn't the threatening, abusive, confining, intensely frustrating prison atmosphere make a nasty customer nastier still, raising his testosterone levels in response?

A large body of evidence also ties testosterone to a high general level of activity, the kind of energy usually expressed in sports, rough play, or unfocused running around. American and European researchers fairly routinely find boys more active than girls, engaging in more of what the literature calls "rough-and-tumble play." But the sharp-eyed Melvin Konner, this time collaborating with N. Blurton-Jones, noticed that something else affects energy level, at least in the U.S. and the U.K. The more active girls have higher IQs.

So might activity level express social permission? Fieldwork among the !Kung San, where women work hard and travel long distances, revealed no obvious sex differences; girls were just about as active, and very nearly as rough, as boys. Can it be, as Konner and Blurton-Jones gingerly conclude, that boys and girls simply learn how active, how aggressive, they ought to be? Perhaps Western industrial culture, where generations of women have stayed home to master the art of high-level consumption, teaches girls, but not boys, to sit still?

The idea of social permission seems reasonable on somewhat different grounds. American boys, for example, don't only learn to fight; they learn rules about fighting fair, "picking on someone their own size" (or, more precisely, someone on their own level of approved agility and aggression). American boys are rough, but not indiscriminate ruffians. True American manliness forbids fighting with the obviously smaller or weaker; it thus offers the weak a refuge and defense in their weakness.

One experiment tested aggressivity by also testing the strength of this chivalrous code. Young men and women squared off, both armed with pillow clubs; they could bash opponents all they liked without doing any physical harm. Paradoxically though, a man's effectiveness against a woman opponent had nothing to do with his size or strength or even athletic ability; his attitude was the key. The more authoritarian his view of sex roles, the more traditional his notion of manliness, the harder he found it to see a woman as an equal and thus an adversary, and the harder he found it to hit her, even when she severely violated his beliefs by hitting him first.

Thus, sex differences in aggressivity may not measure physiology but social power. The greatest divergences show up—once again—not in behavioral tests, which show women every bit as willing as men to administer painful electric shocks. Instead the differences appear in self-report tests, which explore "what [people] have social permission to do or be rather than . . . how they actually behave."[29]

But we started out talking about *feelings,* and this idea of social permission violates what we know about them. Emotions, after all, don't ask leave, like children playing "Mother-may-I?," before they take the giant step into consciousness. We don't will ourselves happy, sad, worried, elated, or mad. First we feel the turmoil in brain or belly or bloodstream, and only later give it a name.

Or do we? Are feelings really such clear-cut, independent, identifiable states of excitement? Almost a century ago, the great psychologist, William James, suspected there was something more at work. An emotion, he thought, was a state of excitement *plus* an idea that explains the pounding heart, the sweaty palms, the flushed face, the sudden rush of energy. He even suggested an experiment to test his theory. What would happen, he wondered, if researchers could induce an unfocused state of excitement in an unwitting person? Could they manipulate someone into identifying it as a particular feeling? Might they even convince people to call the very same physiological symptoms by different names?

James, alas, could think of no way to create the symptoms. A test of his theory had to wait many decades for pharmacology to provide it. At last, in 1962, Stanley Schachter and Jerome Singer reported an elegant and convincing demonstration of James's surmise (but one that new rules about the rights of experimental subjects have since made unethical).

The drug epinephrine—which produces physical symptoms similar to high emotion—provided the unfocused state of excitement. Under the pretext of testing a new medicine, Singer and Schachter convinced some college students to take a dose and others to take an inactive placebo. Then they truthfully told some of the students about the symptoms they would soon experience. They told others nothing about what would happen to them, and they misinformed a third group, describing symptoms that would not occur.

At this point, a carefully planned "problem" arose, creating a short delay. The researchers apologetically asked each subject to spend a short time filling out a questionnaire in an adjacent room. In a few minutes, they promised, the experiment would resume. But there, in the waiting room, the unsuspecting students underwent the real experiment. Another "subject," actually an actor in league with the researchers, also sat working on the questionnaire.

And as the epinephrine began taking effect, as the real subjects felt the first symptoms suggesting emotional excitement, the confederate put on an act that culminated in either euphoria or rage (as chosen earlier by the researchers). The confederate tried to draw the subjects into the mood—either throwing paper airplanes and snapping rubber bands, or loudly objecting to the increasingly insulting questionnaire items (which started with name and address, and advanced through "Do you hear bells?" and "Which members of your family do not bathe regularly?" to "With how many men has your mother had extramarital relationships [4 and under; 5–9; 10 and other]?"). Some subjects simply stared at the confederate's antics, some found the moods rather contagious, and some joined in wholeheartedly.

Who did what vindicated James. Sitting in the waiting room with the stooge, the subjects who had received the drug faced an urgent conceptual problem: Why did they feel so strangely excited? Those who knew the truth about their symptoms, also knew they weren't angry or euphoric, but simply reacting to a chemical. Few of them joined in the stooge's outlandish mood. The second group, ignorant of the drug's effects, could ascribe the symptoms either to the injection or to their own feelings. More of them joined the stooge. But the third group, the willfully misled, knew for sure that their excitement had nothing to do with the drug; an authoritative person had told them to expect their feet to tingle. So when their hearts began to race, many came to the next most obvious conclusion: that they, like the stooge, were wildly elated or furiously angry. And they acted exactly as James said they would: they combined a physiological state and explanation for it into a genuinely felt emotion.

But the tendrils tying physiology and cognition into the unity that we call feelings bind even more tightly and more subtly than James suspected. The Schachter-Singer experiment came to a new prominence twenty years after its first publication because it seemed to clarify an important issue of the early 1980s, the tangle of emotional and physical distress christened premenstrual syndrome. Every month, every normal woman between menarche and menopause undergoes a marked fluctuation in hormones. Many women report a corresponding fluctuation in mood and comfort, with irritability, tension, depression, and physical complaints peaking just before or during menstruation.

For many scientists, hormones are reason enough for these feelings. One study, for example, found that a group of women with ovaries but without wombs rode the same monthly emotional roller coaster, even though they technically had no "period." But other scientists look for the answer in a combination of mind and body. Women generally report that they do less well at various tasks during the "time of the month," although objective tests show no loss of performance. Women of certain religious backgrounds—especially Jews and Catholics—and of certain personality types—highstrung, emotionally changeable—report the greatest distress. Women of certain nationalities—Americans, for example—expect and experience more discomfort than Finnish counterparts. A group of Princeton women who merely *believed* their periods were coming (thanks to researchers supposedly testing a new method of predicting periods) reported the expected aches and anxieties.

Scientists who see the monthly mood changes as a flux of organic molecules also tend to see menstruation as an elaborate form of female hay fever—a predictable, recurrent cluster of annoying symptoms. But few American women experience it so straightforwardly. It brings each month, along with backaches and the blues, a tangle of messages from the past and the future. First, it announces, "I am a woman of childbearing age," and then, almost simultaneously, the triumphant or terrible news, "I am not pregnant." And then it whispers all the hopes, fears, grudges, and superstitions that mothers, grandmothers, sisters, and friends have confided about the female mysteries. And finally, it begins again the cycle of hope or trepidation that is the condition of being the vessel of life.

Months before a girl's first period, word often comes from beyond the closed border of womanhood. Mother may have spoken matter-of-factly, or conspiratorially, or distastefully, of far-off babies and bloodstains and low-back pains. An older sister may have advised how to avoid embarrassments when "a little friend" comes to visit or "the curse" begins. School chums have weighed the probabilities and advantages of late and early starts.

In some non-Western cultures, where universal bodily functions are not undignified secrets, whole communities mark the event. They may feast for days to celebrate a new source of life, or seclude the confused young carrier of spiritual danger, or place heretofore desultory marriage negotiations on an emergency footing.

Hay fever never gets this kind of attention. No one slyly jokes about it, calls it by rueful nicknames, invokes it as a distant secret, fears it as a form of pollution, feels secret pride in the power it implies and secret woe at the powerlessness it proclaims. No one sees in it a comment on her nature as human being. So no one should take menstruation at less than its true measure: it is a physiological point where deep and contradictory feelings about femaleness pivot. Menstruation is, therefore, not merely a physical or a psychic moment, but that most human of constructs, an event acted out bodily but defined culturally.

"All very interesting in theory," the biological determinist may object. "Still, the fact is that cultures propose but hormones dispose." But even where hormonal changes have been clearly tracked, the picture remains clouded. Marianne Frankenhaeuser, for example, has spent years studying another point where feelings and physiology flow together. Men and women handle stress, she found, in quite distinctive ways.

The Finnish matriculation exam provided Frankenhaeuser a case in point. This grueling ordeal of five to seven six-hour sittings determines who goes to university. It is the much-feared culmination of the entire school career, and the linchpin of many families' hopes. Men and women score about equally well, but Frankenhaeuser's hormonal tests show that they do so rather differently. During the test, males secreted large amounts of a hormone group called catecholamines—the best known member is adrenaline—involved in coping with emergencies. Indeed, the male catecholamine level correlates positively with success in exams and other competitive situations. But women achieved their equally good scores through a physiologically more "economic" approach; they secreted much less catecholamine, and their secretion levels did not correlate with their outcomes. They paid a much lower physical cost for their success. Indeed, Frankenhaeuser suggests, over a lifetime the more drastic male strategy may account for higher male mortality from stress-related diseases.

On the other hand:

> In psychological terms, . . . the results suggest that the cost was higher for females. They reported more intense negative feelings, indicative of general discomfort, than did the males. At the same time, the females appear to have experienced virtually none of the sense of success and satisfaction that was a rather common feeling among the males. In this context, it is interesting that high discomfort was related to good performance in females and to poor performance in males.[30]

And more interesting still is the fact that the sexes' different combinations of stress hormones translate into different balances of effort and distress.

At first and even second reading, these results, which Frankenhaeuser duplicated among twelve-year-olds and preschoolers, seem to point in a single, unequivocal direction. Males, though perhaps burning their candles at both ends, have hormones naturally adapted to making a brilliant light. Responses as old as the chase on the African savannah seem to equip them to compete at a high pitch but with zest and enjoyment, to spend their efforts in brief but dazzling bursts of accomplishment. Females, less comfortable under pressure, follow in the more moderate footsteps of those distant, plodding ancestral gatherers. In women, adrenaline release remains fairly constant throughout the monthly cycle, but "in males, even mild emotional strain is almost invariably accompanied by a rise in adrenaline excretion."[31]

But before drawing any definite conclusions, Frankenhaeuser looked more closely at what she meant by "females," and made an even more interesting discovery: women who do "male" work—engineering students, Ph.D. candidates, bus drivers, lawyers—"tend to respond to achievement demands by the sharp increase in adrenaline secretion that we found to be typical of males." And women tested in a noncompetitive area of female competence—taking a three-year-old to the hospital, for instance—"secreted as much, or even slightly more, adrenaline, noradrenaline, and cortisol than men."[32] Could it be, then, that the divergent test-taking strategies didn't reflect inherent sex differences in reaction to stress, but differences in the degree and kind of stress that the exams imposed? Did everyone attack them with the same uncomplicated determination to excel, with the same naked fear of failure? Did the chance for university carry the same meaning for all the young men and women chewing their pencils and watching the clock through those exhausting hours?

Clearly it did not. For boys, high adrenaline related positively to both a feeling of success and a set of values that expected it. The girls presented a more complex picture; those with a traditional view of the female role, even when they did well academically, did not experience the catecholamine rise. And even more remarkable, in girls, "self-esteem and sense of fulfilling social expectation are negatively related to adrenaline excretion during the examination."[33]

"Psychological factors are powerful determinants of neuroendocrine stress responses," Frankenhaeuser concludes, although she also admits that "there is no unequivocal interpretation of these results." But they strongly suggest, as do all the disparate facts we've covered in this chapter, that emotion springs not only from synapses and hormones but from our human knowledge of the kind of people we are.[34]

Males and females come equipped with somewhat different bodies and grow toward markedly different futures. Just how different is probably too subtle a question for social scientists to capture in their mathematical nets. But Jan Morris, one of the few human beings competent to say, remarks:

> We are told that the social gap between the sexes is narrowing, but I can only report that having, in the second half of the twentieth century, experienced life in both roles, there seems to me no aspect of experience, no moment of the day, no contact, no arrangement, no response, which is not different for men and women. The very tone of voice in which I am now addressed, the very posture of the person next in the queue, the very feel in the air when I entered a room or sat at a restaurant table, constantly emphasized my change of status.[35]

Children, of course, know this by the time they are two. By three they choose toys that match their—and society's—notion of what boys or girls are like. By five—except for very few exceptions like Morris—they accept their fate as irrevocable and permanent. Just how they come to know what men and women are remains something of a mystery. Certainly the persons they observe and the treatment they receive sharply affect them; still, mothers, the parents who most influence children, sex-type the young much less than fathers do.

For many years social scientists thought that early experience and mimicry sufficed to mold children's behavior. But more recently, theorists as diverse as the hormone expert John Money and the psychological historian Joseph Pleck have suggested a more sophisticated and convincing possibility, and one that mirrors another complex learning process occurring at the same time of life. Children learn sex roles, they propose, the same way that they learn language, through a lengthy and highly original process of reasoning out the rules of a symbolic system. From many samples of speech, each child derives the sounds, the vocabulary, and finally the syntax and semantics, of his or her native language. As a child grows, successive levels of neurological and intellectual development permit increasing understanding and mastery. Children don't exactly copy their parents' speech; children of immigrants usually speak with the accent of their schoolmates, not of their homes.

Eventually, though, the language itself becomes a major factor in individuals' dealings with their surroundings; human beings are built to speak language, but only one or two languages with native fluency. In just the same way, children are built to observe, and eventually absorb, the grammar of the social system they grow up in—to mold their behavior around the template of their culture's values just as they mold their tongues and minds around the template of its language.

But does culture truly mold them into what we know as men and women? Not all by itself, surely, but certainly as physiology's powerful ally. We started this chapter wondering about nurturance and dominance: whether women naturally nurture the weak, whether men naturally dominate them. From the Luo of Kenya, and the streets of Atlanta come two provocative answers. Luo families that lack daughters put boys to work helping with childcare and household chores—boys who grow up "much more like girls in such social behaviors as aggression, dependency, and dominance" than those who never do this work.[36] And in American cities, culture also patterns how we help for the weak. In Columbus, Seattle, and Atlanta, experimenters "inadvertently" dropped pencils in public places. Who helped whom retrieve them tells a provocative story. In Atlanta, only 7 percent of women and 12 percent of men stooped to help a man, but 70 percent of men helped a woman. In Columbus, 23 percent of women helped a man and 32 percent of men helped a woman. Helping, the researchers concluded, was part of a pattern of dependence, and depended on social appropriateness, not any inborn tendency to "nurture."

Of course, much more than aggression and nurturance differentiate men and women in America. There's also calculus and Petrarchan sonnets—the whole universe of intellectual endeavor that seems to split into male and female realms. To find out why, we now proceed to the American version of the Finnish "matric."

9

Different Intellects?

On half a dozen Saturday mornings each year, young Americans gather in high school classrooms across the country, and at American outposts around the world, for a sacral rite of middle-class life. It's an occasion of high solemnity, complete with a meticulous protocol of sealed documents, official passes, and doorkeepers. The apprehensive young congregants come fortified with exercises and incantations, as well as small tokens of comfort that they carefully array on the desktops: wristwatches, rolls of hard candy, newly-sharpened pencils already pocked with converging rows of dents. At last the leader calls for silence, gives a signal, and the ritual begins.

Into this moment, into this Mississippi of American educational life, run the great continental streams of our culture: our belief in fairness, our belief in merit, our belief in opportunity, our belief in measurement, our belief in objectivity, our belief in science. From this event debouches the nation's academic hierarchy. The young aspirants sigh, and shift in their seats, and bend to the mighty task before them. They have begun the College Board Scholastic Aptitude Test.

We Americans live a deep contradiction: an egalitarian ideology in a stratified society. Of course, every complex society has to sort its young among alternate futures. The Europeans and Japanese, for example, pick university students by testing sheer mastery of subject matter. Our decentralized school system, however, rules out any national test of facts. Instead, we rely on a particularly American invention, a notion that we call "academic aptitude." Our experts claim to test an underlying, measurable ability to do school work, and to test it fairly, but without demanding a uniform knowledge of specific facts.

We have a lot riding on those claims, and they run deep into our basic beliefs. We argue for equal opportunity, but live with a very unequal distribution of rewards. We can, of course, explain the racial discrepancies in achievement historically, as results of past injustice. But the sex differences are much more problematic; boys and girls grow up in the same families, attend the same schools, live in the "same" environments; young men and women attend the same universities. But they don't come out the same. So we urgently need convincing reasons why. And these days, for most Americans, the most convincing reasons are "scientific."

And thus arises, thinks psychologist Julia Sherman, our national "fascination" with sex differences in testable intellect. "Hundreds of small sample studies have been published about IQ sex-related differences," she notes, and that is very odd, because "the IQ tests had deliberately been developed in a way so as to eliminate any differences between the sexes in Full Scale IQ."[1] Additional thousands of published and unpublished experiments compare male and female performance on all manner of mental exercises, games, puzzles, tasks, and tests.

Making sense of this great tangle of conflicting results may be the most challenging puzzle of all. In their 1974 *The Psychology of Sex Differences,* psychologists Eleanor E. Maccoby and Carol Nagy Jacklin hacked a painstaking path to conclusions that were quickly accepted as standard in the field. They discarded many less-than-meticulous studies on their way to the consensus position of those who argue for sex differences in intellect. Simply put, Maccoby and Jacklin concluded that women excel in linguistic skills and men in spatial ones (which they believe also explain superior male scores in mathematics). Several subsequent reviews by less prominent authors have come to different conclusions, but none has received as much attention.

The pleasing symmetry of Maccoby and Jacklin's idea may account for its immediate popularity. Intuitively appealing, apparently evenhanded, and just scientific enough to command respect, it has appeared in both scholarly literature reviews and popular magazine articles, textbooks, and talk-show discussions. It enjoyed a tremendous vogue during the early 1980s, when every major science and news magazine carried a cover story on sex differences.

In telling us that women should excel in the arts and parts of speech—that they speak and read more fluently, more correctly, more exactly—researchers simply echo our common experience (without, however, explaining why our major literary figures are nearly all male). Adding that men dominate the frontiers of mental space—that they read maps, run mazes, orient themselves to their surroundings, manipulate imaginary objects, more proficiently than women—researchers merely complete what we already know from experience. But some scientists go further, asserting that these differences express something central to human gender, indeed, that they fulfill the retroactive predictions of evolutionary theory.

When our ancestors ranged across trackless savannahs to hunt with darts or spears, they ate partly through their ability to guess where a missile would fall and which horizon hid their camp. No man could attain full majority who did not, sometimes at least, contribute to the downing of dinner. It's clear that utter ineptitude at finding his way or aiming a projectile must have seriously cut into a man's chances of adding his genes to the next generation. The spatial argument goes further, though, and argues, implicitly at least, that in every generation the superior hunters fathered more, and presumably better-fed, offspring. Their mates, of course, rarely had to fell calories on the hoof; but women did cross the same trackless distances to provide their children's main subsistence diet. The spatial theory ignores this and sees a woman's main task as negotiating her own and her children's survival in a society of men. Ergo, it argues, hunting selects for superior male spatial abilities, whereas mothering selects for superior female social abilities.

But tracing the results of twentieth-century pencil-and-paper tests back to ancient African plains displays a peculiar forgetfulness about the primate past. Our distant ancestors may have hunted on the savannah; *their* distant ancestors undoubtedly lived in trees. With all our primate relations we share an arboreal heritage immensely older and longer than our hominid history as predatory carnivores. To all those generations spent swinging and leaping among branches, we owe central features of our primate selves: the general shape of our bodies; our long limbs; our prehensile fingers and hands; our rather mediocre senses of taste and smell; our expert binaural hearing; our superb, full-color, three-dimensional vision; and, without any doubt, a superior ability to understand space.

Few selective pressures could have been stronger than that favoring individuals who did not fall out of trees. To this day, tree-living primates are born able to cling—literally for dear life—to mother's fur and to balance on her back or belly as she races, leaps, and swings through the three-dimensional landscape of the forest canopy. (Human babies still start life with a grip strong enough to support their own weight.) For their part, tree-living mothers find food, elude predators, mate, give birth, and follow the group in that treacherous world of flexible branches—all while bearing the unbalancing loads of pregnancy or dependent young. Long before our ancestors left their homes in the trees for new ones on the ground, both sexes had mastered the arts of aerial acrobatics—a mastery presumably based on features of the nervous system.

Our ancestors may have come out of the trees with other highly developed skills as well. Present-day vervet monkeys, neither the most intelligent nor the most humanlike of primates, indubitably have "vocal repertoires [that] are far larger than originally believed,"[2] announced UCLA anthropologist Robert Seyfarth, conceding also that the grunts and cries have "gone some way along the road to language." When vervets give an alarm, Seyfarth and Dorothy Cheney reported some years ago, they don't merely cry generalized danger; they select a cry specifying a snake, an eagle, a leopard, or what have you.

But they also grunt a good deal, issuing sounds so apparently indeterminate that "even experienced observers can't tell the difference." Experienced human observers, that is; for vervet listeners it's another story. Seyfarth and Cheney patiently eavesdropped for years, and eventually they began to hear what the monkeys heard: distinct sounds for four events common in simian social life. Vervet etiquette apparently requires a particular grunt when accosting a subordinate, another for greeting a dominant, a third for spotting a neighboring band, and a fourth for notifying a leader that you've heard his order to move from shelter out onto the open plain. Amplified recordings of each grunt elicited appropriate reactions from groups of wild monkeys. Computer analysis of sound patterns revealed differences not unlike those that humans use to distinguish vowels. Of course, vervets don't need grammar because they don't —as far as we know—make sentences. Even so, Seyfarth concedes, "You can't judge the size of vocal repertoire by ear alone." Nor can we judge other species' capacities by what seems obvious to us. And even less can we extrapolate from the dimly understood lives of our distant forebears.

Still, whatever their evolutionary origins, sex differences in test scores persist. Given the centrality of tests in our lives, their meaning has become central to the meaning of gender. But to discover what the differences mean, we must first understand what they are: differences in the *average* performances of males and females past puberty. Now, means, modes, and medians by themselves tell nothing about the size or shape of the data they condense. And we still can make one statement with confidence: the range of performance within each sex far exceeds the differences between them. Indeed, in an article published some years after their book, Jacklin and Maccoby assert:

> The most important point is that there is very little to explain. Recent publications concentrate not on whether a sex difference exists but on how large a difference really exists. These analyses are sobering if we consider the social implications of the work. It is completely impossible to predict an individual's abilities on the basis of his or her sex. Large numbers of both sexes score at the high end of distribution for all cognitive tests—enough to fill society's need for persons of exceptional skill.[3]

The modern verbal/spatial dichotomy began to appear in the psychological literature early in this century. By the 1930s, many scholars had "generally conceded" it, but no one devoted much emotion to the subject. But when, in the 1970s, feminist research-ers began to question this bit of received wisdom, they evoked, in the words of psychologist Hugh Fairweather, "not the earlier dispassion . . . but a closing of psychological ranks, perhaps more in reaction to the manner than the message."[4] Researchers trained in animal studies, by then a powerful segment of the profession, naturally saw shadowed in human behavior the obvious sexual dichotomies—mounting versus lordosis, for example—that their rodent subjects acted out. The verbal, tactile, intuitive female and the visual, spatial male made good logical and possibly good physiological sense. "What had before been a possibility at best slenderly evidenced, was widely taken for fact; and 'fact' hardened into 'biological' dogma."[5]

But bell curves with very similar middles (which the curves of male and female abilities clearly have) can still produce different averages if their "tails" differ. A small number of very high or very low scores can substantially move a mean. And though the males in the middle ranges do little better or worse than their female counterparts, the same can't be said about the extremes; more boys do very badly at verbal tasks and more do very well in math. Every kind of verbal deficit appears more frequently in boys; male dyslexics—who suffer from an otherwise unexplained failure to read—outnumber females by three or four to one. And the decades-long study of very gifted youngsters conducted at Johns Hopkins University has turned up many more boys who achieve astronomical math scores on the College Board math test (SAT-M). "It is clear," write Camilla Persson Benbow and Julian C. Stanley in one of their highly influential and controversial articles asserting a natural male superiority in math, "that much of the sex difference on SAT-M [given as a test of giftedness to bright sixth and seventh graders] can be accounted for by a lack of high-scoring girls."[6] The top scorers, they maintain, are always (or, other experts argue, nearly always) boys.

In its early days, the dichotomy theory concerned matters peripheral to American intellectual concerns—the ability to find one's way through mazes or think up strings of synonyms. But it quickly proceeded to our society's intellectual core: the ability to solve the equations that run computers and launch missiles, the ability to decipher the sentences that fill the newspaper and the tax code.

How did we get from there to here? By way of another evolutionary leap.

Spatial results generally correlate with math results. The two types of instruments, of course, don't measure the same, or even closely related, abilities. But many writers have still extrapolated from the male-spatial/female-social dichotomy to the modern math-verbal split. Thousands of generations spent chucking spears on the savannah, they suggest, might have selected for genes favoring trigonometry; thousands of generations of social chit-chat might have selected for genes favoring reading.

But look at what this superficially obvious connection implies. If there does indeed exist an inborn male tendency to solve quadratic equations or an inborn female tendency to scan quatrains, then natural selection worked, over all those many millennia, to perfect skills that, demographically speaking, hardly anyone possessed until a century or so ago. Even today, a huge fraction of humanity can barely sign its name, let alone read with any proficiency. Even more of our fellow beings are innocent of any calculations beyond those required to trade in the marketplace, stay on good terms with the landlord or commissar, and figure the time of day or year, or perhaps the worth of a dowry. The upper reaches of what American psychological testers test require skills and knowledge so abstruse that they bear almost no relationship to everyday people's everyday accomplishments. How could natural selection possibly have chosen in favor of boys adept at calculus or girls attracted to sonnets? Neither has the slightest bearing on survival or reproduction (although they might correlate sociologically with a high social position and thus with adequate diet). In American society, at least, both have probably correlated negatively with fecundity for at least the past few generations.

Fairweather, an Englishman, suggests a less flattering possibility: "that curious North American disease 'Myopia U.S.A.' "[7] "By far the majority of studies finding significant differences [in reading] originate in the USA," he notes in a major literature review; "in England, and notably Scotland, such differences are hard to find."[8]

But in England and Scotland, grown men play word games on the radio; limericks and anagrams rank as national pastimes; the witty Ronald Coleman, not the stolid Gary Cooper, molded the notion of celluloid sex appeal. Schoolmaster—the admirable Mr. Chips—remains an honorable masculine calling, immune to the scorn Americans heap on ineffectual buffoons like the comic strips' Mr. Weatherbee or television's Mr. Peepers or Mr. Conklin.

British culture has traditionally tied social power and literary skill into a single urbane, upper-middle-class package. It trains young politicians in the crackling debates of the Oxford Union. It signals class and caste by subtleties of stress and syntax. That highly verbal culture—not surprisingly—produces males who do as well as females on verbal tests. But so do Nigeria, where British educational traditions continue, and West Germany, where men often teach in the primary grades.

Can it be that American boys simply don't see verbal skill as very masculine? One insightful study in 1974 found that Americans see reading as womanly—and to a large extent they're right. Among Americans who read a book in the last six months, women outnumber men by almost three to two; and among the heaviest readers, by almost two to one. Men dominate the ranks of the magazine and newspaper readers who rarely read books. Almost two-thirds of female readers read mainly for pleasure; men more often read for career or business advancement, perusing trade papers and newsletters much more often than women do. The statistically heaviest reader in the U.S. is a well-educated white housewife—whose children go from their book-filled home to their female-run school.[9]

Reading comes no less "naturally" to boys than to girls, found the same study. The researchers found out what interested fifth-graders, and then tested their reading comprehension. They found what Fairweather calls "the expected sex difference" only in materials that the boys found uninteresting; boys did as well as girls on subjects they enjoyed. "Boys were apparently poorly motivated on material in which they had little interest, whereas girls performed equally well across the board: a particularly neat example of the intrusion of sex-role into the achievement domain."[10]

But such intrusions happen rarely in the hard-edge world of cognitive psychology. Students of animal behavior need not, as far as we know, consider their subjects' images of suitable hamsterhood. But we humans form ourselves to vastly divergent patterns. Should a boy do his utmost on a grammar test, or would that be sissyish? Should a young woman insist that an experimenter set the rod to absolute vertical, or would that be mannish and aggressive? The entire tradition of psychological testing assumes that people answer questions to the best of their inborn ability. The ambitions, fantasies, hopes, and fears that drive us to our separate fates become experimental contaminants, not windows onto the nature of intellectual achievement.

The authors of the Binet and Stanford-Binet tests, of course, found just such a contamination: in the early days, females scored higher on the IQ. But the test writers didn't ponder the reasons, or plumb girls' backgrounds and motivations to find why they got more factual answers right. They simply sanitized their instrument; exactly contrary to what Terman would do on the M-F tests, they removed the items that distinguished the sexes. (But they left in the items that distinguish social classes.)

A second influential intelligence test, devised by David Wechsler in the 1930s, left the sex differences in, and thus illuminates the workings of achievement. For two decades, women scored slightly higher. By 1955, though, their advantage had disappeared; starting with that year's revision, the scores favored men.

So pronounced and consistent a trend, showing up in a very large sample, indicates more than statistical bias. This highly respected, widely used test was measuring something other than raw intellect. And that something, psychologist Dorothy Kipnis argues, can only be the continental shift in male attitudes toward education that accompanied the remaking of twentieth-century society.

Until the 1940s, few American youths saw school as masculine. Huck Finn and Horatio Alger—and boys who admired them—shunned the sissified schoolroom for adventure in the world of men. For generations, college had catered to the upper classes and the inordinately bookish; men who "got ahead" in life pursued the "gentleman's C." "Joe College," with his saddle shoes, costly raccoon coat, and general sophistication, sprang from a privileged background. Only those aiming at a handful of learned professions really "needed" a degree. (President Reagan, for example, admits to majoring in sociology because it left time for his real interests— football and dramatics.)

Well into this century, apprenticeship was still a common route into law and other professions. Success in business demanded brains, contacts, luck, and stamina, but certainly not a diploma. Even journalism, now as self-consciously "intellectual" as any occupation, disdained book learning. "Almost as many upper middle class or upper class women attended college as did men," observes Kipnis, of the days when the campuses served only a tiny minority of American youth. "In a day when a man's occupational success had little to do with his intellect [or with the portion related to school work], many men were willing to grant intellectual equality to women in the same spirit that they presently might allow them to excel in flower arranging."[11]

Few parents of modest means kept sons in school when opportunity (or a needed extra paycheck) beckoned elsewhere. It was the Great Depression, not any love of learning, that turned high school attendance into a positive social good, and then only to protect desperate breadwinners from the competition of cheap and energetic youngsters. Until 1940, in all age categories, women had more formal education than men (and less than half of girls had even finished high school). The refined woman—often a schoolmarm—who married "beneath" herself starred in a century of domestic melodramas. Lyndon Johnson and Russell Baker are only two of the accomplished American sons whose scholastic ambitions sprang from such frustrated mothers. Wherever the frontier tradition held sway, marks of "culture" like pianos and poetry—or even books of any kind—indicated the presence of a woman.

By 1950, though, young men had more schooling than did women, and the male median had climbed to the beginning of college. The GI bill lured to campus thousands of men seeking an education that would shield them from what the Depression had done to their fathers. Their wives eagerly quit school to earn their "PhT" (putting hubby through). By the mid-1950s, the "organization man," with his paper credentials, began to dominate the business scene, and formal schooling became more and more crucial to career success in the broad reaches of the middle class. Draft policies also encouraged lingering in the ivied halls. Can it be a coincidence that demography anticipated, by only a few years, the scores on Wechsler's intelligence tests? Kipnis thinks not, and concludes that the Wechsler scores measure both education and innate intellect. Thus, she concludes, "whatever genetic differences between the sexes exist must be so slight as to be readily modifiable through exposure to appropriate learning opportunity."[12]

It's obvious, of course, how attitudes and education can account for reading scores, but mazes and mental rotations don't appear in school curricula. They do, however, figure prominently in the informal curriculum of boyhood. American girls, in the city, suburbs and countryside, generally stay closer to home than do their brothers. Prudence, modesty, custom, and fear discourage wide ranging through the neighborhood or across fields and forests. And their games teach them much less about objects in space. They less often hit baseballs, punt soccer balls, catch footballs, throw snowballs, build block cities, make models, race soapbox cars, break down engines, steal second base. They learn less about trajectories, distances, and the relationships of moving parts.

In U.S. culture, at least. Eskimo girls, who hunt with the men across the empty Arctic miles, do as well on spatial tests as do Eskimo boys, Julia Sherman argues. Mexican girls, more closely chaperoned than Americans, lag behind their brothers by a larger gap than U.S. girls do. American Indian women, tested for "field dependence" by measures that really test spatial abilities, score lower than American Indian men but higher than Anglo men.

If spatial abilities do indeed relate to mathematical ones, then math results ought to vary too. An extensive 1967 study obligingly found "large differences in math performances *between* countries; *within* countries boys tended to score higher than girls. But even this is less clear-cut than it seems. Lower-scoring girls of one country . . . scored higher than the higher-scoring boys of another."[13] Surely this proves the natural male superiority, argues psychologist Lauren Julius Harris; cross-cultural studies showing variation in spatial abilities are "dramatic but misleading, for the absence of sex differences in certain cultures is much more the exception than the rule."[14] The male advantage, for example, showed up among maze-running Bhil of India, Alorese of the Pacific Islands, and Chamorros of Mexico, as well as Americans and Europeans. The rod-and-frame test favored French, English, Dutch, and Hong Kong Chinese men. Can a handful of scattered exceptions weigh against the great mass of the evidence?

It can, Peggy Sanday would argue, if the great mass were biased toward male-dominant cultures. If we compare cultures that all treat spatial skills alike, then piling case upon case doesn't constitute comparison. Only comparing cultures that differ on gender roles can really test limits of human possibility. Traveling from France to Britain or Holland to Hong Kong won't provide the real contrast we need, when each society consists of traditionally homebound women and traditionally venturesome men.

But substituting insight for airfare can find cases close to home. Marjorie Schratz, for example, found three divergent approaches to knowledge in a single New York neighborhood; she merely gave a spatial test to the third, fourth, fifth, and ninth grades in three neighboring parochial schools. Her young subjects had the same low economic standing, but very different cultural backgrounds—and the differences told the tale. The groups' average performances differed, but until puberty, boys' and girls' scores within each group did not. The adolescents, though, presented a more complicated picture. White boys and girls followed the "normal" pattern, but the other groups reversed it. Hispanic and black girls both outscored their boys, the Hispanics by the larger margin.[15]

So here, in the crowded tenements of lower Manhattan, the middle-American generalities about intellect don't hold. "But," you might object, "this isn't a normal situation; society skews the results by giving poor city boys no real incentive to go to school." Sanday's point exactly: no situation is "normal"; each arises from the concrete facts of particular lives.

But if there's no "normal" situation, can there be a normal human mind—a normal human way of perceiving the world and organizing what we know? In the early 1960s, Gerald Lesser, Gordon Fifer, and Donald Clark asked a series of subtle and profound questions in an attempt to find out. Young New Yorkers again provided whole worlds in the space of a few city blocks. Three hundred twenty six- and seven-year-olds—from four of the city's self-conscious ethnic groups—took a comprehensive mental test. And beneath their uniform accents, inside their interchangeable jeans and sneakers, the Chinese, Jewish, black, and Puerto Rican youngsters proved to be, in a way that the city's immense scale makes possible and even necessary, true products of their very different cultural memories.

The basic results matched the stereotypes. The two cultures that most strongly emphasize schooling and intellectual achievement produced the highest average scores. In every group, children from prosperous, educated families outscored the sons and daughters of the poor. But the more interesting results cut deeper: not only the level, but the *organization* of abilities varied from culture to culture, and the differences held across social classes. The four cultures very simply appeared to foster different patterns of intellectual strength. Poor children achieved at a lower level, but according to their group's model. Bilingualism made no difference.

The Chinese, with their legendary propensity for science and math prizes, led the spatial scores, followed fairly closely by the Jews, and trailed by the blacks and Puerto Ricans. On verbal ability, the Jews, as "people of the book," came first, followed by the blacks, with their tradition of talk as folk art. The Chinese came next, and the Puerto Ricans behind them. The Jews also led in numerical ability, ahead of the Chinese, Puerto Ricans, and blacks. The Chinese, however, ranked first in math reasoning, followed closely by the Jews and more distantly by the blacks and Puerto Ricans. Jewish girls, unlike those in other groups, bested their brothers both verbally and spatially. Culture, it appeared, had worked at least as hard as the X and Y genes to mold these young minds.

Each September, a substantial slice of the nation's young science and math talent converges on Cambridge, Massachusetts. Valedictorians, math team captains, science fair winners from across the nation stream into town to enroll at MIT, perhaps the most selective, and certainly the most renowned, technical university in the world. Four springs later, these young men—the overwhelming majority of MIT graduates are men—emerge wearing a tangible sign of their notability: an utterly distinctive, immediately recognizable class ring. No colored stone or ornate seal adorns the squared-off, massive, solid metal. On the front, in bas relief, is a beaver building a dam. With industry and ingenuity, with discipline in the service of technical perfection, nature's master technologists, and Cambridge's, reshape the world.

Yes, Techmen say, the ring captures the essence of their undergraduate years, which were spent down the road from, and to some extent in the shadow of, the other great university on the Charles. "As the beaver is engineer of the animal world," they ruefully intone, "the MIT man is the animal of the engineering world." The contrast between the prototypical Harvard man and the quintessential Techie could hardly be more pronounced—the one facile, sophisticated, at home in a world of Georgian halls and literary allusions; the other a "nerd," a hacker, a loner hunched over his computer screen or lab bench, forever, in the evocative but precise student slang, "tooling."

Harvard's proximity probably makes MIT men exaggerate their eccentricity, but many have lived a long time with a sense of social ineptness, even isolation. MIT has made two great contributions to the national collegiate culture: the egg-drop contest, in which an egg thrown from a roof must land unbroken on the ground below; and election of the Ugliest Man on Campus. The one celebrates pride in technical mastery; the other, chagrin at social inadequacy.

But why should gifted young men, with distinguished academic records and promising career prospects, view themselves as hapless social misfits? Because, argues MIT psychologist-sociologist Sherry Turkle, author of a pioneering study of the culture of computers, that vision is integral to the culture of hard science, and very likely to the students' decision to become scientists.

Becoming a scientist involves more than mastering certain subject matter. It also means entering a specific subculture, with very specific values and beliefs. As the scientist-novelist–civil servant C. P. Snow recognized in Britain, the culture of science was one of a pair competing for the allegiance of the ruling classes. In the United States, which lacks a homogeneously educated national elite, other competitors also vie for power. But Snow's central point remains, if anything, even truer here: even more than a body of demonstrated truth, science is a social and cultural system. It embodies a theory of knowledge that has enjoyed essentially unchallenged hegemony among secularly educated Westerners for generations. But from the point of view of the person doing science, or hoping to, it is first and foremost a seductively powerful and prestigious social system that inducts a select number of young persons capable of meeting its norms.

It is, moreover, a social system that mostly fails to recognize itself as such. It doesn't generally distinguish its fundamental tenets from the lineaments of the universal. Of course, all ruling social systems enjoy this right to establish the boundaries of reality: Christianity had a very long run, and managed to silence some notable dissenters. Only the less powerful social systems need notice alternate versions of truth. When religion took formal note of evolution, when Genesis became a metaphor instead of literal history, the hegemony of science was complete. During science's reign, though, no other competing way of knowing—with the possible exception of Oriental medicine—has yet received the compliment of serious attention from scientists.

At the center of the culture and society of science stands a belief in objective reality: a discernible truth exists, separate from the mind of the knower and unaffected by the act of knowing. All "hard" science accepts this statement as transparently obvious; only at the outer reaches of theoretical physics does it apprehend, with some perplexity, any other possibility. But under this apparently commonsensical creed, rather like an angel in an overcoat, lurks a being of an entirely different order. A belief in objective reality, and in the possibility of objectivity, is not an empirical conclusion; it is a philosophical position and a psychological stance.

And from it flow unseen consequences, like an aura from the angel. If objective reality exists apart from and unaffected by the knowing mind, then the knower exists apart from what he studies; the act of knowing involves no reciprocity between knower and known. Only one relationship is possible: domination by the knower. In its Latin root, meaning "thrown at or against," the word "object" has a profound implication of separateness and opposition (another word, meaning "put against," also shares the prefix "ob-"). To be objective, therefore, is to be apart, separate, bounded and impersonal, immune to reciprocal influence.

It is to be, like the "tool" in his laboratory or the "hacker" at his screen, sovereign and alone. Numerous excellent science students told Turkle of their longstanding frustration with the world of the subjective, their awkwardness at personal relationships, their failure to apprehend others' motives and emotions, their annoyance that such illogical entanglements hold power over them, their resulting sense of themselves as in some way socially unacceptable and even weird. An objective world without emotion or relationships—a world in which events occur not because of the incomprehensible vagaries of another consciousness but because of perfect and discoverable rules—a world, in other words, very like that of science—"seems to gratify particular emotional needs," she notes.[16]

This cluster of needs resembles a particular type of masculine personality that develops in cultures like ours—cultures that strongly differentiate the sexes but segregate all children in a female realm. The child's first great love, first great emotional experience, is mother. In psychoanalytic theory, the great drama of a male childhood is separation from that engulfing, tantalizing unity—a separation sufficiently complete for her to recede into "other"; a separation, in other words, that permits a masculine identity. Girls need never rip themselves away so completely. Being female means being like mother, perhaps even *of* mother.

It is society's conception of maleness, rather than any inherent will to isolation, that fuels this urge to separateness. If father exists on the periphery of childish consciousness—as, since the industrial revolution, in nonfarming families of Europe and America, he has; and if the masculine can never resemble the feminine, then becoming a boy means becoming other than mother, the caretaker. The ability to transform experience into object is thus masculine; the capacity to blur the self into others—to achieve empathy perhaps and subjectivity surely—is, in this sort of society, feminine. Some cultures—the egalitarian, deeply esthetic Balinese, for example—make openness to emotional experience a human, not a female, trait. But, in a culture where the masculine is, in the words of Evelyn Keller, who first recorded this insight, what "can never be feminine," masculinity requires eternal vigilance on the boundaries of the self. Only constant policing of the borders can keep the insidious invasion of emotion at bay.

Objectivity, Freud and Piaget agree, requires a firmly established self—a self standing in opposition to encroaching experience, a self impervious to the siren call to blend with other selves. Without doubt this accounts for the difference, exhaustively documented by Carol Gilligan, between the styles of moral reasoning characteristic of young American men and women. A belief in objective, external justice, in the balance of rights and duties, anchors the male style. A wish to mediate suffering, to reduce the pain on all sides, fuels the feminine. Only strict observance of rights keeps borders clear; "good fences makes good neighbors." But where separateness is not an obsession, an occasional excursion into other selves can do no harm.

Should a man who steals medicine to save his wife's life go to prison for the crime? Gilligan put this and other dilemmas to university students. The men most often debated the relative claims of rights to life and to property. The women tended to wander into "side" issues: Why is the pharmacist so heartless that theft becomes necessary? Isn't there some other, less painful, alternative?

In this sense, and in this society, science, the apotheosis of objectivity, is an intensely and intrinsically masculine culture. Its central value re-creates a young man's central struggle. "Everyone knows" this, Keller reports, even her own young son, who told her, a scientist, that "science is for men."[17] The preponderance of men in science, she argues, is at bottom an effect, not a cause, of a set of beliefs deeply uncongenial to many women raised in this society.

Children themselves provide corroboration. Lynn Fox found that, among the stupendously able youngsters identified by the Johns Hopkins Study of Mathematically Precocious Youth, values, not innate ability, distinguish the gifted boys who become math prodigies from the gifted girls who do not. Gateway to the world of serious science, and as perfectly objective a system as the human mind has devised, mathematics shares with science an intensely masculine aura—one centered in the value of theoretical perfection. "Differences in values appear to be related to differences in mathematical precocity," she concludes.[18]

Not merely outstanding intellectual endowments, but the determination to use them in a particular way, precede the prodigiously high math scores. The twelve- and thirteen-year-olds who top the SAT-M scores value "theoretical pursuits" much more strongly than do others of their age, and so they spend their spare time formally or informally studying math. Relatively fewer girls pass solitary but engrossing hours working puzzles, debugging programs, or deriving theorems. They place too much weight on social values, on the desire to keep friends and the esteem of a peer group. The mysteries of relations among people, not among numbers, fire their imaginations. The loneliness of the long-distance hacker may well lead directly to the ugly-man contest at MIT.

But isn't this rather too weighty a result to hang on the slender reed of a psychoanalytic theory? Probably so. A somewhat more mundane cause also contributes to this result: specifically, the simple fact that growing boys and girls inhabit very different worlds. A boy knows that he will grow up to be a man; a girl knows that she will not. Certainly by late childhood or early adolescence—the time when interesting math first appears on the curriculum—observant girls have begun to appreciate the very different means that many women use to achieve their aims. American women, like all in subordinate positions, prosper in large measure by the approval of those holding power over them; even corporate success seems tied to the ability to maintain an adequately feminine persona. Members of the dominant group—the ones with the power to invite, to propose, to bestow social status—have no need to understand the foibles of their dependents. (Hence the legendary unpredictability of women.)

Subordinates, though, live by their mastery of nuance. Blacks, children, women all make careful studies of the quirks and weaknesses of those holding power over them. And sometime during childhood, many girls come to understand that their quickest route to prosperity and esteem is through the approval of males— through the manipulation of appearances to gratify a male's sense of his own maleness. Simply put, a girl smart enough to score 800 on the SAT-M is smart enough to know that a smart girl shouldn't look that smart. Indeed, as early as age three, the more intelligent the child, the more he or she knows about sex stereotypes.[19]

Smart girls thus suffer their own special terror, different perhaps from that of boys—the fear that intellectual pursuits will render them inadequate women, unable to fulfill a young woman's overriding goal of attracting appropriate men. Many smart girls turn their ambition, insight, and intuition (which really is highly developed reasoning from subtle cues) away from academics and toward

a surer path to adult satisfaction, social striving. "As the uncomplicated nature of masculine ambition permits the male to strive for
money, education, and status simultaneously, no choice of objec-
tives is elicited from him. As choice is demanded from the female,
the conventional path is the route to marriage."[20]

What would the testers make of young Suzanne, a bright girl
from a poor family? Prepared from infancy to rise above her origins, she earned high grades at a good high school and high scores
on the SAT. But instead of the good universities she could have
attended on scholarship, she chose instead a high-priced but mediocre girls' college. This obscure institution offered a single advantage, but one that Suzanne carefully sought out: it was very close to
a great medical school. In her sophomore year she accepted the
marriage proposal of a carefully selected and very promising medical student. By her senior year she had achieved her life's ambition:
entry into the upper middle class. At her ten-year high school reunion, her outfit and address proclaimed her progress. Another
classmate, an "intellectual" girl whose high school average had
matched Suzanne's, was just finishing her doctorate after years of
drab academic penury. Can any test of "cognitive ability" say which
girl more wisely used native intelligence?

In American suburban high schools, those crucibles of identity
and ambition, academics rank below sports (for boys) and below
social life (for girls) in the canons of youthful prestige. Even so,
girls do better than boys in both grades and IQs. But at the very top
of the class, where the very brightest and most ambitious ought to
cluster, a remarkable reality plays itself out. In every case studied,
the best girl scholar—the one in each school who most fully embodied the value of intellectual excellence—was less bright than the
best boy scholar. The very brightest girls apparently know better
than to lead the class.

So math and science, and the life of the mind in general, face stiff
competition for young women's loyalty. Unless utterly overpowered by their own intellectual gifts, adolescent girls rarely seek out
the company of the mathematically precocious boys. "Weird,"
"nerdy," said the gifted girls of the boys in the Johns Hopkins
program's accelerated math classes; and this weirdness and nerdi-

ness is what kept the girls away from the courses themselves, they
told Fox.

Are Benbow and Stanley measuring pure ability, as they seem to
believe, or an amalgam of ability and values, as Fox suggests? Ravenna Helson's studies of male and female professional mathematicians strongly support Fox. "Professional" here refers to their educational status, because many of the women in the sample—
including the most able—lacked paying jobs. But they all had
Ph.D.s and journal publications in math. Of the three hundred or
so women mathematicians in the U.S. when she undertook her
research, Helson studied forty-five, including "virtually all creative
women mathematicians" in the country—with creativity rated by
the exacting jury of their peers.[21]

This high and hard-won accolade, however, meant very different
things to men and women. Men considered creative stood at the
pinnacle of American intellectual life, the amply paid, confident,
professionally active occupants of immensely prestigious posts. For
them, a creative career in math meant a culmination of conventional ambition. But the women considered creative had inferior
jobs (one-third had no jobs), less self-assurance, more self-doubt,
narrower social lives, less professional contact, more personal
stress. They crammed their "real" work into the interstices of lives
also devoted to housekeeping and routine teaching; accomplishing
this meant ruthlessly narrowing their interests down to a handful. A
creative female math career meant a lonely, devoted, lifelong struggle against society's notion of womanhood, almost a vow of social
poverty. "The creative women are further removed from social
norms than the [less creative] women [mathematicians], whereas
the creative men do not differ in this respect from the [other]
men,"[22] writes Helson, her dry scholarly prose disguising, but not
hiding, the pain of lives where the pressing demands to take children to the dentist, grade mid-term exams, and cook Thanksgiving
dinner competed for the energy needed to concentrate deeply on
abstract problems.

These women chose lives far outside the American mainstream.
Is it surprising that half the creative women were themselves foreign born, and half of the entire sample of female mathematicians
had at least one foreign-born parent? Indeed, the creative women

came from a very particular kind of home—one strongly biased toward education, dominated by the father, and lacking sons; a home, in other words, that encouraged a talented girl to identify with a male intellectual role, and equally important, with a father who permitted her to do so. After rather isolated girlhoods, these women enjoyed their first—brief—social blossoming in graduate school, where they at last met men attracted to and unthreatened by their talents. They received their Ph.D.s and achieved their first publications at the same age as male classmates, but within a few years fell far behind in prestige of job and numbers of publications.

For them, a creative career meant a harder, lonelier fight, but they persevered against odds that would have discouraged most members of either sex. They possess the personality traits of creativity even more strongly than the creative men. "Among the creative men," Helson notes, "some were original, flexible, ambitious, but essentially conventional individuals. One may suppose that a conventional woman would never develop the 'purity of motive' [or, indeed, the free time] which seems to be necessary for a new symbolic structure to emerge."[23]

Only the strongest of drives could propel a person against such titanic obstacles. Many women of exceptional intelligence would at some point choose, with Suzanne, to achieve their satisfactions elsewhere. For the creative women, unlike the comparably creative men, the work in itself had to constitute the main and often the only reward. They did not achieve their due esteem as mathematicians, and even less as women.

In the starkly masculine upper reaches of science, the very fact of being a female can in itself devalue the work—as witness the famous example of bigotry and vindictiveness described in James Watson's *The Double Helix*. Recounting the work that earned him and Francis Crick the Nobel Prize, Watson heaped such scorn on the appearance, wardrobe, and disposition of the valiant Rosalind Franklin that he felt compelled to append an apology. Cut off from the old-boy network that nourished her male colleagues, and fatally ill, she made—and made available to Watson and Crick—a discovery crucial to their ultimate success. Had she lived, she might well have deserved a share of the prize. In a male scientist of her stature, personal eccentricities—Einstein's indifference to socks, for example—become confirming stigmata of genius, not signs of inadequacy.

So when young persons begin, unwittingly, to narrow their future prospects, the world of science, and its necessary prerequisite, mathematics, hold fewer attractions for girls than for boys. Math and spatial scores begin to diverge at or shortly after puberty, when, as the biological determinists rejoice to point out, the steroid sex hormones flood young people's systems. But something else also floods into the life of a person peering over the horizon of childhood toward the far-off landscape of the adult self—the absolute necessity of becoming a man or a woman. For a boy, there beckons, through the widening path of adolescence, the broad, sunlit plain of manhood; for a girl, a much more perilous and problematic passage to a land of more shadowed promise. "Traditionally devoid of several of the social advantages experienced by a similarly maturing boy, such as athletic prowess, leadership roles, and expectation of occupational success, physical maturation for a girl may carry more explicit sexualized meanings."[24]

Each sign of physical maturity marks a boy's progress toward the freedom and power of adulthood. Each increases his stature among peers and the freedom allowed by parents. Early puberty raises a boy's self-image, but lowers a girl's.[25] Each sign of *her* physical maturity transforms her into a more patently sexual being, and increases her parents'—particularly her father's—protectiveness. Childrearing practices differ most sharply not in the early years of pink ribbons and blue booties, but during high school, when boys take major steps toward independence and girls learn dependence and the arts of relationship. And the change hits a girl months or years earlier than a boy, and—what is crucial to her intellectual future—during a lower school grade.

Precisely when stereotyped sex roles press as insistently as they ever will, serious math courses begin. Numerous studies conducted or reviewed by Julia Sherman clearly indicate that math courses taken and spare time spent studying math account for much of the discrepancy in math scores—and that sex role orientation accounts for a good deal of the rest. A particularly illuminating study of four Wisconsin high schools found a male advantage in only two—and the differences, Sherman writes, correlate with variables that "probably all serve as mediators of sex role influences."[26] In schools that gave girls confidence in the ability to learn math, convinced them of its future usefulness, and encouraged both parents to see girl math learners favorably, girls did as well as boys.

The father's approval is particularly crucial. As much as the mother, he defines womanliness for his daughter; his approval grants her permission to consider a trait or interest feminine. But fathers sex-type behaviors far more than do mothers, and this has crucial consequences for a girl's image of the possible. The girls who grew into mathematicians, and especially those who became creative in that very masculine field, had fathers who strongly approved and encouraged their interest.

But then, in fields as diverse as tennis and neuroscience, those who achieve renown come from a special sort of highly motivated, child-centered, very encouraging homes. In their extensive study of young talent, Benjamin Bloom and colleagues found that family life, not mere native ability, paved the way to success. The high achievers—including Benbow and Stanley's math prodigies—adopt, sometime in early or middle childhood, the social role of the talented child. And like all social roles, this one plays in an ensemble of supporting roles. Parents, teachers, relatives, neighbors, siblings, classmates, friends each have their assigned parts as the gifted child grows into the eminent adult. But do they respond to a girl's intellectual gifts in precisely the same way as they do to a boy's?

All evidence points to a single conclusion: they do not. Boys and girls take different routes to intellectual achievement, found a thirty-year study of eighty-nine children, and they diverge long before the child has any intellectual interests to speak of. "The pattern most likely to lead to involvement in intellectual achievement in the boy is early maternal protection," the Fels Institute researchers found, "followed by encouragement and acceleration of mastery behaviors." Indeed, in the very early days of the Johns Hopkins gifted children study, Stanley found his first subjects as word of his interest in math prodigies spread through Baltimore dinner parties, PTAs, and back-fence chats. Parents eagerly brought forward sons whose gifts they believed matched those of Stanley's first brilliant boy, Joe Bates. To this day, SMPY depends on children coming forward to take the test.

"For girls, however," the Fels researchers continue, "the pattern was quite different. Maternal hostility toward the daughter during the first three years, together with acceleration during age six to ten," produced "adult intellectual mastery in the woman." (Hostility meant a "critical attitude toward the child," not serious rejection.)[27] "The general picture emerging," Dorothy Kipnis concludes, is that "girls who persist in intellectual concern as adults are girls who have resisted (or perhaps been excused from) the traditional sex-role socialization of Western females."[28] Perhaps, indeed, their cool and demanding mothers permit easier and more complete separation than other girls experience. "For males, the picture is the reverse. Males who display strong effort in academic learning or achievement-testing situations are males who have been encouraged to do so by their mothers and who quite possibly are more fearful than most of rough body contact and peer disapproval." Could this warmer, perhaps more smothering, mother make the boy even more determined to establish his masculinity through a sharp separation, but not in the rough and tumble of sports?

A few years ago, the distinguished biologists R. C. Lewontin and Steven Rose and the psychologist Leon Kamin published a profound consideration of biology and behavior. In it, they recount an experiment with corn seed. "Suppose one takes from a sack of open-pollinated corn two handfuls of seed. There will be a good deal of genetic variation between the seeds in each handful, but the seeds in one's left hand are on the average no different from those in one's right." We next plant each handful in specially prepared beds, one full of clean sand enhanced by chemical plant food, the other containing similar sand but only "half the necessary nitrogen." Weeks pass, and the seeds become seedlings, each bed containing plants of varied heights. "This variation within plots is entirely genetic," because the seeds in each plot grew under identical conditions, so "the variation in height is then 100 percent heritable." But when we compare the beds, we see that one has seedlings uniformly taller than the other. "This difference is not at all genetic but is a consequence of the difference in nitrogen level. So the hereditability of a trait *within* populations can be 100 percent, but the cause of the difference *between* populations can be entirely environmental" (emphasis added).[29]

Lewontin, Rose, and Kamin make this statement with confidence because they understand in detail how corn seedlings grow. Neither science, nor, for that matter, religion or art, understands how the human mind grows. Even Arthur R. Jensen, whose views on the inferiority of black intellect sparked a celebrated controversy, has conceded, "No really clear distinction can be made operationally at the level of tests between *intelligence* and intellectual *achievement*, though intelligence and achievement can be clearly distinguished at the conceptual or theoretical level" (emphasis in original).[30]

So what do we know about the differences between male and female minds? Well, long Saturdays hunched over answer sheets seem to turn up evidence that they exist. But what do we know about the nature and origin of those differences—about the likelihood that they spring from biology rather than biography? The short but embarrassing answer is, almost nothing at all. Until we raise all our seedlings in the same bed, until we offer all young minds the same sunlight and nourishment, we very simply cannot say.

But in the meantime, some researchers are seeking answers in another quarter altogether. Male and female abilities differ, they argue, because of different synapses, not different socialization. This is the evidence we will examine next.

10

Different Brains?

We've considered the growth of corn seeds. Scientific theories behave in much the same manner. If they don't fall on fertile soil, they wither. But if they do alight in a favorable spot, it's sometimes hard to keep the riot of blooms inside the bed. Consider, for example, why hardly anyone today knows the name of Marc Dax.

In 1832, this little-known country doctor, soon to die in provincial obscurity, presented, at a meeting of his local medical society, the sole research paper of his life. It aroused absolutely no interest, and would have disappeared forever into a dusty archive, but for a single, extraordinary fact. Dax was first to demonstrate a finding that would, generations later, help revolutionize thinking about the human mind.

Three decades after that forgettable address, a Paris surgeon whose name is famous today, unaware that Dax preceded him, duplicated and expanded his results. And a century after that, a Caltech professor won a Nobel Prize for inventively exploring the ramifications of the idea first reported to a bored audience of GPs. By then, the presses were running overtime to satisfy a scientific and lay public insatiable for the latest from his and other laboratories.

Part of what distinguished the Parisian, Paul Broca, and the American, Roger Sperry, from Marc Dax, was their ingenuity and resolve. But part was that when they spoke, the world had become ready to listen. Indeed, by Sperry's time, the ideas that flow from his stunning experiments seemed to answer a deep yearning in the culture. And in the late 1970s, the insight shared by the three researchers crossed the threshold from physiology journals to up-per-middle-class dinner tables and drugstore paperback racks; it be-came part of what everybody simply knew. As completely as Dar-winism and Freudianism had in their times, it grabbed the attention of the classes that keep current with ideas. And as persuasively as those other theories once had, it seemed to solve an intractable puzzle of nature.

But if Dax had terrible timing, he had quite good powers of observation. Over years of practice, he had noted more than forty cases of aphasia, or loss of speech, and each had coincided with injuries on the left side of the head. Not once in his career did he see aphasia associated with injuries exclusively on the right side. The conclusion seemed obvious: the left half of the brain rules speech. But, unfortunately for his future renown, he presented his overwhelming evidence while the embarrassing memory of one Franz Gall, only eight years in the grave, still stalked scientific cir-cles.

Gall also had had a very good idea, which he had elaborated into a very bad one. His original research into the structure of the brain established the nature of the white matter, and he pioneered the eminently sensible theory that the brain's various parts had special-ized functions. He also proposed that the shape of the brain tissue influences the shape of the skull (a fact exploited by modern paleoanatomists to study the mental equipment of our ancestors). But from this very sound footing he made a daring and disastrous logical leap—he mistook, as your high school English teacher might have put it, "the container for the thing contained." He argued that the bumps on the head accurately predict the brainpower inside. In other words, he founded the pseudo science of phrenology.

Laughed out of the medical profession in his native Austria, Gall established himself in Paris where, like many an industrious quack before and since, he grew rich from consultations to a devoted following. As his bank balance rose, his scientific standing fell. And his reputation so tainted his other, sound, ideas that most scientists simply refused to credit anything he said. Dax simply lacked the prestige (although he had the evidence, if one were inclined to study it) to convince doubters to look again at any concept proposed by the famous charlatan.

But twenty-five years separated Dax's talk from Broca's, time enough for Gall's bad name to fade and his good ideas to gain some prominent support. Medical professor Jean Baptiste Bouillaud, for example, completely agreed with his assignment of speech to the frontal lobes. In fact, Bouillaud put his money where his scientific reputation was, offering "500 francs (a considerable sum at the time) to anyone who could produce a patient with damage to the frontal lobes . . . unaccompanied by loss of speech."[1]

Indeed, in 1861, Bouillaud's son-in-law, Ernest Auburtin, argued this view before a Paris meeting of the Society of Anthropology. Broca, in the audience, thought of an elderly, aphasic patient of his who also suffered paralysis on one side. Broca, like most persons credited with new ideas, had exquisite timing; he invited Auburtin to a joint examination of the man. And the patient had excellent timing too; he obliged Broca the researcher, if not Broca the physician, by dying a day or two later. Broca's autopsy found damage right where Gall and Dax predicted, in the left frontal lobe. Going Dax one better, Broca presented the actual brain to the next meeting, but got a reception as cold as Dax's.

But he persevered. When his practice shortly provided another such case, he braved his colleagues' disinterest and again brought it to the Society's attention. And by now the stars, or Parisian anthropologists' own brains, were in proper conjunction. The second presentation rather inexplicably thrilled its audience. The astonished Broca found himself at the center of a building scientific storm over localization of brain functions. The ensuing waves of criticism and praise may have encouraged him to pursue what began as a rather peripheral interest. He eventually isolated the exact portion of the left frontal lobe involved in aphasia, which we now know as "Broca's area."

Soon, however, word of the research reached Gustav Dax, who had followed his father Marc into the medical profession. He raised the charge of intellectual thievery. Broca claimed innocence, protesting complete ignorance of the name and writings of Marc Dax. Gustav dug up the old paper and published it, establishing his father's priority. But this didn't dislodge Broca's name from the seminal discovery, because, as Sally Springer and Georg Deutsch state in their highly regarded book on the brain, "Eventually, Broca presented a considerably more impressive argument for the association between aphasia and damage to the left hemisphere than had Dax."[2]

And, more importantly in the long run, Broca's work so intrigued and challenged his contemporaries that serious research in brain anatomy picked up briskly. Within a decade of Broca's first talk, two of the basic concepts of modern brain studies were on their way to universal acceptance. The first was lateralization, the notion that the two sides control different abilities. The second was cerebral dominance, or the idea that one half can exercise major influence on behavior.

With the passing years, knowledge of the brain grew ever more extensive and exact. But for a century it still remained an abstruse medical specialty. Until, that is, word began to spread about the amazing doings in Roger Sperry's lab.

The American chapter of this story also begins with a sharp-eyed surgeon. In the late 1930s and early 1940s, Dr. William Van Wagenen of Rochester, New York, felt frustrated by his inability to help certain cases of severe epilepsy, which didn't respond to drugs. Enormous electrical discharges, too large for the hemisphere they originated in, would engulf the whole brain, bringing on violent, uncontrollable seizures. In technical terms, the charges leapt across the corpus callosum, the most important of the bands of tissue (or commissures) that bridge the brain's two halves.

But Van Wagenen learned of a 1940 article reporting a successful treatment in monkeys; the experimenters had cut the corpus callosum, severing the two hemispheres. The operations produced no observable ill effects, and Van Wagenen decided to try commissurotomy (cutting the commissure) on human patients. As in the animal tests, the operations caused no observable changes in the patients' general behavior; unfortunately, though, neither did they always cause changes in the epilepsy. We now know that he performed a number of different procedures under a single name, and that he generally left parts of the corpus callosum intact. No one appreciated the significance of that fact for some years, by which time he had abandoned the procedure as a treatment for epilepsy.

But the little-understood band of tissue continued to interest animal researchers, among them Sperry and Roger Myers. Ten years after Van Wagenen, they collaborated on an astonishing discovery about the eyes of a cat. When they completely severed the animal's two hemispheres, it could no longer transfer information from one half of its brain to the other. Ordinarily, of course, knowledge from each eye is available to the whole brain, through the optic nerves and the corpus callosum. But with the commissure cut, each eye, along with the hemisphere it remained connected to, was on its own.

Specifically, Myers taught cats with completely severed hemispheres to do visual discrimination tasks, distinguishing a square from a circle, for example. Ordinarily, of course, the cat could learn with both eyes open or one eye covered, just as you can see a picture with your right eye and recognize it when you see it again with the left. The information about squares and circles and landscapes simply passes to both hemispheres for the later use of either or both eyes.

But Myers wasn't working with ordinary cats. He forced them to master the tasks with one eye covered. Then he switched the eye patches and had them try again. And then the amazing thing happened: nothing. Cats that had done tasks with ease now failed completely, as if Myers were dealing with a totally different animal. And in neurological terms, of course, he was. The second hemisphere faced a task it had never seen before, and Myers had to teach the very same lessons to the very same cats again from scratch.

But with both eyes open, the split-brained cats, like Van Wagenen's commissurotomy patients, seemed disconcertingly normal. And this apparent normality encouraged two Pasadena surgeons to try the operation on epileptic humans again, this time, however, severing the commissures completely. This small change in procedure produced a major change in results. Everything about the patients appeared to remain unchanged, but their epilepsy improved dramatically.

But Sperry's group looked deeper. A moment like this comes rarely in the steady accretion of small facts that constitutes "normal science"—only once in a while does a door of knowledge suddenly swing open to reveal new and unexpected worlds. Darwin's finches and Freud's Viennese neurotics gave their times such a glimpse of the unimagined realities within ourselves; Sperry's California epileptics seemed to, too.

Though outwardly utterly ordinary, this band of students, housewives, and business persons were living in a way that no human ever had before: with two independently functioning brain systems inside their single skulls. The mystery and power of duality has long fascinated the human race: male and female, yin and yang, day and night, good and bad. They have formed the fabric of our dreams, the foundations of our philosophies. Here, suddenly, were living specimens, men and women who seemed to have two minds inside their single heads—and two minds that weren't on speaking terms. A perfectly intelligent man, for example, couldn't describe in words a picture shown only to his right visual field. He couldn't point with his right hand to a face his right visual field had seen. Sensible, educated persons, when asked to indicate the drawing they had just viewed, would simultaneously say "the one on top"—and point to the one on the bottom.

The disreputable Dr. Gall, of course, had long ago won the localization debate, and science had accepted that different parts of the brain specialized in different abilities. But no one had dreamed of following these facts to their utmost implication: that the two halves of the brain house different systems of thinking. As any biology student now knows, the left cerebral hemisphere controls the right side of the body and experiences the world directly through the right ear and right visual field. It also usually has the language centers. And, as research gradually demonstrated, it tends toward a "linear," "propositional," "analytic" mode of thought. The right hemisphere, master of the body's left side, specializes in spatial reasoning, intuition, and analogies, a "gestalt" mode of thought; it gets the "big picture," not the details. Yin and yang, science and art, day and night—two completely different ways of knowing seemed to cohabit in each human head.

Soon a flood of brain studies was pouring out of the laboratories and a torrent of books and articles off the presses. The split-brain patients, of course, could not make careers as laboratory subjects, and, in any case, it was normal brains that held the ultimate answers about human nature. Psychologists, physiologists, psycholinguists, neurophysiologists, and others raced to devise means of teasing the brain's abilities apart. They generally favored two techniques, tachistoscopy and dichotic listening. These use special screens or earphones to present different stimuli to each ear or visual field. Combined with sophisticated recording and timing devices, they can often reveal discrepancies in the time the two sides take to handle tasks; researchers generally consider the faster side dominant for the ability. With special pictures, tables, projectors, and eye covers, researchers try to mimic one of the effects of commissurotomy—limiting a direct experience to one side of the brain.

In study after study, a familiar consistency emerges: male and female brains appear to respond somewhat differently. It's a question of cerebral dominance or lateralization—of which hemisphere acts more efficiently in a given circumstance. Results of many types of spatial and linguistic tests appear to imply that the same problem takes a different route through the average male and female brain. Of course, the differences within each sex once again dwarf the differences between the sexes, but here at last the biological determinists saw the clue they had long hoped for. Here at last was a physiological difference basic enough to explain intellectual and behavioral differences.

And here, indeed, was news that the entire known universe had seemingly pined to hear. No sooner had the first murmurs of the hemisphere's different tendencies seeped from the lab than they swept through the general culture. Here at last was the answer to a thousand questions: the factor that made Western culture "linear" and Eastern culture "holistic"; that made artists "intuitive" and scientists "rational"; that prevented our "explicit," "deductive," "differential" industrialized selves from experiencing the "tacit," "imaginative," "existential" truths available to members of simpler societies. Readers of best-selling books and popular magazines earnestly assessed their talents to determine "left-brain" or "right-brain" tendencies. Handbooks appeared to guide the excessively "left-brained" to the untapped riches in their underused right hemispheres. The concept of cerebral dominance, long intended to locate the controls over particular acts or thought processes, expanded to describe whole personalities, casts of mind, and even groups of people.

If the twin hemispheres concept seemed to hold the long-sought key to understanding the human mind, surely it could also solve that lesser quandary, the basis of the widely accepted sex differences. In the balance of the brain, it appeared, lay *la différence*, the reason for men's superior spatial performance and women's advantage in things linguistic; for man's rationality and woman's intuition; for the division of power between warriors and mothers.

Scientists, of course, have powers of observation at least as keen as those of publishers. By the score they hastened to this new field of experimentation, testing the laterality of every mental task imaginable. From the great welter of evidence that rapidly accumulated, several tentative hypotheses quickly emerged. In one of the early forays, A. W. H. Buffery and J. A. Gray proposed that female brains were *more* lateralized than male; that in women the left hemisphere dominated for language and the right for spatial tasks, whereas in men both hemispheres participated in both types of performance. They implicitly argued that strong lateralization favored language performance but not spatial performance, but offered no explanation for the discrepancy.

But no one dwelt long on the contradiction. Within a few years, newer ideas swept it aside. The overwhelming weight of recent evidence now finds women *less* lateralized than men. Their brains appear less specialized. They do more spatial and verbal tasks in both hemispheres. Some writers have inverted the Buffery and Gray paradox, suggesting that language impinges on brain space needed for spatial tasks.

But Springer and Deutsch found all the excitement impinging on other brain space, the kind needed to construct clean experiments. During their careful review of the lateralization literature, they report, they developed "a healthy respect for the Type I error [finding a difference where none exists] and the scientific chaos it creates." In many studies, the differences are tiny, hard to pin down, or by-products of some extraneous factor. Nevertheless, Springer and Deutsch do concede that "frequency as well as consistency" argue for accepting this sex difference "at least as a working hypothesis." Very few studies show greater lateralization in females.

"This consistency suggests that there are true differences that are small in magnitude and easily masked by individual variability or other factors that may not be controlled."[3]

Why the two sexes should show different lateralization remains a mystery; indeed, we don't understand why anyone's brain should show any laterality at all. Our two lungs don't breathe differently, nor do our two kidneys specialize in different types of impurities. The animal evidence is inconclusive, with some researchers asserting, and others denying, lateralization in cats or chimps or monkeys. Many of these studies, alas, have lacked both sophistication and respect for animal possibilities. Until very recently, of course, no one suspected that other species had anything resembling linguistic codes, and no human speaks Vervet well enough to construct an IQ test to pinpoint individual differences in communication ability; we don't know if lady vervets grunt more fluently or wittily than their men.

But we can still rest assured that no one else processes symbolic information in the volume or with the subtlety that we do. Members of no other species appear to read music, send Morse code, converse in signs, take shorthand, or speak several languages. Regardless of what even our closest cousins do, therefore, it seems reasonable that the human brain needs separate centers to handle the very different coding demands of reading, music, dead reckoning, computation, and target practice. Brains that read Japanese, for example, must deal with two writing systems in simultaneous use, one based on an alphabet, like English; the other on pictographs, like Chinese. Fluent readers appear to store their two vocabularies in different cerebral regions. An ability to shift between and combine modes of thought would benefit almost any species, and especially one like Homo sapiens, living by its collective wits in desert, jungle, seashore, and rush-hour subway tunnels. The more different ways we can divide up an experience, the more precisely we can react to the exact situation we face. We've already seen how a masculine mastery of space and a feminine propensity for communication would have benefited our ancestors, Mr. and Mrs. Man-the-Hunter (assuming, of course, that our forebears really lived that way—which they undoubtedly did not). Such doubts, however, have not assailed many of the contributors to the brain-lateralization literature. Many books and articles trace the lab results directly back to those far-away camp fires when our gene pool had newly emerged from apedom.

But the reasons for sex differences in laterality may flow from vastly greater distances than the savannahs that made us human. In a series of publications striking in their originality, the Canadian researcher Pierre Flor-Henry traces them back past our mammal heritage, past even the inheritance we share with all vertebrates, to the very sources of our existence as multicelled, mobile creatures. "The evolution of life progressed from spherical symmetry, through radial symmetry, to bilateral symmetry," be believes. What caused us to evolve from little balls of protoplasm to shapes with well-defined tops and bottoms, fronts and backs? A force as basic as life itself: "gravity provided the first lever" for differentiating up from down, forward from backward, and "hence, right and left. However, at a more fundamental level the organization of all living material [such as the amino acids composing our very genes] is asymmetrical."[4]

The first definitive finding of a true sexual dimorphism in the structure of brains, in Fernando Nottebohm's celebrated studies of songbirds, placed singing in the male's left brain—and singing, Flor-Henry notes, relates to both sex and direction. A bird does not sing to brighten our springtime, but to assure the reproductive success of his own. His song announces his location to his potential or actual mate, and the extent of his territory to male competitors.

Sex and direction are a far from coincidental pairing, Flor-Henry argues. You can't have one without the other, because you need to find someone to mate with. Beyond that, of course, finding anything at all, such as food or shelter, requires an ability to analyze space, and a left-right differentiation in the brain would clearly help with that. So, he argues, it follows that "in those species where the male actively seeks the female, the former would exhibit a greater degree of lateralization than the latter."[5] Sex and space should go together, in creatures like ourselves. If, indeed, we spring from a line of creatures whose males hunted more actively for mates—a proposition at present better supported by theory than by evidence —then a male spatial superiority becomes a major selective advantage for many species.

But the brain's laterality goes far beyond telling right from left. With all our fellow vertebrates, we share a crisscross (or decussated) nervous system; each hemisphere controls the opposite side of the body. This we owe not to our gonads but to our eyes—specifically, to our "advanced optical system incorporating inverted lenses" that throw upside-down pictures on our retinas. The brain, of course, flips them back again to read reality right side up. But only by crossing them "can the panoramic visual field be reconstructed intact."[6] Otherwise the two halves of the final picture couldn't connect in the middle. (Why hearing, smell, taste, and touch should follow the same neural routes the theory does not explain.)

But still, the "double brain" appears as early as the fishes, Flor-Henry states, and as vision gains on smell as a major spatial sense, mammal brains increase in size and complexity. The two sides must communicate very clearly and rapidly, of course, so that the animal has a whole 3-D picture, and a whole complex mind, instead of two competing halves. The corpus callosum—our own instantaneous interhemispheric communicator—appears in "hedgehogs, rats, cats, dolphins, and primates," but not in lower mammals or marsupials, and "callosal conductions" increase in speed "as one moves up the primate filiation."[7]

Laterality is a basic element of our most basic behaviors, Flor-Henry believes, but it still must serve the higher interest of a single mind. The normal brain shifts with lightning speed among different parts of both hemispheres as each task requires. But even so, Flor-Henry argues, we carry remnants of our remote, sexual past. His psychiatric practice convinces him that "the differential hemispheric organization of the male and female" put them at risk for different mental illnesses, usually triggered in their weaker hemisphere. Males seem to succumb more readily to left-hemisphere malfunctions like autism, schizophrenia, and psychopathy, females to mood malfunctions controlled on the right.[8]

But an evolutionary theory, even one as sophisticated as this, is not a physiological device. Scientists have long sought the nuts and bolts of brain differences. For some years a special sex-linked gene for spatial ability seemed a likely cause; the hunt centered on a supposed recessive on the X chromosome. Under this theory, excellent spatial ability would thus follow a predictable pattern in families, rather like baldness, and appear in many more men than women. Fathers and daughters, mothers and sons, Turner's syndrome "women" and XYY men solved mazes and mentally rotated objects for numerous researchers. The "trait" of excellent spatial ability, however, obstinately refused to mimic the mathematical models and the elusive gene eventually faded from view.

Conceptually much simpler possibilities now hold center stage. As recently as 1978, psychologist Daniel Goleman could write in a magazine that prides itself on accuracy, "there are no agreed-upon, observable differences in the physical size, structure, or biochemical components of the brain of the two [human] sexes."[9] We now know definitely of several, and as their number grows, so does the likelihood that still more will emerge. In 1982, Christine Lacoste-Utamsing and Ralph Holloway came upon the first: a shape discrepancy in the corpus callosum. Unlike the rather cylindrical male samples, the female samples they examined had a wider, more bulbous shape, especially in the area that involves "interhemispheric transfer of visual information."[10] (A 1985 study by Sandra Witelson found that callosa in right-handers were larger than in lefties or the ambidextrous, but saw no difference between the sexes.) A shape difference has also turned up in the suprachiasmic nucleus of the hypothalamus. And in 1985, D. F. Swaab and E. Fliers reported a substantial difference in the volume of a nucleus in the preoptic area of the hypothalamus—a region that shows marked sexual dimorphism in rats and contributes to the hormonal control of sexual activity in all species.

In rats, birds, and some other animals, clear size and shape differences correlate with equally clear behavioral differences. Amorous male songbirds sing; most females do not. Randy male rats mount; receptive females bend their backs into a distinctive silhouette. Hormonal and neurological manipulations of a kind impossible in living humans have repeatedly shown direct ties between brain structures and behavior. Transplanting male cells to a female brain, injecting androgen into a female infant, removing the testes before they "set" the fetal brain for life, have drastically altered adult sexuality. But humans present a far more difficult research problem.

First, we use sexual signals more subtle and varied than any rodent. Secondly, we can't experiment on each other.

But is dimorphic anatomy the only route to divergent cognition? Consider the simple act of walking down a moderately busy street. In the space of a single block, thousands of sense impressions clamor for your attention. Visual images converge from all sides: the color of the sky, the color of the pavement, the shapes and sizes of buildings and persons, the movement of cars. Sounds bombard your ears: footfalls, car horns, conversation, a passing radio, birdsong, a hawker's cry, children's laughter. And those are only the major senses. What about the smell from an open bakery door, or a trash can at the curb, or a dog squatting under a tree? What about the feel of the pavement under your feet, or the sudden ping as a child's ball glances off your leg?

And, apart from the senses, a hundred avenues of speculation open before you. What drama lies behind the angry faces of a passing couple? What inspired the eccentric dress of the man coming out of that door? What ails the car whose owner peers in dismay under the lifted hood? What sort of accent does that woman in the red jacket have? Is the fruit at the grocery stand as ripe as it appears or has it been dyed and waxed? What is the shortest route to your destination? Is the rain likely to hold off until evening? In a few moments of perfectly routine motion, hundreds, even thousands, of possibilities present themselves to our brains. Clearly, no one could get to the next corner, let alone to the next day, without ignoring all but a handful.

And for some brain researchers, this is the key to cognition: what we pay attention to. They believe that what defines our mentalities isn't the outward shape taken by the billions of neurons inside our skulls, but the inner connections that bind them into a functioning whole. For these scientists, males and females may differ mainly in what holds their attention. If, for example, one stroller on our hypothetical street habitually notices the faces and speech of passersby, and another calculates the dimensions of the buildings, and a third catalogues the plants and animals, and a fourth studies the makes of the passing cars, they would shortly amass very different knowledge about the same stretch of pavement. And each time they returned they would sharpen certain observation skills but ignore many others.

Some evidence already exists that men and women, on average, do attend to different aspects of the same event. The written word, for example, presents two routes to meaning: the look and the sound of the letters on the page. One experiment asked subjects to cross out the letter *e* whenever it appeared in a printed passage. Silent *e*'s most often survived the purge, because people gave great weight to sound as they read. But still they used visual coding as well, because they caught quite a few of the silents.

But men and women differed in even so basic a skill as reading. In a similar task—eliminating *b*'s—males got more of the silents than did females, which the researchers believe indicates a more visual approach. They then asked subjects to decide which of various strings of letters constitute English words. Both sexes rejected obvious impostors more quickly than nonwords that sound plausibly English, but the women took significantly longer than the men. Why? Because, argue Max Coltheart and colleagues, the men tended to begin by treating all the strings by sight—as strings of meaningful shapes to be compared with real words stored in their memories. But the women more often began the analysis with sound, and that added a step. In this experiment at least, the more visual—and more masculine—approach won the day. (An auditory approach to reading is not without advantages, though; hearing sentences in the mind's ear seems to underlie skillful writing.)

A rather more challenging exercise highlighted even more clearly the results of different coding strategies. On two tests of spatial reasoning, women generally followed "more concrete, less efficient, methods," whereas men more often used purely spatial methods in a worldless mind's eye. Women more often framed and tried to solve the problem in words. But, the experimenters emphasize, the difference was relative, not absolute. "Both sexes appear to use spatial strategies less effectively and fall back on less organized, less efficient, more concrete methods."[11] It's just that women did so more often.

But the central question remains: Why should men and women approach the same problem differently? Some argue for pure habit. Let's suppose, for example, that infant girls—who will mature two years earlier than boys born the same day—emerge from the womb ever so slightly more mature, ever so slightly more attuned to the human world of language. And if they pay just slightly more attention to their hearing and boys slightly more to their sight, if the girls respond slightly more eagerly to faces and boys slightly more eagerly to objects, their sensitivities might grow into preferences and the preferences into habits of mind.

Julia Sherman, otherwise severely critical of physiological theories of cognitive sex differences, believes that girls arrive with a slight edge in language ability, and that this "bends the twig toward female preference for verbal approaches to problem solution. This bent is then increased by the verbal emphasis of the educational system and by aspects of sex roles that do not encourage girls' development of visual spatial skills."[12] (The schools, of course, will spend a dozen years or more assiduously bringing boys' verbal skills to the higher female standard, but they will neglect to do the same for girls' abilities in math.)

But Sherman begs the question of *how* baby girls become more verbal and baby boys more visual. Ever since the discovery of hormone receptors in the brain, attention has centered on the possible influences of steroids. As Diane McGuinness and Karl Pribram point out, "receptor sites for sex hormones are concentrated largely in . . . the forebrain, focus for the brain systems that control arousal." The same system that controls attention also affects the intensity of perception, they believe. "Possible sex differences might therefore reflect differences not in inherent abilities but in this intensive dimension of experience."[13] If the signals coming over one channel—sight, for example—were simply more vivid than those coming over another—such as sound—an infant would naturally pay them more attention. "This develops the competence of that channel" at the expense of others. Without affecting structure at all, therefore, sex hormones might "bend the twig."

There are other possibilities too; we'll mention a few. Hormones obviously play some role in the two sexes' different maturation rates. And there's evidence that, for reasons unknown, early maturers do better at language tasks and late maturers at visual tasks. Maybe boys—reaching puberty two years later—are simply late maturers?

Or maybe they mature differently from girls? In her family's shoe store, brain researcher Jerre Levy learned that left and right feet grow at different rates; other paired organs also seem to do the same. In boys, right-brain functions mature first, but not in girls, her data suggest. She rejects social causes, arguing that "fetal sex steroids may play a critical role in determining relative maturational rates of the two half-brains and possibly of other bodily regions as well." Children with reversed lateralization—left-handers, who use the left hemisphere for spatial tasks and the right for language— show the same maturation pattern as righties of their own sex. "Relative hemispheric development as a function of sex was independent of the specializations of the two hemispheres," Levy writes, "and the difference in boys and girls cannot, therefore, be attributed to sociocultural factors that might encourage different abilities in male and female children."[14]

And a third possibility has attracted a good deal of attention lately. It seems that a single, mysterious factor ties together migraine headaches, autoimmune diseases, dyslexia, allergies, stuttering, thyroid problems, and left-handedness. Until a casual comment in 1980, of course, no one imagined that so unlikely a catalogue of complaints had anything in common. But then the late Norman Geschwind, a world-recognized brain scientist, urged dyslexia researchers not simply to track that single disability up and down their young patients' family trees. Rather, he suggested, they should find out if the branches hid any other genetic anomalies. And when the trees were shaken, anomalies in plenty came tumbling down. Most common was a single, very suggestive trait: left-handedness. Southpaws suffered learning disabilities at ten times the rate of righties, and immune-system difficulties more than twice as often. Conversely, autoimmune disease sufferers were significantly likelier to be lefties.[15]

This may seem merely a statistical trick, but not to Geschwind. He and his co-workers had spotted a common thread in this strange and unexpected knot of symptoms. Suppose, they suggested, that a single factor retarded the maturation of both the thymus gland, vital to the immune system, and the brain's left hemisphere, responsible for both language ability and the usually dominant right hand. And suppose that this same factor could account for the preponderance of male dyslexics (although there appears to be no corresponding preponderance of male left-handers). This mysterious factor, of course, was none other than that jack of all physiological trades, testosterone. Precisely why the male-making hormone should have this effect—if indeed it does—remains one of the many mysteries that still, a century after Broca, envelop our understanding of the brain. Geschwind's death unfortunately cut short his own efforts, but others remain in hot pursuit.

So what does this tangle of surmises add up to? A good deal, of course, but probably less than the breathless reporting in the popular press would have us believe.

No one, though, can accuse *Science* magazine of a tendency to gush. This venerable organ, ranking among the world's most authoritative learned journals, has impassively observed the scene in mainline research for almost a century. Each week it issues forth with stately, exacting, utterly emotionless, often soporific reports from leading laboratories.

So in June 1984, when the editors made a rare exception, not even the most poker-faced scientific objectivist could find fault. A world-class laboratory, for years in the vanguard of its field, suddenly announced a finding "so unexpected, so incredible, that they literally do not know how to explain it."[16] Now, *Science*'s contributors hardly ever find themselves at a loss for an explanation—if only a provisional one that but partially covers their data. But this was something special. Two months earlier Fernando Nottebohm, the pioneering student of bird brains, had found what scientists look for least, a bit of evidence "contrary to . . . neurobiology dogma." Indeed, the news overturned a principle enshrined in generations of textbooks: "no new neurons are ever formed after infancy."

But Nottebohm had found, incontrovertibly, in the forebrains of both male and female canaries, "a massive birth and death of neurons . . . well after sexual maturity." Exacting tests revealed that old neurons were constantly dying off, and other, new ones constantly taking their place. And if that were not enough, this unheard-of thing was happening right in an area that in "birds and other vertebrates controls complex learned behavior." And if those two surprises were not enough, the turnover was happening on a massive scale. Indeed, Nottebohm admitted, it was the volume of the replacement that he found "the most shocking."

But he saw no possibility of error. These were unmistakably brand-new, genuine neurons, their identity definitely established in a series of experiments Nottebohm calls "a heroic effort." He suspects that sex hormones may play some role in the process, and suspects that the same thing may happen in humans. That's because "from all we know of nervous systems, we get the impression that principles of function are widespread across taxonomic phyla." But we won't know any time soon if it's going on in our heads too; finding the new neurons meant killing the canaries. On that same lab table also perished an established certainty of neurobiology. Comments Nottebohm, "It is so contrary to anything we anticipated that we are not yet prepared to sound intelligent when we talk about it."[17]

Suddenly a leading neuroscientist, clearly in the Nobel contention even before this amazing discovery, waxes incoherent over bird brains! What, then, can ordinary observers make of the state of our knowledge of human brains? Simply this: it's much too early for definite conclusions of any sort.

In the gigantic ocean of the unknown that constitutes the human brain, researchers today stand perhaps calf deep. In Broca's time, of course, the ripples barely reached the instep. In Dax's, scientists had hardly wet a single toe. The past century has seen tremendous progress, but it will take many years and many more surprises before science can swim confidently in this ocean, and still more before it accurately maps the contours of the depths. So it wouldn't hurt to remember that not all informed opinion accepts inborn brain structure and lateralization as bases for distinctly male and female minds. It's harder to find popular reportage of these doubts, though; the bold assertions of definite answers make better copy. A hundred years of astonishments have trained journalists and readers to look to the latest, most confident, and "hardest" pronouncements from laboratories.

In the flood of studies reporting sex differences in cognition and laterality, for example, Warren Ten Houten's modest efforts got very little attention indeed. He wanted to find factors that predict people's approaches to problems, and he found one that quite reliably foretold "left-" or "right-hemisphere" styles of reasoning. Unfortunately for Ten Houten's future celebrity, though, it wasn't a modern favorite like testosterone. Indeed, it was a rather disreputable old-timer that rarely shows its face in respectable company these days. It was not only outdated; it was utterly discredited. The factor was none other than race.

Now, Ten Houten doesn't propose an updated version of Jim Crow. For him, in modern America, membership in a nonwhite racial group reliably correlates with only one other trait: less-than-elite social standing, or, in his favored sociological jargon, a position of "subdominance." The "normally" feminine superiority in left-hemisphere tasks did show up in some women, but only in a select group: the well-educated and well-to-do. Poor people of all races and both sexes got their best scores on "right hemisphere" tasks. Can it be, then, that other university-based researchers have systematically skewed the results by testing the women nearest to hand, undergraduates and graduates enrolled in psychology courses? Would their results differ if they tested the women who sweep up the labs and computer rooms after the researchers and students have gone home?

Clearly, Ten Houten's results suggest habit, not hormones. And in the current state of knowledge, this idea is far from untenable. Of all creatures, Homo sapiens enters the world with the smallest proportion of neurons given over in advance to particular uses. Rats, for example, emerge from the womb with certain connections "hard-wired" and others impossible to achieve. Even after lengthy training, for example, they can't learn to make out-of-the-way associations, like feeling nausea when they hear a loud noise. They can easily associate nausea with bad smells (so, of course, do we, though we can also learn an enormous number of original associations). But in the rat's small and rather rigid brain, the odor-nausea connection makes both neurological and evolutionary sense, as Melvin Konner argues. Signals from the taste centers and the gut converge on the same portion of the brain; signals from the ears go somewhere else entirely.

Bad smells and bad food also go together in the outside world; the rat that makes the connection might well enjoy better health and longer life (not to mention more offspring) than a slower learner. But "natural selection very likely had no opportunity to favor rats who could associate lights and sounds with nausea."[18] They've never, for example, lain on an operating table contemplating the great, glaring lamp overhead and the procedure that lies before them; they've never connected lights with gut-wrenching fear.

But what does the inflexibility of rodent brains teach us about the possibilities of our own? If the capabilities of lower animals predicted the uses we could make of our own neural tissue, we'd spend a lot more effort looking, smelling, listening, and tasting, and a lot less time reading books and debating human nature. Springer and Deutsch point out that "in lower animals most of the brain is devoted to sensory and motor functions; there is little else."[19] We obviously have learned to smell less and think more. And we have mastered feats beyond the comprehension of our close relations, while still using an organ that looks a lot like theirs.

Lewontin, Kamin, and Rose observe:

> Evolutionary processes are parsimonious with structures, pressing them constantly to new purposes rather than radically abandoning them. Feet become hooves or hands, but we do not conclude that hands behave in hooflike ways. The human cerebral cortex [the part we think with] evolved from a structure that in more primitive-brained forebears was largely the organ of olefaction. This does not mean that we think by smelling.[20]

In a certain, quite influential tradition of evolutionary thinking, these three eminent scientists note, "molecules and cellular activity cause behavior."[21] But learning—another name for the influence of experience on neural cells—has some genuine physiological consequences, both in ourselves and other species. Rats raised in an enriched, stimulating environment have a "thicker cortex with larger neurons having more complex dendritic branching, more spines, and increased connectivity," as compared with their fellows reared in boring isolation.[22] A variety of toys, the freedom to explore, and the company of others appear to "produce metabolic processes that help sustain established synaptic connections during the late fetal and postnatal period of neuronal death," when large numbers of brain cells normally die off.[23] That stimulation makes human babies smarter is now a commonplace of enlightened childrearing. That it does so by affecting the physiology of the brain seems logical, but is rather harder to prove.

Luckily, though, nature has carried out the crucial experiment—a detailed study of what happens to normal human brains that undergo radically abnormal experience. This research design begins in the genes and nerve fibers of tiny babies in their mothers' wombs. It continues as they go through their lives—playing, studying, working, growing, loving, raising families—without hearing sound. It's the lot of certain persons, the congenitally deaf, to experience the world almost exclusively through their eyes. But they succeed; they grow into children who can communicate symbolically and adults who can live in a complex society. They succeed by learning to handle information in ways markedly different from the rest of humanity.

It's hard, in fact, to imagine just how different a world their brains have to deal with. What happens when language is a spatial task, when quickly moving hands, not soundwaves, deliver symbolic meaning? Well, one thing that doesn't happen is lateralization of language to one hemisphere and spatial analysis to the other. Numerous tests on deaf persons strongly suggest that the "normal" pattern arises at least partially from experience; "the developmental course of cerebral specialization may depend on the fact and mode of acquisition of a formal language system."[24]

If our present level of brain knowledge perplexes even Fernando Nottebohm, why have reports of sex differences received such intense interest? Well, admit Springer and Deutsch, "from a theoretical standpoint, the significance of sex differences in brain organization is considerable."[25] From a practical standpoint, though, they presently see almost no significance. We can't confidently extrapolate to normal men and women from the atypical brains of persons who suffer epilepsy so severe that only commissurotomy brings relief. We certainly can't make any predictions about any individual's abilities based on sex alone.

We can't even draw consistent conclusions from theory. Women apparently excel in such left-hemisphere properties as verbal fluency, but not in such left-hemisphere properties as linear reasoning. Men seem to lead in such right-hemisphere techniques as spatial analysis, but not in such right hemisphere qualities as intuition. Experiments have observed a high "tactile sensitivity" (or delicate touch) in women. Researchers have used this to explain feminine superiority in "clerical tasks" like typing, handicrafts like embroidery, and the delicate but repetitive work of the laboratory assistant. Somehow, though, these same superiorities rarely flower into virtuosity on the violin or prowess at brain surgery. (Even typing was a "technical," masculine skill, not a "clerical" feminine one, when, a century ago, the first professional typists used their day's very highest technology.)

To put the matter simply, we're not completely sure of what we know. Scientists, one of their number has observed, have a strong tendency to explain their results in the terms that their experiments suggest. This bias is an honest one; it flows quite naturally from a philosophic belief in objectivity and the personal conviction of having done one's best. Suppose, for instance, that we want to compare the spatial abilities of male and female rats. We might see which learned a maze faster. If, after numerous trials, the males emerge with fewer "errors," few researchers would resist the strong temptation to say that males simply understand space better than females do. But it's the experiment, not the behavior, that forced this conclusion. In human terms, an "error" is a mistake, a misstep on the way to an intended result. But in the experiment's terms, it's merely a turn into a blind alley. Now, female rats in general move around more than males; they make more turns, both correct and incorrect. But this fact didn't figure in the experimental design; not surprisingly, it rarely shows up in discussions of results either.

Fernando Nottebohm muses:

> In our old-fashioned manner, we still tend to think of the male and female sexes as two alternative archetypic forms. This is useful enough for purposes of establishing genetic sex or gross morphology of gonads and reproductive organs. In terms of behavioral phenotypes, some males are more "masculine" than others and some females are remarkably masculine. In this behavioral sense there may be a continuum, and the "maleness" or "femaleness" of the

brain may be more closely linked to this continuum than
to genetic sex.[26]

Thus, he suggests, "variability in measures of hemispheric functioning may be influenced by the shortcomings in sexual typing."
He certainly doesn't counsel abandoning the study of sex differences, or even the search for physiological bases. He suggests perhaps a bit more modesty in interpreting the results.

Which brings us back to where we began—the scientists listening
to Dax with their minds already made up by what they thought of
Gall. In the field of sex differences in the brain, one bemused researcher notes, "Any conclusions rest on one's choice of which
studies to emphasize and which to ignore." Indeed, this whole debate resembles nothing so much as a scientific Rorshach test—an
array of tantalizing, evocative possibilities, and still so undefined
that it tells us much more about the interests, values, and beliefs of
the researchers than it does about the true nature of human gender.

IV

WHAT ARE MALES AND FEMALES FOR?

11

Uses of the Past

Now it's time to make some sense out of all the facts and theories. Many things about hemispheres, hormones, bones, gonads, and cells have already come clear. Less clear is what these things tell us about men and women living in the United States in the last sixth of the twentieth century. In this chapter and the next, we'll try to draw these many lines of argument into a few coherent skeins of meaning. We'll try to see what our genetic and physiological past implies for our social and political present—and future.

At first glance, that looks easy. "Natural selection," writes a primate behavior expert, "of course, is the key." Many of the thinkers we've considered strongly agree. They see our evolutionary past as a series of narrowing options; over eons, our species became better and better suited to a particular style of life, our chromosomes more and more concentrated with useful traits. The choices made then, they assume, limit, even dictate, the choices possible now.

And if those choices mean constricted possibilities for half of humanity, then that, they argue, is no one's fault, but only the unconscious, remorseless working of natural law. Two natural laws, actually: evolution proposes, genetics disposes. Natural selection makes refined choices among behaviors, they argue; heredity then imposes them on individual lives. But is this the way it really works? Our primatologist has his doubts; he continues: "The door which [natural selection] opens, unfortunately, reveals a maze."[1]

A peek behind that door shows just how tortuous the maze really is. A generation ago, the English molecular biologist Sydney Brenner decided to solve one portion of the puzzle; he wanted to understand "the genetics and biochemistry of control mechanisms in cellular development," to lay bare the code and program that guide the building of a living thing. And he proposed a singularly audacious way of finding out: he would document the complete natural history of every cell in an organism's body. If he followed a creature from single-celled gamete to normal adulthood, he reasoned, he'd know where every cell came from and how and when it took up its chores. He'd see genetics in action, watch a genetic blueprint become living tissue. Even considering the modest scale of his chosen subject, the tiny worm *Caenorhabditis elegans,* the scheme was breathtaking.

Today, two decades later, the worm's 959 cells, including its 302-cell nervous system, are the best-understood multicelled system in the world. As *Science* magazine observed, "Brenner and his associates now know the complete developmental history of every one of those cells and can describe every connection within the nervous system."[2] They also know a great many things that can and do go wrong as a mass of cells works at becoming a *C. elegans;* they've followed particular mutations to specific results throughout the creature's "mercifully short 3.5-day life cycle." But they still haven't tracked down what they set out to find: a unified control mechanism.

But that wasn't for lack of skill or perseverance; even a researcher as bold and determined as Brenner can't find what may not be there. When his team started, the best thinking of the time told them to look for an orderly process of growth, a well-planned garden growing under efficient genetic husbandry. But instead of neat rows of plants budding toward a certain harvest, they found a tangled little forest thicket, a slapdash procession of seemingly uncoordinated, makeshift, even random, events that usually resulted in a *C. elegans.* They simply didn't locate any single overall blueprint hiding in the genes, just waiting to be deciphered into worm after well-wrought worm.

They expected that the procedures for building the organs would be reasonably predictable. Instead they watched a long series of coincidences and surprises; the cells simply didn't act with what humans regard as logic. They just didn't divide or combine in a straightforward, workmanlike manner. Organs didn't always grow out of the likely-seeming ancestor cells. "Structures are often assembled piecemeal, with the coming together of cells from several lineages. And, most surprising of all, symmetrical structures are just as likely as not to be constructed in an entirely unpredictable, asymmetrical manner."[3]

It may be, some scientists suggest, that a worm isn't constructed like a building at all, but grown like a forest. Still, life in the woods, though impromptu, isn't wholly lawless. After a forest fire, for example, life returns to the scorched ground in a particular order well known to ecologists. Various plants and animals invade the suddenly uncrowded habitat and establish themselves on a fairly predictable schedule. The new communities of grasses and shrubs and trees even pass through a set of well recognized stages. And eventually, over many years, they will duplicate the kind of forest that stood before the catastrophe.

But does this imply that there exists somewhere an overall "plan" for forest growth? Is the decades-long series of encroachments by grasses, shrubs, smaller and then larger trees; by funguses, insects, birds, mammals, and reptiles, "coded" somewhere? Do someone's genes carry it whole? Clearly not; only individual plants and animals contain genetic material. And if an observer watched a forest with Brenner's care, he'd see no grand scheme, only a procession of apparently random events with causes often unrelated to forest building. Seeds would blow or fall from surrounding vegetation. Birds or squirrels or insects would carry others in. And day after day, most of them would fail to root on the charred forest floor.

But some would sprout and grow, and a few of them even thrive. All manner of fauna, meanwhile, would amble or slither or flap through the area. They would fight rivals, hunt for food, find nesting spots, hide their caches of food, defecate. They, too, would gradually, subtly, change the place. Some individuals would survive and stay on, but most would perish. And all that would "control" this series of events is the coincidence of many creatures needing what this particular spot of ground—this combination of soil acidity, drainage, sunlight, rainfall, temperature, and nearby life forms

—can provide. And so an infinite number of related and even inter-dependent—but causally separate—events would grow a forest. Ecologist Gunter Stent calls this kind of process a "historical cascade." And obviously, the "plan" that makes forests renew themselves in set stages is not "coded" anywhere; it's an abstraction that scientists have imposed on millions of separate events.

But it's no accident that we try to find order in happenstance, Brenner believes. "We tend to be more at home with hierarchical structures and sequential processes and it is common to find these in many models of development and its genetic control," he observes.[4] This is increasingly true as the computer has become a powerful metaphor for natural processes. The computer may not follow nature's way, but it offers us the opportunity to explore many complicated natural events. Through computer simulation we can witness, for example, a forest growing from scorched ground to a mature stand of second-growth trees in minutes, not generations. But this very speed comes at a subtle but significant cost: it can bias us toward a misleading presumption of order. Computers mimic, even predict, outcomes. That doesn't mean, though, that they accurately mirror the intermediate steps as they naturally occur. Computers work by the orderly, systematic logic of binary systems. They also cost a lot to program and run. And so they press toward straightforward, logical, efficient conclusions to problems.

But a growing worm seems rather to resemble the advancing forest. In the woods, some seeds and animals happen to alight in places where they can grow; they become founders of new communities; less fortunate individuals simply wither into the forest floor. Likewise, the growing cells of *C. elegans* harbor countless separate events, and many embryos never become completed worms. (One third of all *human* embryos fail to complete a crucial step in the first weeks of life.) Some embryonic cells, for example, diffuse particular molecules needed for biochemical reactions elsewhere. Like the lucky seeds, some of the molecules may well alight on "appropriate binding sites" and take part in the reactions that build the organism. Others wander off where they're not needed or arrive too late to participate; they "are simply ignored." As in the forest, growth takes the form of a cascade, not a blueprint. "Unlike computer programming," Brenner says, "natural selection is cheap and has plenty of time to work.'"[5] It is cheap in the sense that seeds, cells, molecules cost little and occur in immense quantities. It has plenty of time to work because evolutionary time is endless. No cost accountants demand efficiency. No overseer keeps track of the near misses. And thus, Brenner believes, unlike the sleek models produced by mathematical theory, "Anything produced by evolution is bound to be a bit of a mess."

"A bit of a mess," of course, is not the same as total chaos. Saying that creatures grow themselves like forests rather than run themselves like computer programs doesn't mean that there is no system to development or that the human mind can't encompass it. But it does mean that you can't "explain the properties of complex wholes —molecules say, or societies—in terms of the units of which those molecules or societies are composed."[6] That sort of old-fashioned reductionism won't explain a single worm, much less the human species in its relationship with nature and with culture.

To understand the growth of secondary forests, we need to know that insects, birds, and mammals collect and hide seeds. But the life cycle of bluejays and the dietary habits of chipmunks give no real insight into the survival of stands of trees. That we must study separately and in its own terms. Nor can we expect to predict the gender relationships in human societies by understanding a prototype of human physiology. We can't even always predict the innards of a 900-cell worm by understanding its genes. Each is on a different conceptual level; each requires its own form of analysis. None carries the "program" for the others.

But we still have to achieve this complex understanding within a framework of evolutionary theory. It is still true, it always has and always will be true, that change occurs in living things through changes in the representation of genes from generation to generation. It is also true that natural selection alters the balance of genes by altering the survival and reproduction rates of various types of individuals. But it is not true that these things work according to easily discernible plans, or with the efficiency of mathematical models. It is not true that evolution drives toward perfectly adapted specimens with genes chosen "for" particular ends. Indeed, "evolutionary geneticists are in serious doubt about what fraction of evolutionary change is the result of natural selection for specific characters."[7]

We need above all to keep our analytical levels straight. At the level of the forest or the whole worm, one can certainly speak of orderly systems. Second-growth stands of trees and *C. elegans* clearly both follow recognized life courses. But at the level of the seed-bearing squirrel or the individual cell, those life courses are harder to discern. The higher level of abstraction does not govern events at the lower one, nor do events at the lower level determine events at the higher. No thought of future pines or oaks impels the squirrel to hide, and then forget about, caches of nuts. No considerations of animal appetites make abandoned acorns sprout into seedlings.

In just the same way, we must think clearly about human beings and the human species. A great abstraction like natural selection imposes a conceptual order on the cascading billions of individual events that compose the life of the human species. But it doesn't impose direction on individual lives. They will end by illness or accident or in childbirth or old age for reasons of their own, for reasons involving choice, fate, and circumstance.

Nor does another great abstraction, evolution, necessarily govern the birth and growth of any individual human. Homo sapiens walk upright, talk, and bear their young live. But countless humans will be born today, tomorrow, and every day who lack any or all of those abilities, and none of them is any less a full member of our species, any less a full product of the natural selection and evolution that shaped our species' gene pool. Those two great abstractions describe events at the level of the forest; we live at the level of the birds. We certainly can't predict the fate or behavior of any person or group of persons from knowing the general nature of their genes.

So, in the end, we may know rather less about the workings of evolution in human life than many influential theorists believe that we do. And we certainly know less, as the previous chapters have demonstrated, about the condition of our early forebears than many wishful reconstructions imply that we do. We know a good deal less about the circumstances and forces that made us human and shaped the nature of our humanity than currently fashionable dicta of biological determinism require. But to say that we know less than we thought is not to say that we know nothing.

We do know enough for some judicious guesses, but for those we have to look beyond the peculiarities of our own twentieth-century lives in our own male-dominant society. We have to be open to the experiences of men and women in other times and places, willing to accept their experiences as validly lived examples of human possibilities equal to our own. And this, learned biophysiologist Estelle Ramey, can be rather harder than it looks.

For over a decade, she and associates at the Georgetown University School of Medicine have been investigating one of the most puzzling of modern sexual dimorphisms: why women on average live longer than men. (It's not clear that this was always the case; childbirth used to be a major killer of women in their prime.) She's not interested, as most researchers seem to be, in why men die sooner than women; she wants to know why—which is to say, how —"females of every species resist stress better than the male." For her, this is a highly significant difference, pregnant with possibilities for lengthening both female and male lives, but one generally overlooked. "When I mentioned this to some of my male colleagues, who are all aware of the statistics that women outlive men by about eight years at the present time, I got some responses that were repeated too often to be ignored," she reports. "Oh, well, maybe I'd rather not know," they would say. After a time, Ramey's studies strongly implicated testosterone as a major culprit that "hastens men to an early death. The other answer I sometimes got was 'I guess you'd like to castrate all men.' "[8]

Keep in mind that Ramey's colleagues staff a major medical school, work at the edge of scientific knowledge, and spend their careers trying to extend life. And yet, she says, a prestigious—and typical—search for predictive signs of heart disease exhaustively examined six hundred men and no women. "They had a well-funded study on heart failure. They never studied heart success." At last, the researchers agreed to take in two hundred fifty female subjects as well. "One of the chief investigators was so furious that he said in a meeting, 'We have been trying to find out how to keep men alive longer. Maybe by taking women into the study we can find out how to kill them off faster.' "

Over the years, Ramey's research has taught her many things about survival. For example, she no longer marvels that information potentially useful in saving many lives meets with such resistance. There's a good—or at least an explanatory—reason: "When that man said to me 'Maybe I'd rather not know,' he was talking about something bred into the bone of society. How could women be superior to men in any respect? When I asked the question of a fellow professor at a medical school, he said, 'Everyone knows why women live longer than men; they don't work as hard.' "9

She thinks the real answer lies in differential concentrations of hormones, but at this point that's still only a belief. Two things she *knows* are that scientists don't always ask their questions without bias, and how they construct a question largely determines the answer. Nowhere is this truer than in questions about gender.

Reasoning about the human species has traditionally consisted of reasoning about males. Generations of medical texts take the male body—a minority of our species—as the human norm. The female body, with its cycles, its distinctive hormonal and chemical balances, its own tolerances and susceptibilities, constituted a special case, not a fully equal variant of humanness.

Most reasoning about the origins of human traits, therefore, has been reasoning about the traits of men. Modern writers, especially those concerned with sexuality, pay lip service and sometimes more to the idea that natural selection treats the two sexes differently. But the notion persists that the traits of male adulthood are the ultimate goals of evolution and thus accurately reflect the trend of natural selection. Thus, as we've seen, most writers theorized that men are taller than women because natural selection chooses for height among fighters. Similarly, men have more lateralized brains because natural selection chooses for better spatial ability, perhaps needed to throw spears.

In both these cases, of course, females represent something less than the culmination of human possibility, which—as in traditional Christian theology—is exclusively male. But the same facts, viewed from a different standpoint, form an entirely different landscape of opportunity and reality. If we take seriously the notion that the two sexes face different selective pressures, our picture's entire perspective changes. In the next chapter, we bring it into focus.

12

The Meaning of Gender

The small face stares from the magazine page or the TV screen, pinched, ashen, the eyes enormous and hollow above the cavernous cheeks. We've seen many such images of privation and despair. We've read the captions or heard the announcers: Carlitos or Kwame or Krishna will die without our help. The need is urgent; a brother or sister has already succumbed to hunger and disease, a parent hangs between life and death. But there is still time for a modest monthly contribution—less than our daily coffee break—to save him. While we live in comfort and safety, can we permit the aberration of this starving child? Can we deny him the birthright of security and hope that rightly belongs to all children?

But our good intentions quickly collide with reality. Try though we might to feed the hungry, to innoculate the vulnerable, we can't make good the implicit promise. There simply isn't enough vaccine or surplus grain in all the world to change a harsh truth about the human condition: except in a very few times and places, a healthy childhood and active adulthood have not been anyone's automatic birthright. We don't now, for example, and probably never will know, enough about the lives of our distant forebears to understand fully the selective pressures (i.e., causes of premature death) that they faced. But we do know a dolorous fact, and it can vastly clarify our thinking. Darlington stated it chapters ago: most of the human beings ever born have not lived long enough to reproduce.

"Nearly everything that is said, written, or thought about children now takes it for granted that children will survive," observes Ann Dally in her shrewd study of the mythology of motherhood.[1] Only that assumption gives the ad its outrage and our age its pervading guilt over intractable poverty. Dickens railed against his age because it assumed nothing of the sort. Indeed, this belief underlies more than our attitudes toward the poor. Our society's small families and intensive, deeply child-centered rearing, our almost universal bias toward controlling fertility, make no sense without the belief that once born, a child has a very good chance of living to adulthood. Nor does much modern thinking about gender. For more than two generations now, in the social circles from which evolutionary thinkers are drawn, the death of a child has been a tragic, and often avoidable, aberration.

But it hasn't always been so. Only in this century, and among a group of societies privileged beyond the dreams of former potentates, has death become an event that mainly befalls the mature. Even now, among the Bushmen—who, of all living peoples, most closely resemble the earliest humans—"peak mortality . . . occurs before the age of five."[2] Throughout the developing world today, and throughout the presently developed world until a mere historical moment ago, death reaped a constant harvest of little children. In much of the world a child born today has less than a fifty-fifty chance of reaching what we consider school age. In eighteenth-century Britain, one child in four died before its first birthday. Even royal families struggled to assure a single living heir. The whole history of Tudor Britain pivoted on Henry VIII's inability to produce a healthy crown prince.

In the earliest days in America, then a poor community on a hostile frontier, things may well have been worse. In one colonial generation, for example, the Sewall and Mather families, social leaders of their time, produced twenty-eight children. Only three outlived their fathers. Of Cotton Mather's fourteen offspring, seven died shortly after birth, one at age two, and five in their twenties. Cotton's father bore the Christian name Increase; this obviously embodied his parents' fond hope, not their realistic expectation.

And his parents knew that the chief obstacle to his success wasn't the difficulty of conceiving children, or even the dangers of bearing them, but the long odds against keeping them alive. And this has been true for nearly all of human history. In a world of mortal danger, whether on the African savannah, the Kalahari desert, or Plymouth Plantation, "the adaptiveness of child behavior for survival *as a child* is clearly as important as its function as a prelude to adulthood" (emphasis added).[3] But most of the individuals who die in childhood never even live long enough to act on their own, adaptively or not. The care given to infants, in short, may very well determine who lives and who dies. And because—as all theorists of every stripe readily agree—the responsibility for childcare falls first to women, the quality of mothering early in life weighs heavily in ultimate "fitness."

That mothering can make a real difference has received very little theoretical attention. Men who write about childcare without having tried it see mothercare as "instinctive" and "emotional" and therefore easy, mindless, "natural," and automatic. They've long ignored the amount of knowledge, skill, devotion, and effort needed to keep a child alive in most of the circumstances that human beings have had to endure. Their easy assumption that "nurturing" consists of hugs and baby talk obscures the much greater need to provide sufficient wholesome food, potable water, clean clothing, and tolerable shelter. They know nothing of the judgment and stamina it takes to nurse a young child through the recurrent serious illnesses that still plague even the pampered young of the developed world.

That effective mothering clearly makes a difference in that most crucial of adaptive abilities, survival, shows clearly in American demographic data. To take one simple example, between 1911 and 1916, Jewish immigrants living as poor newcomers in crowded tenements had an infant mortality rate of 54 per 1,000. Native-born whites, often living in rather more favorable conditions, had the next lowest rate, 94. Other foreign-born whites, many of them slums residents, had a rate of 127. And the nation's poorest and most deprived families, the blacks, lost 154 of every thousand babies born alive.[4]

A finer-grained analysis more clearly isolates the effects of mothering. In those days, many infant deaths—from defects, from birth-related infections, from labor gone disastrously wrong—simply exceeded the capacities of medical science. But against many others,

meticulous mothering had a fighting chance. Many diseases go easier on well-fed children; others respond reasonably well if the
symptoms are spotted early and acted on immediately. So if mother
could simply cook and scrub diligently enough, and stuff enough
nourishment down young throats, and catch the warning signs of
sickness soon enough, and know what to do in an emergency, her
children's "fitness" rose. And any illness that could be forestalled
by compulsive cleanliness, scrupulous overfeeding, unceasing vigilance, and obsessive interest in symptoms, struck the children of
immigrant Jews less often than other children. From gastric, intesti-
nal, and respiratory infections—still the world's largest killers of
children—they had a death rate half that of native-born whites. So
our old friend, that pushy, vulgar, relentless woman transplanted
from her native *shtetl,* that tireless busybody trained by generations
of European oppression to work as her husband's equal, that con-
noisseur of danger now caricatured as the grotesquely overprotec-
tive "Jewish mother," demonstrates how it is that a woman increases her own, her children's, and her husband's fitness: she fights
hard enough to keep alive the children she bears.

A woman's "fitness" therefore depends less on how many children she bears than on how many children she rears to reproductive
maturity. A man's "fitness" might well depend less on how many
women he impregnates but on how wisely he chooses them—and
on how much help he can give them in their mutual project of
seeing their progeny into the next generation of adults. Understanding this basic symmetry—this equality of the sexes before the
laws of nature—brings a great deal else into focus.

Much theorizing about parenthood has assumed an immense dis-
proportion between the investment of males and of females because
a male copulates for a moment and a woman carries a pregnancy for
nine months and then nurses a child for a year or more. And if
human fitness were only about childbirth, that would be so. Katherine Ralls observes in a widely read paper:

> Unfortunately, parental investment is impossible to mea-
> sure. Male parental investment in mammals may take sev-
> eral forms, such as direct care and provisioning of the
> young; the defense of the young or of the group to which

it belongs, against predators; or the indirect provision of resources by the exclusion of conspecific competitors from an area used by the female and young.[5]

In human foraging societies, male parental involvement takes all these forms, and more. Seeing the female as the indispensable link in species survival solves the mysteries of the human division of labor. Males, suggest anthropologists Jane and Chet Lancaster, undertake the tasks of hunting, mining, smithing, and defense not because of their own natures but because of the nature of the work. All these jobs are unpredictable and dangerous. So is the care and pursuit of large animals. And if a father dies on the job, his loss threatens his children rather less than would the loss of their mother. Women do the less risky jobs that allow them to keep small children nearby, under supervision, and at the breast. By splitting the labor, men and women could gather enough of the right kind of calories to feed themselves and their several "weaned juveniles right up through puberty. . . . This uniquely human arrangement permits humans to reap the benefits of carnivorousness without the costs [unlike the lions, for example, who put their females at risk in hunting while the males defend the young] and furthermore, marks the highest level of male parental investment known among mammals."[6]

But why does it pay a male to stick around and help rear his children? Even in terms of Trivers's theory, it makes good sense. Foraging societies, unlike mathematical models, do not provide a man with a large number of alternative mates. His reputation for reliability must weigh heavily in any woman's (or her parents') decision to choose him. His best chance of leaving numbers of descendents, therefore, is to keep alive those he already has.

The same goes for a woman. Helping children survive is much cheaper, in the strict sense of parental investment, than having new ones. Trivers defined investment as effort invested in one child that cannot be invested in another. Well, as every mother knows, the marginal cost of each child in work, worry, time, and expense falls as the number of children rises. It is much more difficult to cook and clean for one child than for none, but very little more difficult to cook and clean for six children than for five. The more effective a mother, therefore, the less investment (in Trivers's technical sense) that she has in the care of each child. And the more it pays her (and her mate) to maintain and increase that effectiveness.

So what happens to the passive, retiring, irrational, loquacious, sedentary female of legend and fable? What happens to her mythical mind? Could natural selection possibly have been choosing for her? If she had to bear and rear her children in the egalitarian, mobile, industrious, self-reliant society of foragers, obviously not.

The !Kung live what seems to us slaves of clock and paycheck a quite leisurely life. They have no need, or even use, for the ceaseless toil of peasants or industrial workers. But neither have they any surplus of food or possessions or resources that gives one adult power over another. Indeed, even if they could gather food to fill needs beyond the horizon of the next few days, they would have no way of preserving, storing, protecting, or transporting it as they made their nomadic way through the year. And so, being sensible people who can count on fairly reliably filling their modest daily needs, they gather only what they can use in the very near future. So every adult must continually make an adult-sized contribution to the larder. And that's what keeps them egalitarian and independent.

But other ways of making a living do, of course, produce surpluses, and surpluses are the snake that corrupts egalitarian society; they permit one person to control another. And because of the nature of the work they do, men usually come to possess them. (Not always, of course; remember Ancient-Bodied's daughters.) There are also other instructive exceptions; much of present-day Africa is one. In the rural areas, the means of self-sufficiency, if not of wealth, have fallen by default into the hands of women. Throughout the continent, women do the vast bulk of the farm labor, living with their children in countryside almost devoid of adult males. The able-bodied men are in the cities or the mines, living in bachelor squalor on their often meager wages and visiting home only briefly from year to year. So the survival of children here too depends heavily on the initiative and energy of women. But in the world that for thousands of generations shaped our humanness, simply getting enough food into young and old took the enterprise of both sexes.

So what did natural selection design the human female for? For the three abilities she needs to do her part in a foraging life. She must keep herself alive, bear her children, and keep them alive until they can fend for themselves (by which time she often has a new baby at the breast). To meet these challenges, she must profit from good times and weather the bad, withstand recurrent lean seasons, get by on relatively little, adapt to change, withstand stress, and recover from injury. She must be built for economy and durability.

An engineer designing a machine to these specifications would specify two features: compact size and what is technically known as redundancy—the presence of spares or back-ups for essential components. Compactness we've already discussed. Redundancy ensures long-term dependability.

Now every human body is somewhat redundant; we have two kidneys and two lungs, although we can—and some persons do—get along quite adequately on one. But the female body is much more redundant than the male—and in the department that counts most.

Herbert Lansdell of the National Institute of Health was the first to understand this more than twenty years ago. His insights, like Sperry's, grew from attempts to help epileptics cope with the violent mystery of their defective brains; Lansdell did this by removing part of the temporal lobe. After many years of observing the operation's results, he was able to predict what would happen: patients who had lost tissue from the right side of their heads would lose some of their visual and spatial ability, and those minus tissue from the left would have lost some verbal ability.

His prediction proved exact, but only for men, and other researchers made similar findings. Male and female stroke and tumor patients, given the Wechsler test for IQ, showed strikingly divergent results. For men, the location of the lesion strongly influenced abilities. A right-side injury translated into a larger loss in spatial or performance IQ than in verbal IQ. A left-side injury, conversely, damaged his verbal score much more than the performance score.

But the women simply didn't show as much of what researchers call "effect of side of lesion." "Their verbal and nonverbal IQ scores were not significantly different for damage to the left or the right side," Springer and Deutsch report. Damage to the left side of the brain robbed men of speech three times as often as women.[7]

In far less dramatic brain damage, we see the same effect. Now, we know that healthy American men generally score better on spatial tests than do women and not as well on verbal ones, with a larger spread between the male scores. But Marjorie Fabian and her associates assessed the damage from a slow, steady insult to the brain. The scores achieved by alcoholics surprised them, but probably shouldn't surprise us. The men did noticeably poorly on visual and spatial tasks. The women did worse than nonalcoholic controls, but still showed no significant impairments in either space or language. They had none of the specialized, "hemisphere-specific" loss common among men. The female brain, or at least female performance in neurological adversity, simply seems more resilient than the male.

The double brain, Pierre Flor-Henry writes, is an insurance policy, just like our redundant lungs and kidneys. In a crisis, theoretically at least, "each hemisphere can reconstruct the world."[8] The neurological literature teems with reports of persons who shouldn't be able to do what they can, whose injuries or congenital defects make their actual accomplishments theoretically impossible. The immeasurable and saving plasticity of human nerve tissue has permitted persons seemingly condemned to mere vegetation or irremediable idiocy to recapture part or all of their heritage as thinking, learning beings. But these miracles usually happen early in life, before the brain has irrevocably committed itself to a specialized plan.

Two chapters ago we said a lot about these irrevocable commitments. At that time we called them lateralization or cerebral asymmetry, and noted how the male brain's greater concentration of tasks on one side or the other may have given men their small apparent advantage in visual and spatial abilities.

Now we will call these commitments something else. We will call them gambles that sometimes go bad. The double brain may provide insurance against disaster, but only the more symmetrical, less lateralized models carry double indemnity.

To fully understand this truth, we have to enter the world of Carlitos, Kwame, and Krishna, the world where catastrophe is commonplace and prosperity a miracle bestowed by a distant demigod. Our prosperous age admires expertise, so we forget that specialization exacts a heavy price. Brain and cognitive research has so intently pursued the logic of the expert—the assumption that tiny marginal increments in ability are worth big investments—that it has largely ignored any other possibility. In good times—such as the instant of human experience we now enjoy—doing a few things somewhat better than others can pay handsomely. But in bad times —such as the eons of travail that the majority of our predecessors, our contemporaries, and our successors know all their lives—you're better off doing lots of things reasonably well and continuing to do them come what may.

The ability to calculate a trajectory slightly better than someone else will not ordinarily mean the difference between your children starving or surviving. The ability to get up from an accident still able to function very possibly could. The advantage that goes to even the best hunter in a group that customarily shares its meat pales beside the advantage to the person who can fall out of a tree and still walk and talk when consciousness returns.

What evolutionary theorists have not widely considered, but what evolutionary logic plainly suggests, is that the female brain is *not* a less refined version of the male brain. It is *not* a less efficient device for throwing spears or doing calculus. It *is* a highly effective engine of survival. By concentrating so exclusively on the selective pressures imposed by what ancestral men supposedly did, many theorists have ignored what ancestral—and modern—women really do: stay alive long enough to see their genes (and their mates') into the next generation. Men may, as the Wild West theorists believe, have been built in part to fight. But women were given the stamina and flexibility to see to the serious business of our species.

This is a fact with ramifications. "Greater plasticity of the young female brain suggests that females may have a lower incidence of developmental disorders associated with possible left-hemisphere dysfunction," Sandra Witelson observes. "Males do have a higher incidence than females of developmental dyslexia, developmental aphasia, and infantile autism, all of which have language deficits as a

predominant symptom."[9] And this even though the male population is at all ages more "select" than the female because more males
die in every period of life except the very end.[10] Not only is the
female brain more redundant. Thanks to the second X chromosome, every cell of the female body is more redundant.

For one season each year, at rutting time, it's clear what red deer
bucks are built for: to battle their fellows for the attention of the
does. The crash of the antlers, the straining, the heroic struggle,
leave no doubt that in the tournament species at least, the theory of
sexual selection—selection for copulation—holds jarringly true.
Among the males who survive to maturity, the rigors of the joust-
ing ground remorselessly choose for size—and in remorseless disregard of what this will cost the next generation of sons.

And cost them it will, we now conclusively know. Among rats,
among birds, among many species besides deer, scientists have observed that the tournament is not the only regularity in species with
males substantially larger than females. Less noticed than the flashy
spectacle of male competition is another, equally important fact: *the
greater the size difference between the sexes, the greater the number of males
that die young.* And they don't die gallantly, struggling for a mate.
They die obscurely and painfully, in the snows of the winters before they come to their full strength. They succumb not to an adversary's superior strength, but to hunger and disease. Quite simply, they starve because they can't get enough to eat.

Robert Trivers and his associates argue that this happens because
winter-hungry mothers simply stop suckling their young when
things get really bad. But the evidence argues otherwise. Among
deer and other ungulates, the male death rate continues higher
even after weaning, when immature animals of both sexes must
search in the snow to feed themselves. It's also higher in the laboratory when researchers impose an artificial winter. When young rats
are reared on an inadequate diet away from their parents, more of
the males die.

T. H. Clutton-Brock and associates followed a herd of red deer
through the frozen scarcity of winter to find out why. The reason
they found lies deep in the economics of growth: "Sex differences
in growth and metabolism are associated with differences in growth

priorities."[11] When the sexes diverge greatly in size, their different bodies simply choose to spend the same nutrients differently. In birds, the smaller sex fledges first, putting protein and calories into feathers and then mobility. In mammals, young males put on less fat (with the single known exception of the Chinese water deer, whose males are fatter and females larger).

This choice has at least two results. First, young males carry a higher proportion of muscle, which will come in handy should they live long enough to square off against a rival. Secondly and more immediately important, they need a larger and more reliable supply of food. Muscle cells take more feeding than do fat cells, so the males have larger and more costly power plants to keep running, and they have fewer fuel reserves to call upon. (They also have less insulation against the cold.) To put it another way, young males run a greater risk of starving when food supply declines, as mortality figures clearly prove. Selection for large adults can therefore push for growth at the cost of sacrificing many young.

So large size proves a somewhat mixed blessing for the young deer that aspires to leave descendents. It's less of a disadvantage, however, for the son of a dominant mother. The doe able to push others around a bit, adept at elbowing her way into a reasonably adequate diet, not only enjoys better conditions and longer life herself, she also produces more calves and sees more of them to maturity than do her more retiring sisters. If the tournament chooses for large males, the winter chooses for resilient, self-reliant females.

And males who reach the tournament must have survived several winters. They must be hardy, canny specimens who know how to take care of themselves. They probably also used their large size to snatch scarce meals from punier competitors. Males who reach the tournament with a showy rack of antlers must be very good feeders indeed; only a well-fed, quite mature buck has big antlers.

So what, in the end, do all these deer and rats and worms tell us about the fate of men and women? Many things possibly, but two things for sure. First, the fearful symmetry of selection, the fact that winter, hunger, and disease, bear down with equal ferocity on creatures of both sexes, has framed the fateful symmetry of two halves forming a single, whole species. And only symmetrical explanations —theories that account with equal truth for the experience of both sexes—can explain the nature or condition of either.

And secondly, the journey that brought us here is infinitely more convoluted than many popular itineraries suggest. It began from a place we do not know, and passed through lands and times unimaginably foreign to our imaginations.

And something else besides: the path that our species followed is different from that which each individual follows. Donald Symons, early in his long determinist argument, pauses to note: "That a given behavior or behavioral disposition has an ultimate explanation does not imply that the behavior has a particular proximate explanation; specifically, it does not imply that the behavior is unlearned or 'innate.' "[12] The human species has an inborn tendency to learn language, not an inborn knowledge of English or Urdu or Chinese. The human species has a similar inborn tendency to mate and rear young and live in groups; but we still must learn the grammar of courtship and matehood, the syntax of being male and female in the terms of a particular world, the semantics of belonging to a specific society. We must adjust the "accent" of our social selves to the conditions that surround us as precisely as we adjust our spoken accent to our native place.

Only with this distinction between species and individual constantly before us does the human past make sense. Evolution, as grand an abstraction as Stant's advancing forest, occurs at the level of the species and the gene pool. Human life occurs at the level of the individual. In evolutionary terms, each individual is simply one of countless expendable and random drops in the cascade. There is no telling in advance what any human will be like, and those who do not alight on a soil that can support their abilities will simply perish and disappear. This blind sacrifice of individual creatures is what Brenner meant when he said that evolution is cheap.

And it's also, in a certain sense, the meaning of his years of work. If we can't explain a one-millimeter worm in terms of an overriding genetic blueprint, then we can't explain human behavior in those terms either. The fact that most or even all human societies follow a certain practice doesn't prove it's genetic. Until a few years ago every human being who ever lived, in every society everywhere, fell downward rather than upward. But their genes didn't tell them to; gravity did. Only when a handful of people slipped beyond gravity's pull could we see that falling-downness had nothing to do with inherent humanness, or even with human survival. It had to do with humanness confined to planet Earth. In the advanced societies, a fraction of humanity has now slipped beyond the technical and social pulls that have confined us for all of human time. Who knows what possibilities exist on the unexplored social frontiers where we now float free? We've slipped beyond the pull of unwanted reproduction, beyond the pull of peasant labor, beyond seasons, weather, and scarcity.

In just this spirit, Robert Goy and Bruce McEwen, whose names are usually associated with the biochemistry of the brain, caution against putting too much credence in the power of general rules to predict individual cases. "A sexual dimorphism found in one species may not be present in another, or may be present but totally reversed in a third. . . . We must be willing to entertain the possibility that some dimorphisms have neither a genetic nor a hormonal basis."[13]

Think back to those gender-changing worms and fish, choosing between male and female based on which offered a brighter future. This idea "obliges us to tolerate a possible like determination of behavioral characteristics typical to each sex." And Goy and McEwen don't speak of swimming and crawling things, but of our ancient ancestors, and of ourselves. "For some highly social species, like the human being, culture may define the types and limits of sexual dimorphism. Worse luck yet, the individual human being may be forced to learn or acquire those dimorphisms that, like the sex-reversing *Anthias squamipinnis,* the behavior of his or her peers thrusts upon him/her." No less than worms, no less than fishes, do men and women live in a world made partially by their fellows. And so, no less than they, do we make ourselves what we are.

So are there kinds of minds, a "female" and a "male," or only individual, variable human minds, working to make the best of particular, concrete conditions? All that we know of gender and evolution suggests the latter. All that we know of human life suggests that each human mind, working in an intricate web of culture and a surrounding frame of nature, weaves and spins the most advantageous life possible at the place where web and frame converge. And because we're human, myth and belief form central strands of that web.

We can be human only within a society, and as part of a society. Culture is not something added to our human nature, but something without which human nature could not exist. This is a literal truth: remember that fire and language made us physically human. The group helped shape our speaking jaw and thinking brain as surely as the ancient treetops shaped our fingers and fashioned our eyes.

But if this is all so obvious, then why did we need hundreds of pages to discover it? For the very reason that culture is central to all human life. Science, our prodigiously fertile way of knowing, developed in a certain kind of society, in certain social circumstances that fostered certain basic beliefs. We humans arise from foragers; but we Americans arise from desert herders; from warrior empires; from irrigated farming; from peasant agriculture; from a moving, aggressive frontier; from factory-centered industrial labor. From sets of circumstances, in other words, that required certain social arrangements and nourished certain social beliefs. From our Hebrew and Greek and Roman and Teutonic and Anglo-Saxon and frontier and industrial background we have inherited certain beliefs about separateness, about duality, about permanence, about emotion, about property.

As other myths have sprung from those legacies—the ten lost tribes, the Trojan war, Jupiter and Athena, Saint Nicholas, chivalry, self-sufficiency, true womanhood, so has sprung the myth of the two innately different—male and female—minds.

EPILOGUE

"And so," people would ask as I worked on this book, "you mean there are *no* differences between men and women?"

No, that's not what I mean. I've learned many surprising things from this inquiry, but that isn't one of them. Clearly there *are* real differences between the sexes—some, like voices and body hair, didn't even fit into this book; others, like women's longer lifespans (in countries where they don't die young in childbirth), involve basic and complex features of physiology. But all of them, I've come to understand, are really beside the main point.

What I *do* mean is that the real differences between men and women count for much less than many people think—than I thought when I started this project. And in fact, the differences we can pin down easily—the obvious things like height, age at puberty, balding pates, hairy chests—have no bearing at all on the great issue that faces our society: how to apportion power, work, and responsibility in late twentieth-century America. Some of these differences, of course, used to matter quite a lot; who had the stronger shoulders, who might unpredictably become pregnant, clearly meant a great deal when work and warfare ran on muscle power and conception lay as far beyond human control as the weather. But now, when every American fingertip commands horsepower by the thousands, when the neighborhood drugstore and clinic offer freedom from fertility, those two great physical differences weigh very lightly indeed in the social balance.

But surely, I can hear readers object, some other, oft-cited differences still hold sway. Don't assertiveness, logical thinking, the ability to comprehend mathematics and technology clearly count as requisites of modern leadership? Of course they do. But what don't count are simplistic, pseudo-scientific theories of their origins. We have no convincing evidence that sex differences in these traits arise from physiology. Until the biological determinists can account for them as elegantly, rigorously, and persuasively as the cultural argument does—as thus far they've utterly failed to do—we're fools to discard half our pool of talent.

So the question that ought to engage us isn't what differences exist, but what we should do about them. For the symbol-making species, of course, *any* difference can take on social meaning. For nearly five centuries, ambitious Latin American men have cultivated moustaches; hairy upper lips advertise descent from powerful, bearded Conquistadors, not from smooth-cheeked, conquered Aztecs or Incas or Mayas. So even a distinction as trifling, as irrelevant to character and intellect as the number of facial follicles, becomes an emblem of privilege when society chooses to enforce a distinction.

But societies can, if they will, also choose to deny the predictive power of group differences. We Americans have done just that as we've reacted to the Japanese economic challenge. We used to lead the world, but now their cars last longer, their computers cost less, their kids score higher in math. Must Yankee ingenuity bow to Yokahama? Do aptitude tests bare inborn intellectual differences? Can their present advantage mirror deep-seated evolutionary truths? (Did spearing sabertooths in the prehistoric bamboo forests require better marksmanship than felling mammoths on the open European steppe?)

Not for one second does the American scientific or industrial establishment entertain any such possibility. Not one penny do they spend on research to find out. Our leaders haven't wasted time musing on antique aerodynamics, haven't dithered over whether our youngsters' brains have the wrong-shaped commissure. No, they've done what Americans under challenge have always done: taken practical action. They've dispatched experts to examine Japanese classrooms and assembly lines; compared syllabi, not synapses;

found out what these competitors do better so that we can do it better still.

The point is really too obvious to belabor. A proud, powerful, embattled American elite is not about to admit *its* inherent biological inferiority to anybody. It will search a rival's culture for clues to success. It will stand on their heads the arguments long used to justify the elite's own traditional preeminence. In short, it will simply refuse to construe anyone else's superior results as signs of more masterful genes or hormones, of better lateralized hemispheres. And just as we refuse to accept Japan's present ascendency as a biological necessity, so we can, if we want to, also refuse to justify as such woman's present subservience.

It took me a long time, laboring through the scientific literature, to reach this conclusion. I had to abandon a major piece of the intellectual equipment I set out with—the deeply buried belief in the social neutrality of "hard" science; I think I must have absorbed it unconsciously, long ago, from the stirring, mythic tales of heroic microbe hunters and astronomers who stood against the powers both temporal and ecclesiastic. But just as no human adult can ignore an infant's cry, I couldn't help but home in on this truth: knowledge about human possibilities can never be "pure" or completely "objective." That fact had an insistence, a piercing rightness, that I could neither deny nor disregard. I almost wish I had been able to decide otherwise; my opinions would have fit more neatly into headlines, slid more smoothly into news stories.

But deeper even than our human propensity for mythmaking is our human need for consistency, for having all the pieces of the known world fit into a coherent whole. So, in the end, my inquiry comes to its inescapable conclusion: science knows a certain amount about our genes, bodies, hormones, tissues, and brains, about our history and evolution, but almost nothing about the limits of either male or female minds.

NOTES

1. WHAT IS GENDER?

1. S. Gordon, p. 42.
2. Gladue et al., p. 1496.
3. Ibid.
4. Goy and McEwen, p. 17.
5. Ibid.
6. Unger, p. 112.

2. WHY IS GENDER?

1. Bell, p. 26.
2. Ibid., p. 391.
3. Charnov and Bull, p. 829.
4. Ibid.
5. Fricke and Fricke, p. 830.
6. Ibid.
7. Ibid.
8. Goy and McEwen, p. 10.
9. Shapiro and Boulon, p. 73.
10. Hall, p. 7.
11. Redican and Taub, p. 248.
12. Quoted in Piel, p. 2.
13. Lehrman, p. 22.
14. Ibid.
15. Ibid., p. 29.
16. Konner, p. 267.
17. Symons, p. 25.
18. Ibid.
19. Goy and McEwen, p. 12.

3. WHAT DO PEOPLE MAKE OUT OF GENDER?

1. Quoted in Sanday, p. 13.
2. Quoted in B. Harris, p. 5.
3. Sanday, p. 3.
4. Ibid., p. 15.
5. Ibid., p. 15.
6. Ibid., p. 60.
7. Quoted in Giddings, p. 313.
8. Zborowski and Herzog, p. 131.
9. Ibid., p. 132.
10. Sanday, p. 164.
11. Howe and Greenberg, p. 39.
12. Giddings, p. 46.
13. Sanday, p. 68.
14. Leakey, p. 5.
15. Ibid., p. 6.
16. Quoted ibid., p. 8.
17. Quoted ibid., p. 9.
18. Ibid., p. 12.
19. Strathern, p. 50.
20. Ibid., p. 49.
21. Ibid., p. 66.

4. WHAT CONSTITUTES A DIFFERENCE?

1. Strathern, p. 52.
2. Unger, p. 90.
3. Hubbard and Lowe, p. 27.
4. Greenwald, p. 13.
5. Fairweather, p. 233.
6. Burstein, Bank, and Jarvik, p. 294.
7. Oakley, p. 60.
8. Alexander, p. xv.
9. Rose and Rose, p. 486.
10. Kuhn, p. v.
11. Ibid., p. 5.
12. Ibid., p. 24.
13. Ibid., p. viii.
14. Archer and Lloyd, p. 168.
15. Kuhn, p. 38.

5. HOW DO WE KNOW A DIFFERENCE WHEN WE SEE ONE?

1. Quoted in Eisenberg, p. 124.
2. Parsons, p. 3.
3. Quoted in Reynolds, p. 85.
4. Quoted ibid., p. 86.
5. Crook, p. xxv.
6. Lewin, "The Victorians," p. 59.
7. Quoted in Hubbard and Lowe, p. 13.
8. Quoted ibid., p. 55.
9. Quoted in Rosenberg, p. 95.
10. Quoted in Lewin, "Folly," p. 160.
11. Quoted ibid., p. 158.
12. Ibid.
13. Quoted in Rosenberg, p. 92.
14. Quoted ibid.
15. Quoted ibid., p. 93.
16. Quoted in Pleck, p. 208.
17. Lewin, "Folly," p. 161.
18. Quoted ibid., p. 162.
19. Ibid., p. 163.
20. Quoted ibid., p. 166.
21. Pleck, p. 171.

6. DIFFERENT BODIES?

1. Krantz, p. 86.
2. Konner, p. 273.
3. Ralls, p. 268.
4. Ferris, p. 121.
5. Ibid.
6. Rosenblatt and Cunningham, p. 80.
7. Leakey, p. 12.
8. Ibid.
9. Chagnon, p. 33.
10. Ibid.
11. Quoted in Sharff, p. 65.
12. Ibid.
13. Frisch, p. 37.
14. Ibid., p. 40.
15. Warren, p. 19.

16. Bennett and Gurin, p. 153.
17. Rensberger, p. E9.
18. Boake, p. 1061.

7. DIFFERENT SEXUALITY?

1. Quoted in Robinson, p. 163.
2. Ibid., p. 114.
3. Symons, p. v.
4. Ibid.
5. Alexander, p. 37.
6. Quoted in Bleier, *Science,* p. 17.
7. Ibid.
8. Symons, p. 177.
9. Ibid., p. 239.
10. Ibid., p. 246.
11. Ibid.
12. Ibid., p. 300.
13. Ibid., p. 292.
14. Krebs and Davis, p. 262.
15. Ibid., p. 247.
16. Alexander, p. 47.
17. Livingstone, p. 111.
18. Quoted in Giddings, p. 46.
19. Quoted ibid.
20. Quoted ibid.
21. Shoumatoff, p. 51.
22. Darlington, "Evolution" (1983) p. 1960.
23. Ibid., p. 1961.
24. Shoumatoff, p. 53.
25. Darlington, (1983) p. 1960.
26. Lewontin, p. 244.
27. Darlington, (1983) p. 1962.
28. Ibid.
29. Hrdy, p. 133.
30. Ibid.
31. Wrangham, p. 908.
32. Hrdy, p. 134.
33. Ibid., p. 46.
34. Ibid.
35. Rowell, p. 178.
36. Ibid., p. 162.
37. Hrdy, p. 141.
38. Rowell, p. 63.

39. Ibid., p. 72.
40. Bernstein, "Primate Societies," p. 465.
41. Ibid., p. 467.
42. Rowell, p. 131.
43. Johnson, p. 643.
44. Smuts, "Special," p. 266.
45. Rowell, p. 62.
46. Ibid., p. 80.
47. B. Lewin, p. 42.
48. Ibid.
49. Clement et al., p. 105.
50. Blumstein and Schwartz, p. 214.

8. DIFFERENT PERSONALITIES?

1. Seward and Seward, pp. 2–3.
2. Quoted in Bleier, "Social," p. 60.
3. Archer and Lloyd, p. 170.
4. Hubbard and Lowe, p. 30.
5. Shields, p. 269.
6. Rossi, p. 11.
7. Ibid.
8. Ibid., p. 15.
9. Ibid., p. 10.
10. Ibid., p. 8.
11. Ibid.
12. Ibid., p. 13.
13. Berman, p. 686.
14. Ibid., p. 680.
15. Ibid.
16. Lamb and Hwang, p. 7.
17. Lamb, "Origins," p. 192.
18. Bleier, Science, p. 95.
19. Archer, p. 249.
20. Bleier, ibid.
21. Katz and Konner, p. 167.
22. Bleier, ibid.
23. Svare, p. 129.
24. Ebert, p. 122.
25. Ibid.
26. Ibid., p. 124.
27. Rubin et al., p. 1320.
28. Ibid., p. 1319.
29. Unger, p. 63.

30. Frankenhaeuser, "Psychoneuroendocrine Sex Differences," p. 158.
31. Ibid., p. 218.
32. Ibid., p. 161.
33. Rauste-Von Wright et al., p. 369.
34. Frankenhaeuser, ibid., p. 161.
35. Morris, p. 148.
36. Rosenblatt and Cunningham, p. 88.

9. DIFFERENT INTELLECTS?

1. Sherman, *Sex-related*, p. 6.
2. Greenberg, p. 356.
3. Jacklin and Maccoby, p. 183.
4. Fairweather, p. 232.
5. Ibid., p. 233.
6. Benbow and Stanley, "Sex Differences in Mathematical Ability," p. 1262.
7. Fairweather, p. 234.
8. Ibid., p. 258.
9. *Reading in America*, 1978, passim.
10. Fairweather, p. 258.
11. Kipnis, p. 97.
12. Ibid., p. 100.
13. Sherman, ibid., p. 59.
14. L. Harris, p. 432.
15. Schratz, p. 265.
16. Turkle, p. 115.
17. Keller, p. 410.
18. Fox, p. 280.
19. Weinraub, p. 1501.
20. Kipnis, p. 110.
21. Helson, "Women," p. 210.
22. Ibid., p. 228.
23. Ibid., p. 217.
24. Tobin-Richards et al., p. 132.
25. Ibid., p. 144.
26. Sherman, ibid., p. 159.
27. Kagan and Moss, p. 221.
28. Kipnis, p. 111.
29. Lewontin, Rose, and Kamin, p. 118.
30. Jensen, p. 205.

10. DIFFERENT BRAINS?

1. Springer and Deutsch, p. 8.
2. Ibid., p. 11.
3. Ibid., p. 127.
4. Flor-Henry, *Cerebral Bases*, p. 10.
5. Ibid., p. 236.
6. Ibid., p. 2.
7. Ibid.
8. Ibid., p. 111.
9. Goleman, p. 49.
10. Lacoste-Utamsing and Holloway, p. 1431.
11. Allen and Hoagland, p. 250.
12. Sherman, *Sex-related*, p. 40.
13. McGuinness and Pribram, p. 10.
14. Levy and Levy, p. 1291.
15. Springer and Deutsch, p. 141.
16. Kolata, "New Neurons," p. 1325.
17. Ibid., p. 1326.
18. Konner, p. 26.
19. Springer and Deutsch, p. 210.
20. Lewontin, Kamin, and Rose, p. 145.
21. Ibid., p. 60.
22. Bleier, "Science," p. 64.
23. Ibid., p. 65.
24. Neville, p. 130.
25. Springer and Deutsch, p. 129.
26. Nottebohm, p. 245.

11. USES OF THE PAST

1. Wrangham, "Ultimate Factors," p. 256.
2. Lewin, "Why Is Development So Illogical?," p. 1327.
3. Ibid.
4. Ibid.
5. Ibid.
6. Ibid.
7. Lewontin, Rose, and Kamin, p. 5.
8. Ramey, p. 75.
9. Ibid., p. 76.

12. THE MEANING OF GENDER

1. Dally, p. 25.
2. Blurton-Jones and Konner, p. 693.
3. Ibid.
4. Patai, p. 412.
5. Ralls, p. 260.
6. Lancaster and Lancaster, p. 193.
7. Springer and Deutsch, p. 177.
8. Flor-Henry, *Cerebral Bases,* p. 12.
9. Witelson, "Sex," p. 426.
10. Sherman, *Sex-related,* p. 28.
11. Clutton-Brock, Albon, and Guiness, "Parental," p. 131.
12. Symons, p. 9.
13. Goy and McEwen, p. 11.

BIBLIOGRAPHY

Abernathy, Virginia. "Dominancy, Feminist Hierarchies, and Heterosexual Dyads." *Behavioral and Brain Sciences,* 4 (1981) 429–30.

Alcock, John. "Beyond the Sociobiology of Sexuality: Predictive Hypotheses." *Behavioral and Brain Sciences,* 3 (1980) 181–82.

Alexander, Richard D. *Darwinism and Human Affairs.* Seattle: University of Washington Press, 1979.

Allen, Mary J., and Randie Hoagland. "Spatial Problem Solving Strategies as Functions of Sex." *Perceptual and Motor Skills,* 47 (1978) 248–50.

Alzate, Heli. "Sexual Behavior of Unmarried Columbia University Students: A Five-Year Follow-Up." *Archives of Sexual Behavior,* 13 (1984) 99–120.

Andersson, M., et al. "Chromosome Y-Specific DNA is Transferred to the Short Arm of X Chromosome in Human XX Males." *Science,* 233 (15 August 1986) 786–88.

Annett, Marian. "Sex Differences in Laterality: Meaningfulness versus Reliability." *Behavioral and Brain Sciences* 3 (1980) 227–28.

Archer, John. "Biological Explanations of Psychological Sex Differences," pp. 241–66 in Lloyd and Archer.

———, and Barbara Lloyd. "Sex Differences: Biological and Social Interaction," pp. 165–77 in Roger Lewin, ed., *Child Alive!* New York: Anchor Press/Doubleday, 1975.

Arendash, Gary W., and Roger A. Grosky. "Enhancement of Sexual Behavior in Female Rats by Neonatal Transplantation of Brain Tissue from Males." *Science,* 217 (24 September 1982) 1276–78.

Aronson, Lester R., ed. *Development and Evolution of Behavior.* San Francisco: W. H. Freeman, 1970.

Ayoub, David H., William F. Greenough, and Janice H. Juraska. "Sex Differences in Dendritic Structure in the Preoptic Area of the Juvenile Macaque Monkey Brain." *Science,* 219 (14 January 1983) 197–98.

Baker, Susan W. "Biological Influences on Human Sex and Gender," pp. 175–91 in Stimpson and Person.

Banks, Edwin M. "Dominance and Behavioral Primatologists: A Case of Typological Thinking." *Behavioral and Brain Sciences,* 4 (1981) 432–33.

Bardin, C. Wayne, and James F. Catterall. "Testosterone: A Major Determinant of Extragenital Sexual Dimorphism." *Science,* 211 (20 March 1984) 112.

Bateson, Patrick. "Uncritical Behavior and Insensitive Sociobiology." *Behavioral and Brain Sciences,* 6 (1983) 102–3.

Beckwith, Barabara. "How Magazines Cover Sex Difference Research." *Science for the People,* 16/4 (July-August 1984) 18–23.

Bell, Graham. *The Masterpiece of Nature: The Evolution and Genetics of Sexuality.* Berkeley: University of California Press, 1982.

Benbow, Camilla Persson, and Julian C. Stanley. "Sex Differences in Mathematical Ability: Fact or Artifact?" *Science,* 210 (1980) 1262–64.

————. "Sex Differences in Mathematical Reasoning: More Facts." *Science,* 222 (1983) 1029–31.

Bennett, William, and Joel Gurin. *The Dieter's Dilemma: Eating Less and Weighing More.* New York: Basic Books, 1982.

Berman, Phyllis W. "Are Women More Responsive than Men to the Young? A Review of Developmental and Situational Variables." *Psychological Bulletin,* 88 (1980) 668–95.

Bernard, Jessie. "The Good-Provider Role: Its Rise and Fall." *American Psychologist,* 36 (1981) 1–2.

Bernstein, Irwin S. "Dominance, Aggression and Reproduction in Primate Societies." *Journal of Theoretical Biology,* 60 (1976) 459–72.

————. "Dominance: The Baby and the Bathwater." *Behavioral and Brain Sciences,* 5 (1981) 419–29.

————. "Motives, Intentions, Science, and Sex." *Behavioral and Brain Sciences,* 3 (1980) 182–83.

Bittles, A. H. "The Intensity of Human Inbreeding Depression." *Behavioral and Brain Sciences,* 6 (1983) 103–4.

Blanchard, Roy, James G. McConkey, Vincent Roper, and Betty Steiner. "Measuring Physical Aggressiveness in Heterosexual, Homosexual, and Transsexual Males." *Archives of Sexual Behavior,* 12 (1983) 511–24.

Bleier, Ruth. *Science and Gender: A Critique of Biology and its Theories on Women.* New York: Pergamon Press, 1984.

————. "Social and Political Bias in Science: An Examination of Animal Studies and their Generalizations to Human Behaviors and Evolution," pp. 49–70 in Hubbard and Lowe, *Genes and Gender II.*

Block, Jeanne H. "Differential Premises Arising from Differential Socialization of the Sexes: Some Conjectures." *Child Development,* 54 (1983) 1225–54.

Blumstein, Philip, and Pepper Schwartz. *American Couples: Money, Work, and Sex.* New York: William Morrow, 1983.

Blurton-Jones, N. G., and M. J. Konner. "Sex Differences in Behavior of London and Bushman Children," pp. 689–750 in Richard P. Michael and John H. Crook, eds., *Comparative Ecology and Behavior of Primates.* London: Academic Press, 1973.

Boake, Christine R. B. "Genetic Consequences of Mate Choice: A Quantitative Genetic Method for Testing Sexual Selection Theory." *Science,* 227 (1 March 1985) 1061–63.

Brooks-Gunn, Jeanne, and Anne C. Petersen. *Girls at Puberty: Biological and Psychosocial Perspectives.* New York: Plenum, 1983.

Brooks-Gunn, Jeanne, and Diane N. Ruble. "The Experience of Menarche from a Developmental Perspective," pp. 155–79 in Brooks-Gunn and Petersen.

Brownmiller, Susan. *Femininity.* New York: Linden Press/Simon and Schuster, 1984.

Bryden, M. P. "Sex Differences in Brain Organization: Different Brains or Different Strategies?" *Behavioral and Brain Sciences,* 3 (1980) 230–31.

Bullough, Vern L. "Age at Menarche: A Misunderstanding." *Science,* 213 (17 July 1981) 365–66.

Callahan, Carolyn M. "Superior Abilities," pp. 49–86 in *Handbook of Special Education,* James M. Kauffman and Daniel P. Hallahan, eds. Englewood Cliffs, N.J.: Prentice-Hall, 1981.

Chagnon, Napoleon A. *Yanomamo: The Fierce People.* New York: Holt, Rinehart and Winston, 1968.

Chapais, Bernard. "Male Dominance and Reproductive Activity in Rhesus Monkeys," pp. 267–71 in Hinde.

Charvov, Eric L., and James Bull. "When Is Sex Environmentally Determined?" *Nature,* 222 (28 April 1977) 828–30.

Cheyney, D., R. Seyfarth, and B. Smuts. "Social Relationships and Social Cognition in Nonhuman Primates." *Science,* 234 (12 December 1986) 1361–65.

Clement, Ulrich, Gunter Schmidt, and Margaret Kruse. "Changes in Sex Differences in Sexual Behavior: A Replication of a Study on West German Students (1966–81)." *Archives of Sexual Behavior,* 13 (1984) 99–120.

Clutton-Brock, T. H., S. D. Albon, and E. F. Guiness. "Maternal Dominance, Breeding Success, and Birth Sex Ratios in Red Deer." *Nature,* 308 (22 March 1984) 358–60.

———. "Parental Investment and Sex Differences in Juvenile Mortality in Birds and Animals." *Nature,* 313 (18 January 1985) 10.

Cohen, Donna, and Frances Wilkie. "Sex-Related Differences in Cognition Among the Elderly," pp. 145–59 in Wittig and Petersen.

Coles, Claie D., and M. Johanna Shamp. "Some Sexual, Personality, and Demographic Characteristics of Women Readers of Erotic Romances," *Archives of Sexual Behavior,* 13 (1984) 187–209.

Coltheart, Max; Elaine Hull; and Diana Slatter. "Sex Differences in Imagery and Reading," *Nature,* 253 (6 February 1975) 438–40.

Conrad, R. "Profound Deafness as a Psycholinguistic Problem," pp. 145–55 in Gunnar Fant, ed., *International Symposium on Speech Communica-*

tion Ability and Profound Deafness. Washington, D.C.: A. G. Bell Association, 1972.

————. "Short-Term Memory in the Deaf," pp. 247–53 in D. M. Boswell and J. M. Wingrove, eds., *The Handicapped Person in the Community.* London: Tavistock, 1972.

Contratto, Susan. "Mother," pp. 226–55 in M. Lewin, ed.

Crandall, Virginia C. and Esther S. Battle. "The Antecedents and Adult Correlates of Academic and Intellectual Achievement Effort," pp. 36–93 in John P. Hill, ed., *Symposia on Child Psychology,* Minneapolis: University of Minnesota Press, 1970.

Crook, J. H. "Introduction—Social Behavior and Ethology," pp. xxi–xl in *Social Behavior in Birds and Mammals,* J. H. Crook, ed. New York: Academic Press, 1970.

Dally, Ann. *Inventing Motherhood: The Consequences of an Idea.* New York: Schocken Books, 1983.

Daniel, William A., Jr. "Pubertal Changes in Adolescence," pp. 51–71 in Brooks-Gunn and Petersen.

Darlington, Philip J., Jr. "Evolution: Questions for the Modern Theory." *Proceedings of the National Academy of Sciences of the United States,* 78 (July 1981) 4440–43.

————. "Evolution: Questions for the Modern Theory." *Proceedings of the National Academy of Sciences of the United States of America,* 80 (April 1983) 1960–63.

Diamond, Jared M. "Birds of Paradise and the Theory of Sexual Selection." *Nature,* 293 (24 September 1981) 257–58.

Diamond, Milton. "The Biosocial Evolution of Human Sexuality." *Behavioral and Brain Sciences,* 3 (1980) 184–86.

Dickason, Anne. "The Feminine as a Universal," pp. 10–32 in Vetterling-Braggin.

Dimond, Stuart J. "Sex Differences in Brain Organization." *Behavioral and Brain Sciences,* 3 (1980) 234.

Doering, Charles H. "The Endocrine System," pp. 229–71 in *Constancy and Change in Human Development,* Orville G. Brim, Jr., and Jerome Kagan, eds. Cambridge: Harvard University Press, 1980.

Duran, Jane. "Nurture Theories: A Critique," pp. 49–59 in Vetterling-Braggin.

Ehrhardt, Anke A., and Heino F. L. Meyer-Bahlburg. "Effects of Prenatal Sex Hormones on Gender-Related Behavior." *Science,* 211 (20 March 1981) 1312–18.

Eysenck, H. J. "Sociobiology—Standing on One Leg." *Behavioral and Brain Sciences,* 3 (1980) 186.

Fabian, Marjorie, Oscar Parsons, and M. D. Sheldon. "Effects of Gender and Alcoholism on Verbal and Visual-Spatial Learning." *Journal of Nervous and Mental Diseases,* 172 (1984) 16–20.

Fairweather, Hugh. "Sex Differences in Cognition." *Cognition,* 4 (1976) 231–80.

Faust, Margaret S. "Alternative Constructions of Adolescent Growth," pp. 105–25 in Brooks-Gunn and Petersen.

Fausto-Sterling, Anne. *Myths of Gender: Biological Theories About Men and Women.* New York: Basic Books, 1985.

Feldman, David. *Marital Relations, Birth Control, and Abortion in Jewish Law.* New York: Schocken, 1974.

Ferris, Elizabeth A. E. "Sex Differences in Athletic Potential," pp. 117–28 in *Biosocial Aspects of Sport, Journal of Biosocial Science,* Supplement 7, 1981.

Field, Tiffany. "Interaction Behaviors of Primary versus Secondary Caretaker Fathers." *Developmental Psychology,* 14 (1978) 183–84.

Flor-Henry, Pierre. *Cerebral Bases of Psychopathology.* Boston: John Wright-PSG, Inc., 1983.

———. "Evolutionary and Clinical Aspects of Lateralized Sex Differences." *Behavioral and Brain Sciences,* 3 (1980) 235–36.

Fooden, Myra, ed. *Genes and Gender IV: The Second X and Women's Health.* New York: Gordian Press, 1983.

Fox, Lynn H. "The Values of Gifted Youth," pp. 273–84 in Daniel P. Keating, ed., *Intellectual Talent: Research and Development.* Baltimore: Johns Hopkins University Press, 1976.

Frankenhaeuser, Marianne. "Challenge-Control Interaction as Reflection in Sympathetic-Adrenal and Pituitary-Adrenal Activity: Comparison Between the Sexes." *Scandinavian Journal of Psychology,* Supplement 1 (1982) 158–64.

———. "Psychoneuroendocrine Sex Differences in Adaptation to the Psychosocial Environment," pp. 215–25 in *Clinical Psychoneuroendrinology in Reproduction (Proceedings of the Serono Symposia,* vol. 22). New York: Academic Press, 1978.

———, et al. "Sex Differences in Psychoneuroendocrine Reactions to Examination Stress." *Psychosomatic Medicine,* 40 (1978) 334–43.

Freedman, Victoria H. "Update on Genetics," pp. 29–37 in Fooden.

Fricke, Hans, and Simone Fricke. "Monogamy and Sex Change by Aggressive Dominance in Coral Reef Fish." *Nature,* 266 (28 April 1977) 330–32.

Friedl, Ernestine. "Society and Sex Roles," pp. 149–58 in *Conformity and Conflict,* James P. Spradley and David W. McCurdy, eds. Boston: Little, Brown, 1984.

Friedman, Richard C., et al. "Behavior and the Menstrual Cycle," pp. 192–211 in Stimpson and Person.

Frisch, Rose E. "Fatness, Puberty, and Fertility: The Effects of Nutrition and Physical Training on Menarche and Ovulation," pp. 29–49 in Brooks-Gunn and Petersen.

Frodi, Ann M., and Michael E. Lamb. "Sex Differences in Responsiveness to Infants: A Developmental Study of Psychophysiological and Behavioral Aspects." *Child Development,* 49 (1978) 1182–88.

Geis, Gilbert, and Ted L. Huston. "Forcible Rape and Human Sexuality." *Behavioral and Brain Sciences,* 3 (1980) 187.

Giddings, Paula. *When and Where I Enter: The Impact of Black Women on Race and Sex in America.* New York: William Morrow, 1984.

Gladue, B. A., R. Green, and R. E. Hellman. "Neuroendocrine Response to Estrogen and Sexual Orientation." *Science,* 225 (28 September 1984) 1496–99.

Glick, S. D., A. A. Schonfeld, and A. J. Strumpf. "Sex Differences in Brain Asymmetry of the Rodent." *Behavioral and Brain Sciences,* 3 (1980) 236.

Goodale, Jane C. "Gender, Sexuality, and Marriage: A Kaulong Model of Nature and Culture," pp. 119–42 in MacCormack and Strathern.

Gordon, Jon W., and Frank H. Ruddle. "Mammalian Gonadal Determination and Gametogenisis." *Science,* 211 (20 March 1981) 1265–71.

Gordon, Susan. "What's New In Endocrinology? Target: Sex Hormones," pp. 39–49 in Fooden.

Gove, Walter R. "Gender Differences in Mental and Physical Illness: The Effects of Fixed Roles and Nurturant Roles." *Social Science and Medicine,* 19 (1984) 77–91.

Goy, Robert W., and Bruce S. McEwen. *Sexual Differentiation of the Brain.* Cambridge, Mass.: MIT Press, 1980.

Graham, Marilyn F., and Beverly Birns. "Where Are the Women Geniuses?" pp. 291–312 in Claire B. Kopp, ed., *Becoming Female: Perspectives on Development.* New York: Plenum, 1979.

Gray, Patrick. "The Influence of Female Power in Marriage on Sexual Behaviors and Attitudes: A Holocultural Study." *Archives of Sexual Behavior,* 13 (1984) 223–31.

Greenberg, J. "The Sophisticated Sounds of Simians." *Science News,* 127 (8 June 1985) 356.

Greenwald, Anthony G. "Consequences of Prejudice Against the Null Hypothesis." *Psychological Bulletin,* 82 (1975) 1–20.

Gregor, Thomas. "Short People." *Natural History,* 88 (1979) 16–23.

Hacaen, Henry. "Functional Hemispheric Asymmetry and Behavior," pp. 119–42 in *Methods of Inference From Animal to Human Behavior,* Mario von Cranach, ed. Chicago: Aldine, 1976.

Hall, Roberta L. "Introduction: Consequences of Sexuality," pp. 3–10 in Hall, *Sexual Dimorphism.*

———, ed. *Sexual Dimorphism in Homo Sapiens: A Question of Size.* New York: Praeger, 1982.

Hamilton, Margaret E. "Sexual Dimorphism in Skeletal Samples," pp. 107–64 in Hall, *Sexual Dimorphism.*

Hapgood, Fred. *Why Males Exist: An Inquiry into the Evolution of Sex.* New York: William Morrow, 1979.

Harris, Barbara J. "The Power of the Past: History and the Psychology of Women," pp. 1–26 in M. Lewin, *In the Shadow of the Past.*

Harris, Ben. "Give Me a Dozen Healthy Infants," pp. 127–54 in M. Lewin, *In the Shadow of the Past.*

Harris, Lauren Julius. "Sex Differences in Spatial Ability: Possible Environmental Genetic and Neurological Factors," pp. 405–523 in *Asymmetrical Function of the Brain,* Marcel Kinsbourne, ed. New York: Cambridge University Press, 1978.

————. "Sex-Related Differences in Spatial Ability: A Developmental Psychological View," pp. 133–81 in *Becoming Female: Perspectives on Development,* Claire B. Kopp, ed. New York: Plenum, 1979.

Harris, Olivia. "The Power of Signs: Gender, Culture, and the Wild in the Bolivian Andes," pp. 70–95 in MacCormack and Strathern.

Harrison, Beverly Wildung. *Our Right to Choose: Toward a New Ethic of Abortion.* Boston: Beacon Press, 1983.

Harrison, Paul H. "Raising the Wrong Children." *Nature,* 313 (1985) 95–96.

Harvey, Paul J., and Linda Partridge. "When Deviants are Favored: Evolution of Sex Determination." *Nature,* 307 (23 February 1984) 689–91.

Haseltine, Florence P., and Susomo Ohno. "Mechanisms of Gonadal Differentiation." *Science,* 211 (20 March 1981) 1272–77.

Heiman, Julia R. "Selecting for the Sociobiologically Fit." *Behavioral and Brain Sciences,* 3 (1980) 189–90.

Helson, Ravenna. "Sex Differences in Creative Style." *Journal of Personality,* 35 (1967) 214–33.

————. "Women Mathematicians and the Creative Personality." *Journal of Consulting and Clinical Psychology,* 36 (1971) 210–20.

Hinde, Richard A., ed. *Primte Social Relationships: An Integrated Approach.* Sunderland, Mass.: Sinauer, 1983.

Hite, Shere. *The Hite Report: A Nationwide Study of Female Sexuality.* New York: Macmillan Publishing Company, 1976.

Howe, Irving, and Eliezer Greenberg, eds. *A Treasury of Yiddish Stories.* New York: Schocken, 1973.

Hrdy, Sarah Blaffer. *The Woman that Never Evolved.* Cambridge: Harvard University Press, 1981.

Hubbard, Ruth, and Marian Lowe, eds. *Genes and Gender II: Pitfalls in Research on Sex and Gender.* New York: Gordian Press, 1979.

Hubbard, Ruth, and Marian Lowe. "Introduction," pp. 9–34, in Hubbard and Lowe, *Genes and Gender II.*

Hull, Elaine, J. Ken Nishita, and Daniel Bitran. "Prenatal Dopamine-Related Drugs Demasculinize Rats." *Science,* 224 (1 June 1984) 1011–13.

Jensen, Arthur R. *Bias in Mental Testing.* New York: Free Press, 1980.

Johnson, Leslie. "Tactics in Reproduction." *Science,* 229 (16 August 1985) 643–44.

Johnson, Olive, and Carolyn Harley. "Handedness and Sex Differentiation in Cognitive Tests of Brain Laterality." *Cortex,* 16 (1980) 73–82.

Juraska, Janice M., Constance Henderson, and Jutta Muller. "Differential Rearing Experience, Gender, and Radial Maze Performance." *Developmental Biology,* 17 (1984) 209–16.

Kagan, Jerome, and Howard A. Moss. *Birth to Maturity: A Study in Psychological Development.* New York: John Wiley and Sons, 1962.

Kaplan, Alexandra G. "Human Sex-Hormone Abnormalities Viewed from an Androgynous Perspective: A Reconstruction of the World of John Money," pp. 81–91 in Parsons, *Psychobiology.*

Katz, Mary Maxwell, and Melvin J. Konner. "The Role of the Father: An Anthropological Perspective," pp. 155–86 in *The Role of the Father in Child Development,* Michael E. Lamb, ed. New York: John Wiley and Sons, 1981.

Keller, Evelyn Fox. "Gender and Science." *Psychoanalysis and Contemporary Thought,* 1 (1978) 409–33.

Kidd, Kenneth. "The Genetics of Sex and Its Consequences," pp. 401–26 in *Becoming Female: Perspectives on Development,* Claire B. Kopp, ed. New York: Plenum, 1979.

Kipnis, Dorothy McBride. "Intelligence, Occupational Status, and Achievement Orientation," pp. 95–122 in Lloyd and Archer.

Kolata, Gina Bari. "Math and Sex: Are Girls Born With Less Ability?" *Science,* 210 (12 December 1980) 1234–35.

———. "New Neurons Form in Adulthood." *Science,* 224 (22 June 1984) 1325–26.

Konner, Melvin. *The Tangled Wing: Biological Constraints on the Human Spirit.* New York: Holt, Rinehart, and Winston, 1982.

Krantz, Grover. "The Fossil Record of Sex," pp. 85–105 in Hall, *Sexual Dimorphism.*

Krebs, J. P., and N. B. Davis. *An Introduction to Behavioral Ecology.* Sunderland, Mass.: Sinauer, 1981.

Kuhn, Thomas S. *The Structure of Scientific Revolutions* (2nd ed.). *International Encyclopedia of Unified Science,* vol. 2, no. 2. Chicago: University of Chicago Press, 1970.

Lacoste-Utamsing, Christine de, and Ralph L. Holloway. "Sexual Dimorphism in the Human Corpus Callosum." *Science,* 216 (25 June 1982) 1431–32.

Lamb, Michael E. "Early Contact and Maternal-Infant Bonding: One Decade Later." *Pediatrics,* 17 (1982) 763–68.

———. "On the Origins and Implications of Sex Differences in Human Sexuality." *Behavioral and Brain Sciences,* 3 (1980) 192–93.

———, and Carl-Philip Hwang. "Maternal Attachment and Mother-Neonate Bonding: A Critical Review," pp. 1–33 in *Advances in Developmental Psychology,* vol. 2., Michael E. Lamb and Ann L. Brown, eds. Hillsdale, N.J.: Lawrence Erlbaum, 1982.

Lancaster, Chet S. "Sexual Rivalry in Human Inbreeding or Adaptive Co-operation." *Behavioral and Brain Sciences,* 6 (1983) 109–10.

Lancaster, J. B., and C. S. Lancaster. "The Division of Labor and the Evolution of Sexuality." *Behavioral and Brain Sciences,* 3 (1980) 193.

Landau, Barbara, Henry Gleitman, and Elizabeth Spelke. "Spatial Knowledge and Geometric Representation in a Child Blind from Birth." *Science,* 213 (11 September 1981) 1275–77.

Leakey, Richard. *The Making of Mankind: A Five-Program Series about Human Prehistory and Its Implications for Modern Man,* Program no. 5. Kent, Ohio: PTV Publications, 1983.

Lehrman, Daniel S. "Semantic and Conceptual Issues in the Nature-Nurture Problem," pp. 17–53 in Aronson.

Leibowitz, Lila. " 'Universals' and Male Dominance among Primates: A Critical Examination," pp. 35–48 in Hubbard and Lowe.

Lesser, Gerald S., Gordon Fifer, and Donald H. Clark. *Monographs of the Social Research in Child Development,* 30/4 (1965).

Leutenegger, Walter. "Sexual Dimorphism in Nonhuman Primates," pp. 11–36 in Hall, *Sexual Dimorphism.*

Levy, Jerre, and Jerome Levy. "Human Lateralization from Head to Foot: Sex-Related Factors." *Science,* 200 (16 June 1978) 1291–92.

Lewin, Bo. "The Adolescent Boy and Girl: First and Other Early Experiences with Intercourse from a Representative Sample of Swedish Adolescents." *Archives of Sexual Behavior,* 11 (1982) 417–28.

Lewin, Miriam. "Psychology Measures Femininity, 2: From '13 Gay Men' to the Instrumental-Expressive Distinction," pp. 180–204 in M. Lewin, *In the Shadow of the Past.*

———. " 'Rather Worse than Folly?' Psychology Measures Femininity and Masculinity, 1," pp. 155–78 in M. Lewin, *In the Shadow of the Past.*

———. "The Victorians, the Psychologists, and Psychic Birth Control," pp. 39–78 in M. Lewin, *In the Shadow of the Past.*

———, ed. *In the Shadow of the Past: Psychology Portrays the Sexes.* New York: Columbia University Press, 1984.

Lewin, Roger. "Is Sexual Selection a Burden?" *Science,* 226 (2 November 1984) 526–27.

Lewontin, R. C. "On Constraints and Adaptations." *Behavioral and Brain Sciences,* 4 (1981) 244.

———, Steven Rose, and Leon J. Kamin. *Not in Our Genes: Biology, Ideology and Human Nature.* New York: Pantheon, 1984.

Livingstone, Frank B. "Do Humans Maximize Their Inclusive Fitness?" *Behavioral and Brain Sciences,* 6 (1983) 110–11.

Lloyd, Barbara B. "Social Responsibility and Research on Sex Differences," pp. 1–25 in Lloyd and Archer.

———, and John Archer, eds. *Exploring Sex Differences.* London: Academic Press, 1976.

Lowe, Marian, and Ruth Hubbard. "Sociobiology and Biosociology: Can

Science Prove the Biological Basis of Sex Differences in Behavior?" pp. 91–112 in Hubbard and Lowe. *Genes and Gender II.*

Lund, R. D. *Development and Plasticity of the Brain: An Introduction.* New York: Oxford University Press, 1980.

Luria, Zella. "Sexual Fantasy and Pornography: Two Cases of Girls Brought Up With Pornography." *Archives of Sexual Behavior,* 11 (1982) 395–405.

Maccoby, Eleanor E., and Carol Nagy Jacklin. *The Psychology of Sex Differences.* Stanford, Cal.: Stanford University Press, 1974.

————, and Carol Nagy Jacklin. "Sex Differences in Aggression: A Rejoinder and Reprise." *Child Development,* 51 (1980) 964–80.

MacCormack, Carol P., and Marilyn Strathern. *Nature, Culture, and Gender.* Cambridge: Cambridge University Press, 1980.

MacLusky, Neil J., and Frederick Naftolin. "Sexual Differentiation of the Nervous System." *Science,* 211 (20 March 1981) 1294–1301.

Marx, Jean. "The Two Sides of the Brain." *Science,* 220 (29 April 1983) 488–91.

Masters, William H., Virginia E. Johnson, and Robert C. Kolodny. *Human Sexuality.* Boston: Little, Brown, 1982.

McClintock, Martha K. "Menstrual Synchrony and Suppression." *Nature,* 229 (22 January 1971) 244–45.

McCown, Elizabeth R. "Sex Differences: The Females as Baseline for Species Description," pp. 37–83 in Hall, *Sexual Dimorphism.*

McEwen, Bruce S. "Neural Gonadal Steroid Actions." *Science,* 211 (20 March 1981) 1301–11.

McGee, Mark G. "Human Spatial Abilities: Psychometric Studies and Environmental, Genetic, Hormonal, and Neurological Influences." *Psychological Bulletin,* 86 (1979) 889–918.

McGlone, Jeannette. "Sex Differences in Human Brain Asymmetry: A Critical Survey." *Behavioral and Brain Sciences,* 3 (1980) 213–27.

McGuiness, Diane. "Sex Differences in the Oganization of Perception and Cognition," pp. 123–56 in Lloyd and Archer.

————, and Karl H. Pribram. "The Origin of Sensory Bias in the Development of Gender Differences in Perception and Cognition," pp. 3–56 in *Cognitive Growth and Development,* Morton Bortner, ed. New York: Brunner/Mazel, 1979.

Miller, Patricia Y., and Martha R. Fowlkes. "Social and Behavioral Constructions of Female Sexuality," pp. 256–73 in Stimpson and Person.

Morris, Jan. *Conundrum.* New York: Harcourt Brace Jovanovich, 1974.

Naftolin, Frederick. "Understanding the Bases of Sex Differences." *Science,* 211 (20 March 1981) 1263–64.

Nash, Sharon Churnin. "The Relationship Among Sex-Role Stereotyping, Sex-Role Preference, and Sex Difference in Spatial Visualization." *Sex Roles,* 6 (1975) 15–33.

Neville, Helen. "Electroencephalographic Testing of Cerebral Specialization in Normal and Congenitally Deaf Children," pp. 121–31 *Language Development and Neurological Theory*, Sidney Segalowitz and Frederick Gruber, eds. New York: Academic Press, 1977.

Nicholson, John. *Men and Women: How Different Are They?* Oxford: Oxford University Press, 1984.

Nordeen, E. J., and Pauline Yahr. "Hemispheric Asymmetries in the Behavioral and Hormone Effects of the Sexually Differentiating Mammalian Brain." *Science*, 218 (22 October 1982) 391–93.

Nottebohm, Fernando. "A Continuum of Sexes Bedevils the Search for Sexual Differences." *Behavioral and Brain Sciences*, 3 (1980) 245–46.

Oakley, Ann. *Subject Women*. New York: Pantheon, 1981.

O'Brien, Maria. "Comment." *Biosocial Aspects of Sport. Journal of Biosocial Science*, Supplement 7 (1981) 129–31.

Parsons, Jacquelynne E. *The Psychobiology of Sex Differences and Sex Roles*. New York: Hemisphere, 1980.

———. "Psychosexual Neutrality? Is Anatomy Destiny?" pp. 3–26 in Parsons, *Psychobiology*.

Patai, Raphael. *The Jewish Mind*. New York: Charles Scribner's Sons, 1977.

Petersen, Anne C. "Biopsychological Processes in the Development of Sex-Related Differences," pp. 31–56 in Parsons, *Psychobiology*.

———. "Pubertal Change and Cognition," pp. 179–201 Brooks-Gunn and Petersen.

———, and Brandon Taylor. "The Biological Approach to Adolescence: Biological Change and Psychological Adaptation," pp. 117–58 in *Handbook of Adolescent Psychology*, Joseph Adelson, ed. New York: John Wiley and Sons, 1980.

———, and Michele Andrisin Wittig. "Sex-related Differences in Cognitive Functioning: Developmental Issues," pp. 1–17 in Wittig and Petersen.

Pfaff, Donald W., and Bruce S. McEwen. "Actions of Estrogens and Progestins on Nerve Cells." *Science*, 219 (18 February 1983) 808–14.

Piel, Gerard. "The Comparative Psychology of T. C. Schneirla," pp. 1–16 in Aronson.

Pleck, Joseph H. "Masculinity-Femininity: Current and Alternative Paradigms." *Sex Roles*, 1 (1975) 161–78.

———. "The Theory of Male Sex Role Identity: Its Rise and Fall, 1936 to the Present," pp. 204–26 in M. Lewin, *In the Shadow of the Past*.

Plumb, Pat, and Gloria Cowan. "A Developmental Study of Destereotyping and Androgynous Activity Preferences of Tomboys, Nontomboys, and Males." *Sex Roles*, 10 (1984) 703–12.

Poizner, Howard, Robin Battison, and Harlan Lane. "Cerebral Asymmetry for American Sign Language: The Effect of Moving Stimuli." *Brain and Language*, 7 (1979) 351–62.

Poizner, Howard, and Harlan Lane. "Cerebral Asymmetry in the Perception of American Sign Language." *Brain and Language,* 7 (1979) 210–26.

Polani, P. E., and M. Adolfi. "The H-Y Antigen and Its Function: A Review and Hypothesis." *Journal of Immunogenetics,* 10 (1983) 85–102.

Presser, Harriet B., and Virginia S. Cain. "Shift Work Among Dual-Earner Couples With Children." *Science,* 219 (18 February 1983) 876–79.

Ralls, Katherine. "Mammals in Which Females are Larger than Males." *Quarterly Review of Biology,* 51 (1976) 245–76.

Ramey, Estelle. "Making a Difference in Research." *Journal of the American Medical Women's Association,* 39 (1985) 74–76.

Rauste-Von Wright, Maijaliisa, Johan Von Wright, and Marianne Frankenhaeuser. "Relationship Between Sex-Related Psychological Characteristics during Adolescence and Catecholamine Excretion during Achievement Stress." *Psychophysiology,* 18 (1981) 362–70.

Reading in America. Washington, D.C.: Library of Congress, 1979.

Redican, William K. and David Taub. "Male Parental Care in Monkeys and Apes," pp. 203–58 in Michael E. Lamb, ed., *The Role of the Father in Child Development* (2nd ed.). New York: John Wiley and Sons, 1981.

Rensberger, Boyce. "Two Kinds of Male Salmon Found." *Wshington Post* (16 February 1985) E9.

Reynolds, Larry T. "A Note on the Perpetuation of a 'Scientific' Fiction." *Sociometry,* 29 (1966) 85–88.

Robinson, Paul. *The Modernization of Sex.* New York: Harper and Row, 1976.

Rogers, Lesley. "Male Hormones and Behavior," pp. 157–84 in Lloyd and Archer.

Rose, Steven, and Rose Hilary. " 'Do Not Adjust Your Mind, There Is a Fault in Reality." *Cognition,* 2 (1973) 479–502.

Rosenberg, Rosalind. "Leta Hollingworth: Toward a Sexless Intelligence," pp. 77–96 in M. Lewin, *In the Shadow of the Past.*

Rossi, Alice S. "Gender and Parenthood." *American Sociological Review,* 49 (1984) 1–18.

Rowell, Thelma. *The Social Behavior of Monkeys.* Baltimore: Penguin Books, 1972.

Rubin, Robert T., June M. Reinisch, and Roger F. Haskett. "Postnatal Gonadal Steroid Effects on Human Behavior." *Science,* 211 (20 March 1981) 1318–24.

Ruble, Diane N., Jeanne Brooks-Gunn, and Anne Clarke. "Research on Menstrual-Related Psychological Changes: Alternative Perspectives," pp. 227–43 in Parsons, *Psychobiology.*

Sade, Donald Stone. "Human Sexuality: Hints for an Alternative Explanation." *Behavioral and Brain Sciences,* 3 (1980) 198–99.

Salzman, Freda. "Aggression and Gender: A Critique of the Nature-Nurture Question for Humans," pp. 71–90 in Hubbard and Lowe, *Genes and Gender II.*

Scarr-Salapatek, Sandra. "Genetics and the Development of Intelligence." *Review of Child Development,* 4 (1967) 1–57.

Schachter, Stanley, and Jerome Singer. "Cognitive, Social, and Physiological Determinants of Emotional State." *Psychological Review,* 69 (1962) 379–99.

Scholes, Robert J., and Ira Fischler. "Hemispheric Function and Linguistic Skill in the Deaf." *Brain and Language,* 7 (1979) 336–50.

Schratz, Marjorie M. "A Developmental Investigation of Sex Differences in Spatial (Visual-Analytic) and Mathematical Skills in Three Ethnic Groups." *Developmental Psychology,* 14 (1978) 263–67.

Seward, John P., and Georgene H. Seward. *Sex Differences: Mental and Temperamental.* Lexington, Mass.: Lexington Books/D. C. Heath and Company, 1980.

Shapiro, Douglas Y., and Ralf H. Boulon, Jr. "The Influence of Females on the Initiation of Female-to-Female Sex Change in a Coral Reef Fish." *Hormones and Behavior,* 16 (1982) 66–75.

Sharff, Jagna Wojcicka. "Sex and Temperament Revisited," pp. 49–64 in Fooden.

Sherman, Julia. "Book Review." *Sex Roles,* 6 (1975) 297–301.

———. *Sex-related Cognitive Differences: An Essay on Theory and Evidence.* Springfield, Ill.: Charles C. Thomas, 1978.

Shields, Stephanie A. "To Pet, Coddle, and 'Do For': Caretaking and the Concept of Maternal Instinct," pp. 257–73 in M. Lowe, *In the Shadow of the Past.*

Shore, Eleanor G. "Making a Difference in Academia." *Journal of the American Medical Women's Association,* 39 (1985) 81–83, 106.

Shoumatoff, Alex. "The Mountain of Names." *The New Yorker* (13 May 1985) 51–101.

Simmons, Roberta G., Dale A. Blyth, and Karen L. McKinney. "The Social and Psychological Effect of Puberty on White Females," pp. 229–72 in Brooks-Gunn and Petersen.

Smuts, Barbara. "Dominance: An Alternative View." *Behavioral and Brain Sciences,* 4 (1981) 448–50.

———. "Special Relationships between Adult Male and Female Olive Baboons: Selective Advantages," pp. 262–66 in Hinde.

Springer, Sally P., and Georg Deutsch. *Left Brain, Bright Brain* (rev. ed.). San Francisco: W. H. Freeman, 1985.

Star, Susan Leigh. "Sex Differences and Dichotomization of the Brain: Methods, Limits, and Problems in Research on Consciousness," pp. 113–30 in Hubbard and Lowe, *Genes and Gender II.*

Stimpson, Catherine R., and Ethel Spector Person. *Women: Sex and Sexuality.* Chicago: University of Chicago Press, 1980.

Sutherland, Stuart. "Sex in Society." *Nature,* 307 (23 February 1984) 764.

Svare, Bruce. "Psychological Determinants of Maternal Aggressive Behavior," pp. 129–46 in *Aggressive Behavior: Genetic and Neural Approaches,* Edward C. Simmel, Martin E. Hahan, and James K. Walters, eds. Hillsdale, N.J.: Erlbaum, 1983.

Swaab, D. F., and E. Fliers. "A Sexually Dimorphic Nucleus in the Human Brain." *Science,* 228 (31 May 1985) 1112–15.

Symons, Donald. *The Evolution of Human Sexuality.* New York: Oxford University Press, 1979.

Ten Houten, Warren D. "Social Dominance and Cerebral Hemisphericity: Discriminated Race, Socioeconomic Status, and Sex Groups by Performance on Two Lateralized Tests." *International Journal of Neuroscience,* 10 (1980) 223–32.

Tobach, Ethel. "Genes and Gender Update," pp. 7–28 in Fooden.

Tobin-Richards, Maryse H., Andrew M. Boxer, and Anne C. Petersen. "The Psychological Significance of Pubertal Changes: Sex Differences in Perceptions of Self during Early Adolescence," pp. 127–54 in Brooks-Gunn and Petersen.

Tomlinson-Keasey, C., and Ronald R. Kelly. "The Deaf Child's Symbolic World." *American Annals of the Deaf,* 123 (1978) 452–59.

Turkle, Sherry. *The Second Self: Computers and the Human Spirit.* New York: Simon and Schuster, 1984.

Udry, J. Richard. "Female Sexual Adaptability: A Consequence of the Absence of Natural Selection Among Females." *Behavioral and Brain Sciences,* 3 (1980) 201–2.

Unger, Rhoda K. *Female and Male: Psychological Perspectives.* New York: Harper and Row, 1979.

Van den Berghe, Pierre L. "Human Inbreeding Avoidance: Culture in Nature." *Behavioral and Brain Sciences,* 6 (1983) 91–102.

Vetterling-Braggin, Mary. *"Femininity," "Masculinity," and "Androgyny": A Modern Philosophical Discussion.* Totowa, N.J.: Littlefield-Adams, 1982.

Waber, Deborah. "Cognitive Abilities and Sex-Related Variations in the Maturation of Cerebral Cortical Functions," pp. 161–86 in Wittig and Petersen.

Wallen, Kim. "Influence of Female Hormonal State on Rhesus Sexual Behavior Varies with Space for Social Interaction." *Science,* 217 (23 July 1982) 375–77.

Warren, Michelle P. "Physical and Biological Aspects of Puberty," pp. 3–29 in Brooks-Gunn and Petersen.

Weinraub, Marsha, et al. "The Development of Sex Role Stereotypes in the Third Year: Relationship to Gender Labeling, Gender Identity, Sex-typed Toy Preference, and Family Characteristics." *Child Development,* 55 (1984) 1493–1503.

Westney, Ovida E., et al. "Sociosexual Development of Preadolescents," pp. 273–300 in Brooks-Gunn and Petersen.

Wickert, Gabrielle. "Freud's Heritage: Fathers and Daughters in German

Literature (1750–1850)," pp. 27–38 in M. Lowe, *In the Shadow of the Past.*

Williams, George C. "Some Questions on Optimal Inbreeding and Biologically Adaptive Cultures." *Behavioral and Brain Sciences,* 6 (1983) 116–17.

Williams, Walter L. *The Spirit and the Flesh: Sexual Diversity in American Indian Culture.* Boston: Beacon Press, 1986.

Wilson, Jean D., et al. "The Hormonal Control of Sexual Development." *Science,* 211 (20 March 1981), 1290–1.

Witelson, S. F. "The Brain Connection: The Corpus Callosum is Larger in Left-Handers." *Science,* 229 (16 August 1985) 665–68.

———. "Sex and the Single Hemisphere." *Science,* 193 (30 July 1976) 425–27.

Wittig, Michele Andrisin, and Anne C. Petersen. *Sex-related Differences in Cognitive Functioning: Developmental Issues.* New York: Academic Press, 1979.

Wolff, Peter H. "A Difference That Makes No Difference." *Behavioral and Brain Sciences,* 3 (1980) 250–51.

Wrangham, R. W. "Drinking Competition in Vervet Monkeys." *Animal Behavior,* 29 (1981) 904–10.

———. "Ultimate Factors Determining Social Structure," pp. 255–62 in Hinde.

Zborowshi, Mark, and Elizabeth Herzog. *Life is With People: The Culture of the Shtetl.* New York: Schocken, 1952.

Zihlman, Adrienne L. "The Sexes Look at Sex." *Nature,* 294 (5 November 1981) 43.

INDEX